HIGH PRAISE FOR STUART ZADEL'S SEMINARS

"Journey to financial freedom"

"Stuart has really helped me to get traction on my journey to financial freedom. I have been able to maintain an additional income of around $1,000 a month, whilst living a normal lifestyle and maintaining full-time work, achieved within five months of seeing Stuart live."

Thomas Kovacs, Queensland

"The finest people, mentors and champions"

"After attending my first seminar with Stuart Zadel, I was astounded at the result I achieved in such a short period. The learnings I gained from these experts found my income nearly doubling in just eight weeks from the seminar. Now many months have passed and I cannot express the personal growth, associations and experiences I have enjoyed by maintaining close association with some of the finest people, mentors and champions you are ever likely to meet."

Brett West, South Australia

"I would recommend Stuart Zadel's seminars"

"Since arriving home from university in the United States and attending one of Stuart's seminars, I have been involved in a number of business ventures and begun contracting under my own company. As a 19-year-old there was a lot to learn from Stuart and his team. Having applied the necessary teachings and taking what was essential to me, I have been able to position myself very positively in my industry. I would recommend Stuart Zadel's seminars to any up-and-coming entrepreneurs that want to evoke positive change. Stuart has an incredible ability to captivate his audience and I thoroughly enjoyed my experience."

Nathan Kinch, Queensland

"Just phenomenal the success"

"Nine months ago I attended one of Stuart Zadel's conferences in Perth. At that stage I had an investment property that wasn't making me any money and was costing me about $7,000 annually to own so I wasn't getting anywhere. One of the tools Stuart gave me was a goal setting tool where I set myself a goal for 12 months. That goal was to achieve $10,000 within that period through property investment. What I actually did was ending up earning $80,000 from a property sale within nine months. It's just phenomenal the success I have had from just that one little exercise that Stuart does and he's got so many more to share with everybody."

Jason Chittenden, Western Australia

STUART ZADEL

THE <u>NEW</u> WAY TO MAKE MONEY IN PROPERTY <u>FAST!</u>

FREE BONUS DVD PLUS LIVE EVENT TICKETS INSIDE

DISCLAIMER

The information, strategies, comments, concepts, techniques and suggestions within this book are of a general nature only and do not constitute professional or individual advice in any way. You must seek your own independent professional advice relating to your particular circumstances, goals and risk profile if you intend to take any action as a result of reading this publication. The publisher, authors and experts who participated in this project do not accept any responsibility for any action taken as a result of reading this publication. Every care has been taken to ensure the accuracy of the material contained in the book.

National Library of Australia Cataloguing-in-Publication entry:

The New Way to Make Money in Property Fast! / Stuart Zadel.

First published 2012
ISBN: 9780980769807 (pbk)

1. Real estate investment – Australia.
2. Real estate business – Australia.
3. Finance, Personal – Australia.

332.63240994

Email: stuart@stuartzadel.com
Websites: www.stuartzadel.com
           www.TGRProperty.com.au

CONTENTS

DEDICATION

To all my amazing team, crews and
volunteers right around this great country,
my eternal thanks and gratitude for your
quality, quantity and spirit of service.
You inspire me!

Stuart Zadel

PREFACE

A wise man once said to me: "Once you've spent your money, you can always make it back but once you've spent your time, it's gone forever."

That thought has driven me ever since - both personally and professionally.

My company was created to inspire Australians to raise their awareness, find their purpose and achieve financial freedom – fast and ethically.

You see, there are two ways to do something – the smart way or the not-so-smart way. I want to teach people the smart way because that's how to make best use of your time.

It is said: "An hour's conversation across a table with a successful person in any field is worth a whole year's reading on the subject." If you had the choice to spend an hour with someone who has achieved what you want to, or a year's study on your own, which would you choose?

If you'd choose the former – just like me – then that's why you've picked up this book.

There are common denominators of success and learning from the masters is one of them.

Scottish-born, American businessman and philanthropist, Andrew Carnegie, was once the richest man in the world, making his fortune in the steel industry.

He wrote an epitaph for his grave that read: "Here lies one who knew how to get around him men cleverer than himself."

In other words, he surrounded himself with people who knew more than he did; he leveraged their time and expertise. He sat on the shoulders of giants, in the process becoming one himself. That's the model my business is built on.

The New Way to Make Money in Property Fast! contains the expertise of seven property experts who have done the hard yards for you. Reading each chapter of this book is just like having a one-on-one session with its author – a successful, creative, smart property entrepreneur. How does it get any better than this?

Their proven, step-by-step strategies will work for anyone, anywhere, in Australia and most other countries where people are allowed to own and trade property. These members of my inner circle have made sure of it.

Which brings me to another key success indicator – the power of the mastermind team.

Wealth-generation is a team sport. As individuals, we can't possibly know all there is to know, nor do we necessarily want to. It's far easier, quicker, cheaper and more effective to build a team of experts, working in harmony towards a pre-determined goal.

Since 2006, I've been building my own team of staff and wealth-generation partners to help achieve five big goals. We call it our 2020 Vision.

"Without vision, the people will perish."
King Solomon

By the year 2020 our Vision is to:

1. **Inspire 1,000 prosperity millionaires**: These millionaires come from a place of abundance; they create massive value, are charitable and leave a legacy. They create wealth for themselves and those around them. Every prosperity millionaire creates 10 jobs; every prosperity billionaire creates 10,000 jobs.
2. **Distribute one million books**: Not a week goes by that we don't receive a message from someone whose life has been transformed by one of our books. We believe strongly in the power of self-education and have already distributed more than 320,500 books in Australia and internationally.
3. **Educate 50,000 people at live seminars**: Remember, one hour learning directly from a successful person is worth a year's reading. We offer a smart learning option.
4. **Donate one million dollars to worthy causes**: The principle of tithing is not new though many consider it to be a money subtracter. I believe it is a money multiplier when carefully deployed. Think "hand up, not hand out".
5. **Plant one million trees**: I'm spiritual, not religious. But I know God encouraged us to go forth and multiply; he also instructed us to replenish the earth. I see lots of multiplying going on but not much replenishing! We think planting trees benefits everyone.

Wealth is noble, spiritual and good in the hands of noble, spiritual and good people. It cannot and will not make you something you are not; it can only take on the characteristics of the person whose hands in which it resides.

We all want to live in a wealthy nation. However, a wealthy nation is not one in which all the money is concentrated in the hands of a few. It is one in which all its citizens have the opportunity to participate in abundance and drink from the well of wealth. After all, wealth is your birthright.

The information in this book can lead you to the well of wealth but only you can drink from it. I encourage you to read it from cover to cover and to learn from the masters. Allow us to join and guide you on *your* wealth-generation journey.

Now, before you even turn the page to get started, I encourage you to register for both your FREE DVD and free live event tickets, details of which are at the front of the book.

Finally, in order to transform your intention to generate wealth and develop a prosperity mindset into something tangible, download our "Prosperity Millionaire Commitment" from **www.TGRProperty.com.au/commitment.** Print it out and place it wherever you'll see it regularly; beside your bed, on the bathroom mirror or on the fridge door – anywhere that will remind you that you really can choose to experience financial abundance and live the life of your dreams. What else is possible?

In the meantime, I trust you will enjoy *The New Way to Make Money in Property Fast!*

Stuart Zadel

Stuart Zadel

INTRODUCTION

"Ninety-four per cent of all failure is as a result of the system, not the people."

Dr William Edwards Deming

The old way of doing property - buy, hold, hope and pray - was good, but it's not enough. In this new economy, what worked in the past will not work in the future; in fact, it's not even working now!

Australian Bureau of Statistics figures confirm 63 per cent of all property investors are negatively-geared, losing on average $9,000 per annum. Many get out at a loss, never to return. The days of property doubling every seven to 10 years just by holding it as a passive investment are probably gone forever.

What will work in the new economy is the new way to make money in property, fast. These active strategies enable a far greater amount of control of the outcome of your investment by applying your skill and knowledge that can enable you to attain financial freedom in five years or less.

There are a couple of tides at play right now. The first is that the way property is being bought and sold is changing. Due to high prices, changing banking practices, spending habits, interest rates, global debt, lack of investor confidence and any other number of factors, people are having to become way more flexible in the way they both buy and sell houses.

Secondly, by 2014, Australia will be an estimated 308,000 dwellings short of housing its population, according to The Real Estate Institute of Australia.

So, if demand and supply drive an industry, do you think property investing might have a prosperous future in this country? You betcha!

Did you also know that more millionaires make and hold their fortunes through, and in, property than by any other means? So, long after the natural resources have been mined from beneath our feet, one thing will always remain rock solid – property.

What if, however, the old buy-and-hold property model no longer produces the results it once did? What if it is no longer the right system?

Enter *The New Way to Make Money in Property Fast!*

Would you believe me if I told you it was possible to make enough money from just one renovation project to fund the purchase of an entire new home?

What about making a six-figure profit just from changing the legal title of an investment property?

Did you know there is a smarter way to increase the value of your superannuation by building a property portfolio, either by yourself or with others?

How does earning five times the average wage for less than three hours' work sound?

Can you imagine buying a house for only $1 and without a bank? Or getting the keys to a property within hours of agreeing to purchase it?

Do you know the secrets of the ultra wealthy that allow them protect their assets for future generations, regardless of economic circumstances?

Does it surprise you to hear that the Tax Office can give *you* a refund for creating wealth through property? And that less than one per cent of accountants are even aware of how to maximise the laws?

In *The New Way to Make Money in Property Fast!,* you'll meet seven property entrepreneurs who make amazing profits in their chosen niche. You'll also discover four unique strategies to go from zero to financial freedom in five years of less, plus two approaches to minimise tax and bulletproof your assets.

With this knowledge, you too can become a prosperity property millionaire by learning and applying the closely guarded secrets of these masters! It's easier than you think once you "crack the code" of their strategies. Here's what you have been waiting for…

In the first chapter, I'll reveal to you, possibly for the first time ever, your mind-money connection, the critical role it plays in manifesting your results as well as why you're not already where you want to be financially. I'll also share with you what to do about it plus a couple of extremely powerful processes proven by millions to create precisely the experiences in life you wish to live out.

Next, Australia's Top Renovator, Cherie Barber, will let you in on how she regularly makes hundreds of thousands of dollars *per* renovation. She'll show you how to add value in either a rising or falling market – all without throwing a tool at a wall in frustration! Turn to chapter two for her eight-step, high-value, low-risk strategy – and her top 10 renovation strategies.

It's so simple yet so profound that you'll wonder why you never thought up Sam Sagger's philosophy: "Profits are better than wages." In chapter three, Sam shares his all-new guides to property buying cycles, property finance, town planning, house and land packages, mining markets, self-managed super funds and property management.

Then, the "Dealmaker", Bob Andersen, will show you how to leverage the time and expertise of other property professionals to make up to five times what they do without spending a day at university! You'll find his nine-step successful property development system and seven "no money down" strategies in chapter four.

Rick Otton is famous for buying houses for just $1 and without a bank! He introduced creative financing techniques and super cashflow concepts to the Australian market in 1990. If you don't believe it's possible to create cashflow from scratch, just wait until you get to chapter five.

In chapter six, barrister Dominique Grubisa reveals how the ultra wealthy protect their assets and why you need to do so urgently against the current background of changing world dynamics. If you want to minimise your asset exposure and prosper in future economic climates, don't miss this.

Finally, what's the point of creating wealth if you can't keep and use most of it? Adrian Hill will uncover what more than 99 per cent of accountants don't know – how you can make the tax man work as hard as you do! Chapter seven will make and save you thousands.

So, there you have it. An introduction to the latest members of my hand-picked team of rich – and smart - property entrepreneurs. Learn and replicate their creative, proven systems and become one of our new 1,000 Prosperity Millionaires.

To your success!

Stuart Zadel

Stuart Zadel

"Start small, stay focused, grow strong!"

STUART ZADEL

STUART ZADEL

Wealth educator Stuart Zadel is an author, speaker, publisher, entrepreneur and Director of Australia's premium wealth education company.

His purpose is to inspire people to raise their awareness, find their purpose, and achieve financial freedom.

Stuart is renowned for his authentic, humorous and sometimes controversial style that packs a powerful inspirational punch.

He has five big goals that he and his team are working towards:

1. Inspire 1,000 prosperity millionaires
2. Distribute one million books
3. Educate 50,000 people at live seminars
4. Donate one million dollars to worthy causes
5. Plant one million trees.

Combining entrepreneurship, skill, drive and his specialised knowledge of the mind-money connection, Stuart teaches more than 8,000 people each year about financial prosperity, personal leadership, sales success and peak performance.

He has authored his own series of cutting-edge wealth-creation books, and co-authored three others on sales, leadership and public speaking.

As a successful business owner for more than 20 years, Stuart also actively practices several of the strategies his wealth-generation team members teach.

He has a clear vision to encourage everyone to experience an abundant life – and uncompromising integrity.

MIND-MONEY CONNECTION

DISCOVER THE TWO KEY CONCEPTS THAT WILL PROPEL YOU TOWARDS FINANCIAL PROSPERITY FASTER THAN ANY OTHER

"Whatever the mind can conceive and believe, the mind can achieve".

Andrew Carnegie

Welcome! I am so thankful you are reading these words and as a reward, in a minute, I'll reveal to you the very real but little-known mind-money connection and the critical role it plays in manifesting better results. I'll also show you two powerful and proven processes to create precisely the experiences in life you wish to live out. And I'll introduce you to the second key principle of success: that of the mastermind team.

But first, I'd like to establish a scaffold for your advancing success when you finish this book. You see, I've been speaking and educating audiences now for quite some time. In fact, I've personally trained in excess of 25,000 people and have discovered a few things that work and a lot more that don't!

One of those that does is my principle of "start small, stay focused, grow strong".

You see, people inherently don't like change, even when it's clearly for their own good. For example, I have seen people willingly go to an early grave rather than change their eating, smoking or drinking habits. And as with anything new, there can be a period of discomfort, adjustment and what I like to call "learning experiences".

In learning and implementing *The New Way to Make Money in Property Fast!*, it will be no different, especially if you are used to doing property the old way (work hard, save, save some more, eventually buy, hold, hope and pray it goes up in value).

However, if you use my scaffolding, and allow yourself to first "start small" you'll not only avoid putting too much pressure on yourself too early, you'll also avoid the potential of major career-ending learning experiences. An example of this could be developing a simple lot subdivison into two dwellings as opposed to tackling a 50-unit development.

Next, through "staying focused" you'll repeat all of the little things with which you "started small" and, through the power of repetition and compound experience, you'll ultimately "grow strong".

But of course, I am getting a little ahead of myself and it's time to go back to the beginning and understand that just about everything we were taught to think about money was wrong…

MONEY

> *"Money is a good servant but a poor master."*
> **Dominique Bouhours**

Money is an idea. Understand it's not the paper or plastic in your wallet, the coins in your pocket or the numbers in your bank account. These are all just representations of money, not money itself. Why? Because money is an idea!

Money is neutral, neither good nor bad, just neutral. It has no characteristics except those we project onto it. It has no life, no language…it's neither dirty, evil, nor good nor… ?

Money is a tool. As such, like a hammer, it can be used to build or destroy based on the intent of the user. The effectiveness of its expression is totally dependant on the skill and belief of the person using it.

MORE MONEY

"There is no such thing as something for nothing."
Napoleon Hill

It can be useful to consider money as a reward received for service rendered. If you want more money you are going to have to render more and better service. Presumably your purpose in reading this book is to create a financial surplus for yourself and your family, and the fact that we are using property to do this, is incidental. If you want a million dollars, you need to render a million dollars worth of service. That could mean one deal for a one million dollar profit, or 100 deals at ten thousand dollars profit. Your income and reward will be in direct proportion to the quality, quantity and spirit in which you render service to the market. An entrepreneur understands this. They simply endeavour to take something of a lower value and turn it into something of a higher value according to the needs of the marketplace. When you get this right, you may be rewarded handsomely for your efforts.

MORE PROSPERITY MILLIONAIRES

"I've been rich and I've been poor, rich is better".
Sophie Tucker

Prosperity Millionaires have a prosperous mindset and so attract wealth and opportunity because that's what they are looking for. They are entrepreneurial and come from a space of abundance, good stewardship and common sense. They are good money managers as they value, protect, multiply and share a portion of every dollar that passes through their hands. They always seek to add massive value and engage only in transactions that benefit all (win/win). They continually grow, learn and seek out specialised knowledge of how to be of more service and, in the process, make more surplus to leave a legacy and increase the pie for all.

In contrast, Poverty Millionaires have a poverty mindset and they come from a space of lack and limitation, believing the supply of money to be restricted. This scarcity mentality causes them to hold on tightly to every dollar they have for fear of loss and lack of confidence in replacing it. Poverty millionaires always seek to drive hard bargains, while advancing only their own interests at the expense of others (win/lose).

So now that you can see that not all millionaires are created equal, you will understand why the world could be better off for the presence of more Prosperity Millionaires. For me, inspiring 1,000 new Prosperity Millionaires, dedicated to contributing a portion of their wealth and energies to worthwhile projects, as part of our 2020 Vision, is a goal worth striving for. By doing so, we will achieve our purpose of raising the conscious and financial awareness of the planet.

DECIDE... BELIEVE... BEGIN...

"Tell the world what you intend to do, but first show it".
Napoleon Hill

Just about everything we were taught about money is wrong.

It doesn't take money to make money.
It doesn't take a university degree to make money.
It doesn't take high intelligence to make money.
It doesn't take good grades, good looks or even good ideas.
You don't need a good job. In fact, you don't need a job at all.
You don't need friends of influence and to be "connected".
You don't need to come from a wealthy family.

None of these things matter. But you know what does? A decision. Yes, that's right. The only thing that matters is that you make an irrevocable decision to commit and see it through, no matter what. That's it.

So right now, before we even start, I'm asking you to commit. I'm asking you to become one of our next Prosperity Millionaires. What'll it be? Yes or No?

The moment you make your decision and commit it to writing you will have made it tangible. Now make that commitment by signing here:

Stuart Zadel's Prosperity Millionaire Commitment

I _____ (name) hereby make an irrevocable commitment to becoming a Stuart Zadel Prosperity Millionaire, so that I can attain total financial freedom, serve, inspire and share my success with others and live a full life.

_____

Signed

_____/_____/ 20_____

Date

Next I want you to go to www.TGRProperty.com.au/commitment and download your free Stuart Zadel Prosperity Millionaire Certificate. Print out several copies, fill them in and place them where you'll see them around your home or workplace many times a day.

As US success author, Napoleon Hill wrote, "Somewhere in your make up (perhaps in the cells of your brain) there lies sleeping, the seed of achievement, which if aroused and put into action, would carry you to heights, such as you may never have hoped to attain."

That seed has now been planted. It has begun...

CLARITY IS POWER

"The highest reward for a person's toil is not what they get for it, but what they become by it".
John Ruskin

Congratulations! I'm so grateful you've decided to join us. Let's get started...

For some inexplicable reason, I have always wanted to be a Prosperity Millionaire. Ever since I can remember, I always wanted to have influence so that I could make a difference and inspire others. The ideal and only way I thought to achieve that when I was young was to become a professional soccer player. I figured the fame would give me influence so people would listen and the money would give me the means to do good. So I trained hard, played and showed enormous potential in my early teens. I even earned the nickname there for a while of "Franz", after the legendary German soccer player, Franz Beckenbauer.

As the years went by, I trained harder and harder yet didn't seem to progress; if anything, I may have gone backwards. So I did the only thing I knew to do, which I got from watching my parents struggle through life… I trained harder. I even went to the lengths of getting my own Olympic running coach, working in a gym part-time to get stronger, and dropping out of university to spend more time training and, so I thought, following my dream.

Against the odds and in record time, I overcame what surgeons thought was a career-ending knee injury. Again, I did it by working hard and letting my obsession push my body, all the while completely oblivious to the messages the universe was sending me. Despite playing a few more seasons, my dream to be a professional soccer player never came true (later I discovered it was never my dream to begin with). What annoyed me most when it was all over was that I didn't know why I didn't make it, especially when I was prepared to give everything for the chance.

Years later, I finally discovered the answer to my question: willpower, no matter how strong, will never overcome imagination or conditioning.

Let's start to understand why.

There are only three things you need to be successful in any sport.

1. Skill
2. Fitness
3. The right mindset/psychology.

As a soccer player, my skill level was average; I was neither the best, nor the worst. My fitness, however, was definitely superior. I was one of the fittest athletes in the league, if not the country at the time. The third and final element came down to my personal mindset and psychology. And that's where I let myself down. Outwardly you couldn't pick it, but inside something wasn't congruent with my goal. Later I would learn that in any field of achievement, experts unanimously agree that 80 per cent or more of a person's success comes down to their mental attitude, mindset and thoughts. This became more evident to me when I opened my first business…

OBSERVATION IS POWER

> *"No problem can stand the assault of sustained thinking".*
> **Voltaire**

Shortly after my departure from the soccer field, I redirected that drive, energy and my desire to help people into establishing my own fitness club. Through my part time-work as a fitness instructor, I found I really enjoyed helping people improve their lives. I noticed when they started to get their act together physically, many other areas of their lives improved as well.

But the results were inconsistent. Why was it that some excelled while others were mediocre at best? How is it that two people start out with the same information, the same equipment, the same experience level, similar circumstances and environment, yet one achieves and the other doesn't? What makes the difference between success and failure?

Again, I found that success in the gym came down to just three things.

1. Exercise
2. Nutrition
3. The right mindset/psychology.

Are you starting to see a pattern here? I did. At best, most people only focus on the physical components of any success equation, such as skill plus fitness or exercise plus nutrition or intelligence plus application. What they lack is the most important component of all – the understanding that success and achievement in any field of endeavour starts and ends with the mind.

BE CONGRUENT

"There's a big difference between wishing for a thing and being ready to receive it. No one is ready for something until they believe they can acquire it. The state of mind must be belief and not mere hope or wish."
Napoleon Hill

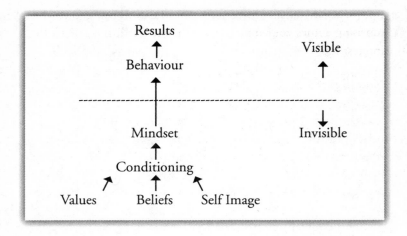

Take a look at the diagram above. You'll notice the word **results** is at the top of the hierarchy. Results are the name of the game and this applies to any area of your life, be that wealth, health, relationships or happiness. It's both normal and natural for every human being to seek more in life and to grow.

Now notice that results are created by **behaviour**. For example, Arnold Schwarzenegger pushes weights. Clearly that behaviour produces a certain result.

Beyond your behaviour however is where all the magic happens. Here is where we now cross over from the visible world into the invisible world, from the tangible world into the intangible world, from the physical world into the metaphysical world. You see, it's your underlying and prevailing **mindset** that motivates your behaviour on a moment by moment basis.

Your mindset is like the weather in that it can change at any moment and frequently does. For example, how often have you told yourself you should go for a run in the morning, but when morning comes your mindset has changed? Hmmm…Isn't that interesting?

Now for the really tricky part. What creates your mindset? Refer to the previous diagram once more and you'll discover it. The ultimate influence on your mindset, and therefore your behaviour and results – is your **conditioning**. Conditioning refers broadly to what you have been brought up to think and believe about the world you live in and yourself. It consists of three key elements: **values**, **beliefs** and **self image**.

According to psychologists, an estimated 90 per cent of your conditioning and indeed, your personality, are formed by the age of seven. This could be good or bad depending on your experience in those first seven years. Secondly, most of this conditioning is below your level of awareness, or what we call subconscious, much like the majority of an iceberg is hidden below the surface of the water. It is invisible and intangible.

So if this was all formed so long ago, and it's invisible, and you're not aware of it - yet it controls **all** your behaviour and is responsible for **all** your results - the million dollar questions have got to be: How do you know what you have been conditioned with and how do you change it?

> *"By their fruits ye shall know them".*
> **Matthew 7:15**

The answer to the first question is simple – just look at your results. Your results broadcast loud and clear to the world your conditioning. It can be no other way. Just like a river that has been dammed momentarily can, and will, find a way around it to the sea, so too your values, beliefs, and self image will always find their natural expression.

So if you want to see what you have been conditioned to believe about money, just check your bank statement. The amount of money you earn each year is, in fact, what you feel you are worth, and not a cent more or a cent less. Take a look at your health and your relationships while you're at it. The state of each will tell you exactly what you have been conditioned to believe.

Since you're presumably reading this book to make financial improvements, let's drill down to see how values, beliefs and self image relate to money.

Values - Everyone has a hierarchy of values. When it comes to finances, you will recognise your values by how you earn your money, how much of it you have and what you do with it. Make sense?

Beliefs - Recognise that your beliefs are not necessarily fact or even true. They are simply what they are, and can broadly be split into two categories: limiting beliefs and empowering beliefs.

Some limiting beliefs might be:
- the money supply is limited. For me to get more, others have to go without;
- money is the root of all evil;
- if this really worked, somebody would have already done it.

Some empowering beliefs might be:
- money is abundant. The more I create the more there is to share;
- the *lack* of money is the root of all evil;

- if it's working for them, it'll work for me.
- ask and ye shall receive.

Self Image - Scientists have determined the overriding cause of success or failure in life to be our invisible self image. This invisible force works much the same as a thermostat on a heater. Let's say the thermostat is set at 20 degrees. When the temperature of the surrounding air drops below this set point, the thermostat reacts to the drop and sends a message to the heater to heat the room; if the temperature of the surrounding air rises above the set point, the thermostat reacts to the increase and sends a message to the heater to switch off. Your self image works in the same way.

Anyone who has ever struggled with a weight problem will be familiar with this process. Dieting may shed pounds for a while but eventually the set point mechanism reacts to the dropping weight, causing the dieter to change the way they feel, change the way they behave and, ultimately, return to their pre-diet weight, or more.

How about financially? Do you think you have a set point there as well? You'd better believe it! The amount of money you earn is a direct reflection of what you feel you are worth. This is why somewhere between 70 and 95 per cent of major lottery winners squander their sudden fortunes in two years or less. The unexpected windfall is way in excess of their financial set point, causing them to subconsciously repel it.

To raise your financial and other set points you not only have to take the right actions in the physical world, but you also need to adjust your in-built thermostat. Both need to be congruent: the visible and the invisible, the tangible and the intangible. You must repeatedly now see yourself as a highly prosperous person. You must create a new set point. Here's a powerful process and exercise that will help you...

THE MIND MOVIE PROCESS

"Any idea that is held in mind, that is emphasized, that is Feared or Revered will begin at once to clothe itself in the most convenient and appropriate form that is available".
Andrew Carnegie

First, put yourself in a completely relaxed state. Next, choose a goal that you would like to achieve, such as becoming a wealthy property entrepreneur. Then, create a short mental movie of yourself enjoying your goal NOW. Be sure you are fully in the picture, the star of the show! Allow yourself to feel the feelings you would expect to feel when you are living out this goal for real. Imagine what this would be like in exact detail. Repeat this mind movie several times a day.

THE GOAL CARD EXERCISE

On a 7cm x 12cm card write an abbreviated version of your mental movie, commencing with the words: "I am so happy and grateful now that..." An example might be: "I am so happy and grateful now that I earn an income of $10,000 per month as an entrepreneur." This is your Goal Card. Carry your goal card in your pocket or purse so that whenever you touch it from now on, the image of your mental movie will flash onto the screen of your mind. Remember to start small, stay focused and grow strong, and when you achieve this goal, you can redo the process with an increased amount.

Goal Card

I am so happy and grateful now that....

_____
_____
_____
_____
_____
_____

The Mind Movie process and the Goal Card exercise really work. Just as a seed is planted into the soil and begins to attract all things necessary for the fulfillment of its growth and potential, so too your goal has now been planted into the deep resources of your subconscious mind where it too has begun to germinate and attract to you all that is required for the accomplishment of your goal.

Once completed, it's now very important that you be open to the messages and opportunities that the universe will present you. The all-powerful universe works in feather touches, and gently suggests to you to go certain places, meet certain people, do certain things, most of which you will have no clue as to why, but if it feels right and light, do it. Follow the trail wherever it leads you.

Realise, the universe can't do it for you, it can only do it with and through you, so be alert and follow your intuition. If you get an inclination to walk into a certain shop, or start a conversation with the person next to you, do it. Don't shut it down by not responding or by letting fear stand in your way.

I admit, this can be a little bit uncomfortable at first, but soon you'll be in awe at how things just seem to "fall into place". Oh, and another tip, it will never be hard work. The universe is effortless in its accomplishments (of which you are one), and will bring to you the people and resources required for your fulfillment.

THE MASTERMIND TEAM

The next big idea I'd like to share with you is that of the **mastermind team.** Since there's genius in simplicity, let's simplify all achievement down to just three key ingredients. You need:

1. A Dream
2. A Theme
3. A Team.

I'm going to assume that you have a **dream** in mind, perhaps to become one of our 1,000 new Prosperity Millionaires? And, given you are reading this book, your **theme** is likely to be that of property. So, the one thing we need to discuss now is your **team**.

The business of property and wealth-generation are team sports. In the following chapters, you'll hear time and time again the experts talk about assembling a team. This has been the secret of my success and the key principle behind this very book. Recall now Andrew Carnegie's epitaph for his own grave that read, "Here lies one who knew how to get around him men cleverer than himself." Carnegie was renowned for working with the very best people. Here's his six essential characteristics for picking them.

The six characteristics of top mastermind team members

1. **Honesty and Loyalty**

   Carnegie placed both honesty and loyalty at the very top of his list for a good reason. Honesty and loyalty breed trust, and trust is the foundation upon which people do their best work. Specifically, he said, "If a person doesn't show loyalty to those that are entitled to it, I want no part of them". Of course, loyalty is not an automatic right and is not something you should ever take for granted. You have to earn the loyalty of your team members by proving to them that you're somebody who is worthy of it.

2. **Dependability**

   This comes in at number two, although dependability, honesty and loyalty are pretty much equal. After all, what good is a loyal person if you can't depend on them? The whole point of developing a team is so you can step back into more of a management role and allow those with the specialised skills you've chosen to do the hands-on work. It's a system that can only function correctly if you are able to assign a task and know that it's going to be done to a standard that will meet your requirements. If somebody comes back to you with a half-finished job and a list of excuses, they're the wrong person for your team.

3. **Ability to do the job**

   This is probably the easiest one to detect but that doesn't make it any less important. It's absolutely essential that you surround yourself with people who actually know how to do what it is that you need them to do. It might seem reasonable to assume that a real estate agent would know everything necessary to successfully complete a property transaction or that a qualified tax accountant will be able to pick up all the deductions you're entitled to but experience has shown these things can't be taken for granted. Still, it's interesting that Carnegie placed this quality in third place behind honesty, loyalty and dependability.

4. Positive mental attitude

Speaking very broadly, there are just two types of people in life: optimists and pessimists. It's been my experience that optimists have, by far, the better end of the deal. They are positive, encourage others and always look for the opportunity in adversity. Attempting anything in life above mediocrity is going to attract both adversity and criticism, often from those who are close to you. Therefore, it's important to surround yourself with positive people who will be able to encourage and support you. I find the "can do" attitude of optimistic people means they're far more motivated and are always keener to get going, which is good for business and excellent for customer service.

5. Willingness to go the extra mile

You'll know you've got a truly excellent team member when you find somebody who not only does the job that is required of them but goes that extra distance to make sure it's done to the absolute highest standard possible. This type of person is incredibly hard to find and well worth holding onto once you have them. I'm talking about the kind of person who will do extra jobs for you, whether or not they are stipulated in their contract, and who will spend their weekend feverishly working on a project they've been given at short notice without any complaint. It can be challenging to find such people but by no means impossible. I know this because I have a number of them in my own team.

6. Applied faith

Let me start by saying this has nothing at all to do with religion. It's about individual minds discovering themselves and establishing a working relationship with the lawful power of the universe, known in this case as infinite intelligence. There's a very important distinction that needs to be made here, between applied faith and mere belief. Simply believing in something is far too passive and no more potent than daydreaming when it comes to achieving your goals. Applied faith is all about action. The more action, the better, not only on your part but that of your mastermind allies as well.

When you've found someone with all six Carnegie characteristics, you're in the presence of royalty. And if they are lacking in just one, you'll need to be careful. Your job from here is to maintain perfect harmony between your team members and discover how to utilise them for maximum effect. Learn the strengths and weaknesses of each member in your team so you can help them reach their potential and, in doing so, achieve your own.

KEEP THEM IN MIND

"If a person advances confidently in the direction of their dream, and endeavours to live the life they have imagined, they will meet with success unexpected in common hours".

Thoreau

We've now covered two of the most important keys to financial prosperity: the mind-money connection and the mastermind team. This chapter has been deliberately placed at the beginning of the book because understanding both concepts will propel you towards your goals faster than any other.

So, with that firmly in mind, let's discover the four unique property strategies to go from zero to financial freedom in five years or less...

FREE BONUS GIFT

Stuart Zadel has generously offered a FREE BONUS GIFT valued at $1,491

Three (3) FREE tickets (worth $497 each) to **The Ultimate Property Entrepreneur and Investors Conference National Tour.**

Visit the website below to receive this free gift
www.TGRProperty.com.au/NEWPROP

Chapter 2
RENOVATING FOR PROFIT

"I can't afford to have a job."

CHERIE BARBER

CHERIE BARBER

Cherie Barber is a full-time professional renovator and highly sought-after public speaker. In 2001, Cherie threw in her full-time marketing job at the end of her first renovation, which saw her earn more money on the weekends renovating than her full-time employment.

In the first year of her professional renovating career, Cherie bought, renovated and sold six houses with a combined value of $6.3 million. She did this with no stable income, no job and little money behind her. Having gained a first-year profit of $1.15 million, this phenomenal result lead Cherie to take on property investment, renovation and development as a serious business. With over a solid decade now behind her as a full-time renovator, Cherie has personally renovated over 30 properties (most of these major structural renovations) and been involved in countless property deals well in excess of $50 million.

The tremendous success achieved by Cherie is attributed to a disciplined, business-like approach to her property projects, complimented by a systemised step-by-step system she personally developed to enable her to follow a logical process in the projects she undertakes.

Unrivalled in what she does, Cherie is Australia's top renovator, continuously averaging a staggering $300,000 to $600,000 profit on every property she touches.

In 2009, she established Renovating For Profit, a company designed to teach everyday Australians the nuts and bolts of renovation as a profession. She now juggles full-time renovating with her national public speaking, media and business commitments and believes that once you have the right knowledge, anyone can do this!

RENOVATING FOR PROFIT

HOW TO EARN LUMP SUM CASH PROFITS BY SPRUCING UP OLD HOUSES!

It's official: renovating is the second love affair of most Australians. As a nation, we're fascinated with the concept of renovating with most people blissfully unaware that everyone will undertake a renovation in some form at least once in their lifetime. But what is it that's so alluring? Is it the hopeful concept of turning old properties into gold? Are you searching for that diamond in the rough that will send you on your way to financial freedom? Perhaps you want to create your own financial future and not have this dictated to you by a boss or perhaps you want to renovate purely to make your existing place more comfortable and enjoyable. Whatever your motivation is, welcome to the wonderful world of renovating - one of the most aggressive wealth-creation property strategies available today.

We've all seen the TV renovating shows that make it look so easy. Properties are transformed in the blink of an eyelid with no apparent fuss or effort. Now for the reality. The truth is that to renovate and do it successfully, you'll need expert property knowledge and to work to a system to ensure you bring home a lucrative profit at the end of it all. After all, profit is the name in the renovating game.

Anyone can renovate but not everyone knows how to make amazing profits from it. Inexperienced renovators underestimate their costs and overestimate their selling price. Time blows out and costs spiral out of control, leaving nothing more than a battered ego and huge loss at the end of it all. So why is it that so many renovations are doomed before they even begin? Quite simply, it's nothing more than a lack of knowledge on all of the critical steps involved in the renovation process. Like anything, renovating is a business. Your aim is to get your renovation done as quickly and efficiently as possible and with insight into what buyers or renters want. And you want to do this whilst adding the most value possible at the least cost. This can be the difference between a loss or profit at the end of your project.

This chapter explains the different types of renovation projects you can undertake, the basics of my systematic approach, along with key strategies that will put you a step ahead of others who don't take the time to educate themselves with such powerful knowledge. The strategies I've listed are just a small sample of the hundreds I have. They are tried, tested and used on a daily basis in all my projects to find, buy and renovate properties for a great profit. As such, this chapter focuses on the buy, renovate and sell strategy where an unrenovated property is purchased with the intention of flipping it for a profit - a great strategy for people who need to create or boost their equity position rapidly in the shortest timeframe possible.

My first renovation was 95 per cent cosmetic with a touch of structural work. From there, I moved rapidly into full-blown major renovations with increasing amounts of structural work, often involving partial demolition of the property. If you're seriously considering renovating as your wealth-creation vehicle, determine where your comfort level lies in respect to the type of renovation you do and the amount of work you'll undertake in each project. Typically, the more work to be done to a property, the larger the profit up for grabs. And if the thought of alterations and additions causes you to lose anything more than 10 minutes' sleep, start with cosmetic renovations and slowly move into more challenging projects as your skill, experience and confidence develops. Ease yourself into it; don't try and win any architectural awards on your first project.

So what sort of person does an amateur or professional renovator need to be? Definitely someone who is not happy to sit back and "wait" for things to happen. Renovators want results now, not in 2, 5 or 10 years' time waiting for capital growth or their development deals to pay off. Renovators take action, many of them rolling up their sleeves to do large portions of the work themselves. Often coined "Sweat Equity", renovation is the fastest way to get quick cashflow. And once your equity starts to build after every successful renovation, you should step back a little, project manage and let other people do the sweating for you.

For the last three years in my career as a public speaker, it amazes me the breadth and variety of people who want to buy old houses and do them up. On a daily basis, I hear the same thing "I would love to buy and renovate old houses, how do you do it?" In fact, if I had a dollar for everyone who's said this to me, I could own half of Sydney right now. Renovators come in all shapes, sizes and nationalities – young to the old, educated to the not so educated, those with absolutely no money to those with too much of it, young adults starting out, couples, daughter and dad teams, older couples looking to complete a reno before retirement, corporate folk looking to throw in their day jobs, young guns wanting to be the next Donald Trumps of the world, best friends who go into business together, women who want to claim their own financial independence outside of their hubbys, single parents looking for an alternate occupation that allows them to earn a decent income whilst juggling kiddie commitments, tradies looking to take the next step up to professional renovators and others who simply want a reno project on the side to supplement their current day jobs. One thing is for sure: anyone can be a renovator. What determines if you will become one is the desire within you to make it happen. One of my recent students is a lovely lady who, at the ripe old age of 87, has decided to become a professional renovator. What a wonderful outlook and mindset this woman has. She's living the adage "you're never too old to start something".

Renovation is and always will be one of the safest, most reliable and least volatile property strategies you can use. It offers investors the ability to add value, regardless of whether the property market is rising or falling. More importantly, renovation is extremely low risk. For starters, you only need to sell one property as opposed to selling 30 units in your development deals. Renovation also offers shorter lead times that allow you to sell your property in a predicted market. Unlike other property vehicles, it is far easier to estimate your selling price in two months' time as opposed to two years' time. What I like best is the fact that I have total control over my properties. The outcome I achieve is a result of my direct actions and input, no one else's. And lastly, property renovation gives you the choice to keep costs down by simply electing to do more or less of the work yourself. This is something you don't often get with other property vehicles. What better way for you to get started in property? You'll soon discover it's not as hard as you first thought. Anyone can do it, you just need to be shown how.

For me, renovating is in my veins. I'm one of the few people that can truly say I love what I do and it doesn't feel like work. Achieving huge profits is real and achievable; I'm living proof of that. You can also achieve this simply by having the skills, faith and motivation to get out there and make it happen. Throw any procrastination you may have in the mini skip bin!

So what are you waiting for? Hold on and fasten your seatbelt for you're about to take the renovation rollercoaster ride. No doubt you'll have many ups and downs, as well as a few curly twists along the way. You'll feel so exhilarated at the end that you'll want to do it all over again. So jump in, let's go for a ride. It's going to be fun!

WHAT EXACTLY IS RENOVATION?

People love to talk about renovation but its meaning can differ greatly from one person to the next. So before we go into any further detail, let's clarify the two most common definitions of renovation used today. They are:

1. Cosmetic renovations
2. Structural renovations.

Cosmetic renovations are improvements made to a structurally sound property to give it a makeover or facelift. Just like humans, properties become old and tired-looking with age, so work needs to be done to give them a new-found appeal. This is done through simple cosmetic enhancements that, ideally, add more in perceived value than actual cost. The most common methods of cosmetic improvements are painting, removing or replacing floor coverings, tiling, polishing floorboards, fixing or replacing window coverings, updating kitchens and bathrooms, landscaping and any other general repair designed to fix a property and portray a clean, modern appearance. Cosmetic renovations do not involve any change to a structural element of a property – adding rooms, removing load-bearing beams etc. – and therefore require a much lower skill level. As a general rule, cosmetic renovations should account for no more than 10 per cent of your property's purchase price.

Structural renovations are improvements aimed at either preserving the integrity of a property or reconfiguring it to add space and maximise its overall use and efficiency. Many structural renovations include partial demolition of the property with approval for new alterations and additions. Rarely is an old house so derelict that it has to be completely demolished. Unlike cosmetic makeovers, structural renovations need council approval and permits to carry out the work. As structural renovations can be major changes to a property, there is no industry average as to what you should and shouldn't spend although there are formulas that you should apply to each area (that I teach in my three-day workshops) to ensure you don't overcapitalise. With structural renovations, it's simply a case of analysing each property on an individual basis and assessing your return on investment against the amount of work to be performed.

COSMETIC RENOVATIONS vs STRUCTURAL RENOVATIONS

COSMETIC RENOVATIONS	VS	STRUCTURAL RENOVATIONS
Doesn't Require Council Approval		Does Require Council Approval
Low Level Skill Required		Medium to High Level of Skill Required
Minimal Investment		Minimal to Major Investment
Shorter Timeframes (<6 Weeks)		Longer Timeframes (2-12 Months)
Active / DIY Role		Project Management Role
Smaller profits		Larger profits

Any property that is completely demolished or starting from scratch is defined as new construction and does not fit in with the realm of renovation.

THERE ARE TWO TYPES OF RENOVATORS:

1. Owner-occupier renovators
2. Professional renovators.

Owner-occupier renovators focus purely on improving the home they currently live in. Undeterred by the thought of having no shower, kitchen or dust-free clothes for a period of time, owner-occupier renovators focus on one thing – what *they* want. They create a wish list of things that will increase their comfort, then set out to transform their property. They commonly take a long-term view on the property and make decisions based on emotion and what personally appeals to them. While they're likely to have a renovation budget, it's not uncommon for an owner-occupier's budget to blow out simply because they splurge on items they desperately want. They have to juggle their full-time job, can easily take 10 months to finish the three-month renovation, usually come close to getting divorced and often end up with something entirely different to what they first planned. It's not their fault, they're simply inexperienced and approaching the renovation with a different mindset. While not all owner-occupier renovators are totally tragic, it's members of this group that are most likely to amuse us all with their tales of being traumatised by tradespeople and inexplicably going from mild-mannered people to uncontrollable maniacs within a short space of time.

Professional renovators, on the other hand, are concerned with just one thing. Make no mistake; it's all about the profit. Professional renovators are business savvy people who analyse the implications and merits of every decision they make in the renovating process. They have intimate knowledge of their market and know what buyers want, sometimes when buyers don't know themselves. They are well-organised, thorough and don't change their mind 30 times when deciding what colour tiles to put on the floor. Professional renovators have the "buy and add value" mentality etched firmly in their brains. For them, lost time is lost money. As each deal is done, they increase their renovation knowledge to make their next project even better. Most importantly, professional renovators never get emotional about their projects. As the last ones to be paid in the deal, their greatest love is the thrill of seeing their bank balance rise a few levels on settlement day.

WHY RENOVATE?

The thought of getting dirty and living in mayhem is enough to turn most people off renovating. I wonder if the opinions of those people would change, though, if they knew it was possible to make six-figure profits in relatively short periods of time? Renovation is unarguably one of the easiest ways to make your start in property. What's more fantastic is the fact that it's within the skill level of the average person.

So if you're seriously considering property renovations, congratulations! My first tip is to make sure you know what you're going to do with a property *before* you buy it. The path you head down will be determined by how much cashflow you have available to you to start. The three options below have differing attributes and will require a different renovation approach. The key is to have a clear vision right from the start. Changing your strategy mid-way through a renovation is fraught with danger so have the goal set before you start and don't deviate away from that.

The **buy, renovate, reside** strategy deals with the owner-occupier renovators we've described above, who renovate their primary place of residence. They make up a huge proportion of the renovation real estate market. Most cosmetic renovations do not require the approval of council while owner-occupier renovators undertaking a structural renovation can obtain one owner-builder permit every three to six years (depending on which state of Australia you live in). It's a great way to get a start in property if you're short on dollars and don't mind putting in some sweat equity. The key advantage here is that your costs are kept to a minimum and whatever profit you make is totally tax-free, provided the home is used as your primary place of residence. While that all sounds great, you need to face the reality. Unless you have a relationship more solid than the CaesarStone® bench top you've been dreaming of, you should be careful about facing the challenges of living together with your family in a construction zone. Like it or not, renovating can be the quickest path to divorce. I struggled with it as much as anybody and it took me years of flying off the handle, numerous break-ups and a few narrowly-missed shots to the head with the closest tool I could reach to finally develop a strategy that allowed my partner and I to diligently and peacefully renovate together.

The **buy, renovate, sell** strategy deals with novice and professional renovators who buy property, add value to it and sell with the intention of generating a profit within short timeframes. Sometimes referred to as "property traders" or "property flippers", the buy, renovate and sell strategy is all about supply and demand. You want to identify a gap in the market and buy a property that can be transformed to satisfy that demand. These properties also need to strike an emotional chord with buyers, so it's important renovators in this category understand the buyer psychology in the local market. The buy, renovate and sell strategy is my specific area of expertise and the remainder of this chapter largely focuses on this.

The **buy, renovate, rent** strategy targets investors who renovate their properties for the purposes of not only creating instant equity but also attracting a rental tenant. This type of renovation does add value but normally doesn't maximise the full potential of the property. More so, properties are held to increase equity through longer term capital growth. The ultimate goal of the property owner is to emotionally attract tenants, get the highest rental revenue and have minimal maintenance issues that detract from their rental return. Cosmetic renovations are fantastic in this scenario. Renovations focus on tenant needs, practicality, long-term durability of fixtures and fittings, and an appropriate level of style and quality to match the rental income of the property. Leave the "wow" factor for properties you intend to buy, renovate and sell. Renovators in this category need to be diligent in keeping costs low to avoid overcapitalising on the property beyond the rental return they'll receive.

THE BASICS OF RENOVATING

We all know that one of the quickest ways to make money in real estate is to buy a property that no one wants (i.e. the dump), magically transform it, put it back on the market and hopefully have buyers competing for it. Although the plan sounds extremely simple, it's a lot easier said than done. In essence, the three basic elements in the buy, renovate, sell strategy are:

Know the true value of a property when buying doesn't always mean buying the property for less than it's worth or below the vendor's asking price. In some instances, you can afford to pay more for the property than its current market value if the property can turn an increased profit from a different or better use. The key here is not to have tunnel vision when assessing properties. Confidently know what can be done with the property and how you are able to fully maximise its potential without being detrimental to others. Once you know this, you can determine what the property is worth. Property developers commonly assess property values in this way.

Renovate for the least cost possible to achieve the desired result. Renovations do not always have to be done on the cheap. What is important is that the quality of the renovation reflects the value of the property being re-sold and the expectations of buyers. A luxury home in a wealthy suburb will fail to sell if you paint the kitchen cupboard doors or install cheap fixtures and fittings. Recognise that different properties, at different price points, in different suburbs, require different renovation strategies.

Sell at the highest price possible in order to maximise your profits. Give consideration to the time of year you go to market. For example, December and January are typically great months to buy property but (almost) never to sell. Again this is suburb dependent. In suburbs such as Byron Bay, in northern NSW, selling your property over the Christmas/New Year is the best time. People go on a holiday and unintentionally come back with a holiday house! Ensure you have a great selling agent working for you and always present your property professionally. Doing this creates an illusion that emotional buyers are lured into.

THE SECRET TO MY SUCCESS

This is it, the nuts and bolts of what it takes to be a professional renovator. My process is designed to guide you through the three basic renovation elements listed above. Though it's somewhat time consuming initially, you should aim to follow each and every step in my process. These steps are in the correct sequential order that you would follow in a real life renovation project. Miss one step and you'll expose yourself to risk.

Many other property experts reduce the number of steps in their renovation theory. I take the opposite approach. I pride myself on being thorough. The more detail I have, the less chance of an oversight that could potentially cost me thousands.

I'm an honest person so will happily admit that for the first few years of my renovation journey, I winged my way through my renovations, getting ripped off by many, paying way too much for goods and materials, accepting poor behaviour and workmanship from tradies and undertaking tasks that added no value. Did I forget to mention that I came close to killing my partner every single day too? I made great profits up to that point but knew I could be far better, so decided to get serious about my renovation processes one day and set out to consciously document and refine them to perfection. I feel that anyone who possesses this knowledge, gained through my hard learning curve of experience, will have a serious advantage over others who don't learn how to renovate right. Like it, hate it, debate over it if you want to. The reality is that my process is tried, tested and proven. It's no fluke I make hundreds of thousands of dollars profit on *all* my renovation projects in relatively short timeframes. Use my process religiously, it will be what safeguards your profits regardless of whether you're in a boom or gloom real estate market.

You will notice that the first five steps of my renovation process focus on the "buying" phase of the renovation. Considering this, it's fair to say that 63 per cent of the renovator's work is done (five out of eight steps) before you even pick up a hammer. Many people get so caught up in the actual renovation work they lose sight of where their skills are best utilised. There's an old saying: "Work on your business, not in it." For structural renovations this is especially relevant and incredibly important. Learn to be a good project manager and let tradespeople do what they do best. Focus your efforts on where it will make a difference.

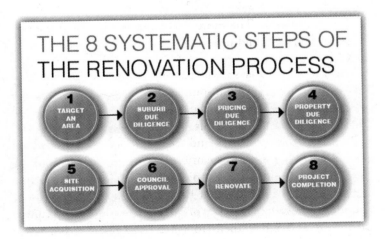

There are hundreds of strategies, methods and tricks of the trade within my eight-step renovation process – far too many to detail at length in just one chapter. With this in mind, I'm going to share some basics with you on just the first four steps of my system including some workable strategies for some of the steps. Take comfort in knowing these strategies are what I use each and every day to make unbelievable profits. They are realistic, achievable strategies you can successfully implement today.

If you're starting to feel exhausted just looking at my model and are thinking it's all too much hard work, let me share a little secret with you. Steps one to six, as well as step eight, are the ones you need to carry out regardless of whether you're a professional renovator, developer, property options trader or anyone else who dabbles in property. My model is a universal system that can be applied to literally any type of property deal. It's purely the use of this strategy that distinguishes the people who are successful in property from those who aren't. Those who skip steps increase their chances of failure. I have never lost money on any of my projects because I am thorough. It's as simple as that.

STEP ONE:
TARGET AN AREA

Let's start at the very beginning. The Australian property market is not one market. It's made up of literally thousands of markets and submarkets. Think macro and micro marketing theories. Some suburbs in Australia are currently in despair while others are still achieving record prices. Why? Because every suburb in Australia is unique and characterised by its own environment and set of circumstances. Therefore, your role as a professional renovator is to select the best suburbs you can possibly afford, then seize and capitalise on the renovation opportunities that lie within them.

So where do you start? If you're smart, you'll realise it's better to be an expert in a few suburbs instead of stretching yourself too thin and not doing anything particularly well. Don't try to focus on 10 suburbs; less than three is a good number and even that will keep you busy. Specialising in a small number of suburbs will give you four things: education, knowledge, specialisation and, ultimately, results.

The great news is that I became a property expert in my target suburbs in just less than three months. That's all it takes. Every Saturday I got up early, made a list of all the properties that were open for inspection and off I trotted to view them all. I inspected 20 to 40 properties every week from the budget priced to the most expensive, sprawling waterfront mansions. I went through them all. Yes, it was time consuming but it was also a fantastic way to learn the property values across the whole suburb quickly.

By doing this every weekend, and then attending the respective auctions, I learned which properties were overpriced and which represented good value. I learned what types of properties sold quicker than others, which ones pulled higher prices, what property styles people paid higher money for and, most importantly, who the buyers were. The supply and demand became more and more apparent to me. I'm sorry to say that simply sitting at your computer clicking buttons on the Internet will not give you this level of knowledge. If you truly want to be a property expert in your area, you have to get your bum off your seat and inside other people's homes. This is the quickest and easiest way to becoming an expert in property values.

Many property experts will advise you to start in suburbs you are already familiar with, one you are already living in or one close to the area where you grew up. That's good advice, though if you're confident enough there's nothing to stop you going for a complete change, particularly if you have a hunch that a suburb has good prospects. Either way, the key is to get into the suburb and do your homework on it. It's not just about location, location, location; it's also about research, research, research.

Which suburbs you target as your new playground will depend on some key variables:

- **Affordability** – Where you can afford to buy, using your money, the banks' or other people's money;

- **Supply versus demand** – The ratio of properties available for purchase weighed against the number of potential buyers in the marketplace;

- **Capital growth prospects** – Home buyers ultimately want to buy in suburbs with good capital growth potential;

- **Availability of unrenovated stock** – Some suburbs, like new housing estates, don't have any unrenovated properties so ensure you invest your time in suburbs where genuine opportunities lie.

The beauty of property renovation is that there are plenty of fixer-upper opportunities everywhere, regardless of whether you're in a prime inner city suburb or a remote outback area. It will be a relief for many to know that opportunities exist in affordable outer suburbs just as much as in the more affluent areas. You just have to be certain that demand exists for a particular type of property within those areas, then create that product to meet that demand.

Here's just two out of my 15 suburb profile examples of where property renovations can work.

LIFESTYLE ZONES

- Suburbs typically located in the inner city fringe ring, metropolitan and outer metropolitan areas.
- High dominance of lifestyle facilities including cafés, restaurants, bars, trendy shops etc.
- Desirable suburbs with limited stock causing pent-up demand.
- Buyers are prepared to pay extra to be closer to these amenities.

LOW-COST HOUSING IN OUTER CBD AREAS

- Cosmetic renovations in metropolitan, outer metropolitan and regional areas.
- Target suburbs and estates where good standard housing exists.
- Choose suburbs where owners take pride in their homes and have pleasant streetscapes.
- Bring poor quality homes up to equal or better standard than current homes in these areas.
- Look for areas where land supply is exhausted.

TIP: Your local council often sells suburb maps for a small fee. These maps are a great way to mark out pockets within suburbs and enable you to view the area in one easy glance. These maps often contain details about zoning, suburb boundary lines, infrastructure routes and, if you're lucky, even individual property boundaries. Buy a copy and hang it on your wall at home for constant reference or as a source of motivation for you to keep taking action.

STEP TWO:
SUBURB DUE DILIGENCE

"Due diligence" is the formal name professional renovators, developers and investors give to the research they carry out on a property. You need to know everything about a particular area so you become a property expert in it. Your aim is to have better knowledge than most real estate agents in your area. They don't often go through other agents' properties but you can, which puts you in a great position to minimise risk by not making assumptions on any aspect of a property transaction. If you know your market well, there's a greater chance you will buy wisely (because you know precisely what an unrenovated property is worth) and will more accurately estimate your selling price (because you also know what renovated properties sell for in your suburb).

By the time you've finished step one, you should have a rough idea on a couple of suburbs you'd like to target. Now you need to drill down a level and explore those suburbs in intimate detail. There are some suburbs that look rosy on the outside but present a much bleaker picture once you scratch the surface and find out what's going on inside.

So how do you become an expert on your chosen suburb? Again, there are exhaustive lists on what things you can do to increase your knowledge of a suburb, as well as an abundance of books that focus purely on this topic. To save you the effort of trawling through all of them, I'll highlight just four easy things you can do, starting today, to become an expert in your target suburbs:

- If you can afford it, live in your chosen suburb. To know what the suburb is really like you need to wake up inside it every morning, walk around the local parks, eat breakfast in the local cafés and see the type of people who live there.

You need to find out when the suburb is at its busiest and quietest, which parts suffer traffic congestion, which parts are the noisiest and so on. Some of these factors can affect property values so it's better to personally experience them before you buy.

- Have a firm grasp of the resident demographics in your suburb. Normally, people looking to buy in the area will be a similar demographic to those people already living there. For instance, in my chosen suburbs, I have three identifiable demographics. The first group is 28 to 35-year-old young professionals with high disposable incomes and no kids. The second demographic is 35 to 50-year-old professional families who moved into the suburb in their late 20s or early 30s and have stayed there ever since. The last demographic is the 70-plus age group, down-to-earth, Aussie battler types who've lived in the area their whole lives. You see, my target suburbs used to be poor man's territory, where blue collar workers lived in virtual slums. It definitely wasn't an area you would have wanted to live in at the time. At some stage, though, the suburb began to transform (suburb gentrification) until it finally became trendy and desirable, with a matching increase in property prices. Most of those 70-year-old battlers are now sitting on properties that are worth anywhere between $1 million and $3 million, simply through capital growth alone. I specifically target the second demographic, the young professional families who have money to spend and no time or patience to renovate themselves. It's how I make such large profits and have almost a guaranteed sale before my property is even finished. The moral of this story is for you to get the detailed knowledge that will allow you to match your renovated property to active buyers.

- Familiarise yourself with the property types and styles of housing within your target suburb. This is easily done by simply jumping in your car and driving the streets. Is 90 per cent of the housing in your target suburb freestanding houses or a mix of houses and semi-detached dwellings? Are properties typically weatherboard, brick veneer, double brick or a combination of all of these? You need to uncover what the norm is in your suburb with respect to the style and construction of dwellings. One of my early students, (prior to attending my workshop) told me that she almost bought an unrenovated weatherboard semi in an inner city location. When I asked why she pulled out of the purchase, she replied: "Because the house wasn't brick. It was weatherboard and I thought I'd automatically be on the back foot." I told her that 80 per cent of the dwellings in that suburb were weatherboard and so buyers are already conditioned to expect that type of housing in that particular suburb.

- Develop good relationships with agents in your area, preferably the best agent or sales director of each local agency. Explain to them the specific type of unrenovated property you want to purchase and the price range you're looking at. If you say to them, "I'm serious, bring me the right deal and I'll buy immediately if it meets my criteria", it confirms you're a qualified buyer, ready to act now. When an unrenovated property does become available, you want the agent to bring it to you first before the general public gets wind of it. Agents are no different to the rest of us; they want to get a deal done quickly too. Agents love it when they bring you an unrenovated deal; you buy it then resell the renovated property back through them. In effect, they get to double dip by drawing two commissions out of the same property in a relatively short time. If the relationship you have with your agent is good, you'll be able to talk comfortably about the real estate market and how it's performing in your area. After all, you aren't talking to buyers directly, the real estate agents are.

Once you've established a good understanding of your suburb(s) in terms of demographics and the property types that lie within them, it's time to look at the property values within your suburb. This is step three called pricing due diligence.

STEP THREE:
PRICING DUE DILIGENCE

It's easy to buy a great house in a great suburb but it's a lot harder to avoid a great house in a poor performing street within that suburb. To put it another way, you should be aware that property values can be very high in one street but substantially lower the next street over. You'll often find pockets of streets within a suburb that hold higher values than others. As a professional renovator, you need to be aware of these price pockets. Otherwise you may grossly overestimate your selling price and put yourself at risk of a loss.

Three ways for you to intimately know and track property values in your target suburb are to:

- Establish a due diligence research system, one that enables you to record information on the different properties you've inspected in your market. I'm proud to say I developed my own unique due diligence system that I believe can't be rivalled in this country. It's a system I hold close to my heart and one that I only share with people who undertake my Renovating For Profit three-day workshops. My due diligence system is somewhat labour intensive but the information I have at my fingertips (in terms of market pricing and property condition) is phenomenal. I attribute a large part of my success to my system. As they say, knowledge is power! You can use my system (if undertaking my workshops) or aim to create your own research system so you too can accurately know property values in your area.

- Visually inspect all properties within your target area, across all price ranges, property types and sizes. This will give you fantastic knowledge on the difference in price values between 1, 2, 3, 4 and 5-bedroom properties, which is particularly important for structural renovators. It will also help you tackle such questions as federation style versus contemporary, garage versus no parking, apartments versus houses and so on.

- Attend as many auctions as possible to see who the real buyers are. Unlike everybody else, when I go to auctions, I don't watch the auctioneer; I'm checking out the buyers. I want to know who they are, how old they are, whether they're a single buyer or a family unit. These visual inspections will give you a number of clues, enabling you to:
  - start learning the value of properties in your area;
  - be able to recognise good value properties and tell them apart from those that are over-priced;
  - be able to recognise the reasons why some homes are in higher demand than others;
  - know what price you should expect to pay for unrenovated properties and, more importantly, what you'll be able to sell them for when fully renovated;
  - have the benefit of personally seeing the condition, style and features of the property with your own eyes rather than relying on glossy marketing material from agents which only ever show the best parts of a property, not the worst; and

- have an excellent way of collecting renovation ideas. If you walk through someone's house and a particular room or feature emotionally draws you to it, think about including something similar in your next renovation project.

WORKABLE STRATEGY: FOUR WAYS YOU CAN SECURE UNRENOVATED PROPERTIES

1) **Door knock** – Drive or walk around the streets in your area and you'll soon identify properties that have renovation potential. Don't be scared to knock on people's doors and ask if they're interested in selling. In my experience, people don't get offended or irate and will often take it as a compliment. It all depends on your approach. If you're friendly and humble, it will be all right but if you go in there wearing your developer's hat, you may get a personal introduction to the family dog. If property owners aren't interested in selling, always leave your business card. People's circumstances do change over time. I bought one property, off market, from a man who I door knocked two years earlier.

2) **Letterbox drops** – If you don't feel entirely comfortable knocking on random doors you might like to try a letterbox drop. A personal letter or greeting card always goes down well, especially because you've taken the time to handwrite it. When I use this method (as opposed to a photocopied letter) I always receive a courtesy call back from property owners. I once received a call from an older gentleman who wasn't keen to sell me his property, but he made sure to mention he had another property that might be up my alley. Turns out it wasn't but that's irrelevant, it could have been! For an example of my letterbox drop letter, see the next page.

3) **Monitor council DAs** – If you're keen to do a structural renovation there's no better way to source your deals than by

monitoring the development applications already in progress through your local council. Property owners sometimes have no intention of renovating, they simply want to sell their property "development or building certificate approved". Get in contact with owners and ask if they're interested in selling, before these unrenovated properties are advertised publicly. Remember, the early bird gets the worm!

4) **RP Data search** – It pays to subscribe to RP Data, an Internet site that allows you to view individual property information. This facility allows you to view houses from above via aerial photograph mapping. It enables you to quickly and effortlessly identify which houses are on under-utilised blocks. It's perfect for structural renovators who want to add substantial value through alterations and additions. Once you've identified the most desirable property opportunities, go and knock on the door or, at the very least, send that letter.

> Dear Property Owner,
>
> I am a local resident and noticed your house when walking by. I would like to point out that I am not a real estate agent nor want to be. I am simply someone who is looking to buy a house in this suburb and took great interest in your property when walking by a few days ago. I really like your property and was wondering if there is any chance I could buy it from you?
>
> If so, I would love the opportunity to meet with you for an informal chat. I am prepared to pay a good price for your property as a private sale. This will also save you thousands upon thousands of dollars in not having to pay advertising costs or real estate agent commission fees.
>
> If you have been thinking of possibly selling now or in the not too distant future, could you please call me? I am a serious buyer and I promise to respond to you immediately.
>
> I sincerely hope to hear from you and have attached a card with my personal details for you to call me if you like. Thank you for your time today in reading my letter.
>
> Kindest Regards,

An example of one of my personal handwritten letters used to acquire unrenovated properties. The language is kept simple, while the tone is friendly and relaxed so the property owner feels comfortable calling me.

STEP FOUR:
PROPERTY DUE DILIGENCE

So how do you find that "diamond in the rough"? Unfortunately, there's no magic formula to finding the perfect property however there are criteria. Buying any old rundown shack simply isn't enough these days; you need to be able to identify which fixer-uppers represent high profitability potential for you. That's what this step is all about.

It has two facets. The first is to thoroughly research a property before you buy and the second part of the equation is to understand how you can unlock potential and add value to the property to maximise its full resale price.

Let's look at the research of a property. Buying a property is one of the most stressing and hardest decisions for most people to make. Am I buying the right property? Is there anything bad about the property that I've missed? Is it going to get me good capital growth? Is it a property I could easily resell at a later date? These are all the sort of questions that run through our heads when making a property purchase. The reality is that most people don't know how to do thorough research on a property (the immediate street and physical characteristics of a property) before they buy, and this lack of knowledge itself creates an element of fear in people. Do they teach us these basic life skills in school? No!

In my insatiable quest to develop the ultimate property investment system, I've developed a property due diligence checklist that contains 59 key things you should always check before you buy a property. Do you know what these 59 research tasks are? Don't worry, you're not alone. You might be thinking 59 things to research sounds exhausting but, my friends, it isn't. In fact, students in my program can complete thorough due diligence on a property within 24 to 48 hours if they follow my system. By default, my students buy good properties not real estate lemons simply because this part of my system weeds out the good deals from the bad.

At a high level, let me give you some basic pointers for you to consider when assessing unrenovated properties at the street and individual property level. In an ideal world, always aim to purchase unrenovated properties that:

- are in established residential streets that are fully built-out;

- have no adverse property (factories or industrial zones) in the surrounding area;

- preferably have a higher concentration of owner-occupiers instead of renters;

- are in close proximity to public transport (but not too close);

- are not on blocks of land smaller in size than the suburb average;

- have a pleasant and consistent streetscape;

- offer appropriate parking (particularly relevant for inner city properties where space is in short supply);

- are not in narrow streets (inner city people know the hassles this can cause);

- offer good quality neighbouring homes (if your renovated project is the only decent looking property in your street, it will struggle to sell);

- do not have any adverse property features, such as a steep driveway or a home that is below street level.

As a renovator, the perfect scenario for your property is to have as fewer buyer objections (negative aspects associated with a property) as possible. The less buyer objections, the greater chance you have of reeling in a buyer at the end of your renovation project.

So now let's look briefly at how you add value to a property and unlock potential. If you've done your homework on steps one, two and three, you should already know the types of property that are in demand in your suburbs. The rest is therefore simple: buy a property that can be renovated to fulfil the shortage of stock in your local market (i.e. demand). Think of your renovations like a normal business product. Failing to get the buyer/product connection right will mean your renovated property may sit and sit on the market, desperately awaiting an offer from somebody. After failing to sell, you'll be desperate to get an offer from anybody so invest time in my first three steps to get this part of the renovation equation right.

UNLOCKING POTENTIAL IN COSMETIC RENOVATIONS

Cosmetic renovations still need to address the issue of supply and demand in your area. There is no point buying and renovating a two-bedroom home if the other homes in your area typically have four bedrooms. The key to unlocking potential and adding value in cosmetic renovations is to lift the condition and quality of the property, raising it to at least equivalent standard of other high priced homes in your area in the shortest time possible.

With cosmetic renovations you need to think creatively about how you can create the perception of higher value for a low actual cost. There are hundreds of ways to do this which I teach in my three-day workshops. Whenever I do a cosmetic renovation, I initially look for effective ways to enhance the property by studying the internal and external floor plan.

(Semi to the right): One of my early cosmetic renovations. Nothing more than a lick of paint inside and out, ripping up the carpets and sanding the floors. It brought me a modest net profit of $23,000 for just three days' work.

What to look for when analysing an internal floor plan

- Can I significantly beautify the property internally?

- Can I make it look new internally?

- Can I give the property a boutique feel?

- Can I add any items, fixtures or fittings to the property to increase perceived quality?

- Can I make the internal space unique in any way?

- Is the kitchen close to the family and dining rooms?

- Can walls be easily removed to create more open family areas?

- Can small family/living rooms be increased in size by removing unwanted rooms?

- Can I open up rooms to make them seem larger and more appealing?

- Can I squeeze an extra bedroom in the floor plan without sacrificing the quality of other areas?

- Can I reduce a larger area into two smaller, higher value areas by adding a party wall in?

- Can I get whatever the property is missing into the space somehow?

- Can I add features that help to better define rooms?

- Can I re-design and enhance existing features?

- Does the house have an entry/foyer/hallway of some form? If not, can this be added?

- Is there enough light in the house? If not, can this be rectified by skylights or other means?

- Does the property have adequate ventilation? If not, can this be rectified?

- Can I upgrade fixtures and fittings to improve perceived quality?

- Can I give the house strong owner-occupier appeal?

- Can I add any special features to the property that will emotionally draw people to it?

- What value adds can I include to maximise the price?

An extra bedroom is easily created in one of my renovations simply by bricking in the existing wall arch. An additional bedroom in my area can add $200,000 to $400,000 in added value to a property, especially in inner city suburbs where space is at a premium.

This is one of my recent structural renovation projects. Unrenovated for over 60 years, this property has fantastic bones that make it ideal for cosmetic or structural renovation. At the rear of the property is an old barn that was approved for business use over 40 years ago. Most buyers would not have realised this approval was still in place. I undertook a cosmetic renovation to the particular area shown in the photo and have converted it into a 10-person home-based office, adding significant value to the property at minimal cost. If you think outside the square, cosmetic renovations can pull huge profits by utilising rooms well.

What to look for when analysing the external footprint

- Can I significantly beautify the property externally?

- Is there good access to the front of the property?

- Is there good access to the rear of the property?

- Can I easily install a carport to increase value?

- Can existing carports be cosmetically rejuvenated by becoming enclosed?

- Can outdoor entertaining areas be easily created?

- Can an outdoor kitchen/BBQ area be easily installed?

- Can fencing be installed to define boundaries and provide security?

- Can pathways be added in critical points where needed?

- Can planting be added to boost the kerb appeal of the property?

- Can outdoor storage areas be included?

- Can anything be done with the roof to make it look new?

- Can any external features be added that strike an emotional chord with buyers?

- Can I add bulk and scale to the property to increase perceived value?

This renovation shows how a property can have substantial value added to it through simple property enhancements, in this case, paint, render, new roof sheets, tiling, plants and a new picket fence.

The crucial thing to remember is that you want to add more in perceived value than the improvements cost. Don't spend $3,000 on new carpet that only adds $2,500 in value. Instead you're better off to spend $3,000 ripping up and polishing the floorboards, which are likely to add more than $5,000 in value to the property. Can you see how one decision results in a profit, while the other incurs a loss? By planning ahead, before you start your renovation, you'll eliminate costly errors of judgment during the actual process.

With cosmetic renovations, things that can't be seen tend not to add value. Of course, there are exceptions and you need to know when to spend money on hidden things that will contribute positively to the value of a property. For instance, installing new insulation batts in the roof cavity won't have the same perceived value as a house that's been completely rewired.

With cosmetic renovations, always aim to give the internal space a designer look at the least possible cost, regardless of the property's value. Use items that look expensive but don't actually cost very much. Today there are lots of fake clones of luxury items, all designed to give your cosmetic renovation the illusion of quality. Tiles are a great example. Real travertine tiles cost, on average, $150 m^2. Fake travertine tiles that look virtually identical can be picked up for about $40 m^2. It's a great example of how you can get a champagne look on a beer budget.

Cosmetically, it's best to invest your money in the two rooms of the property that add the biggest value: kitchens and bathrooms. Kitchens sell houses so make sure this room is always perfect from top to bottom. Doing so is the easiest way to lure in emotional buyers. The main aim with bathrooms is to make them look bigger, brighter and better than before. Add features and inexpensive decorative elements into the property that notch up the "wow" factor.

As a renovator, always keep your underlying focus on the numbers so you don't overcapitalise. Keep reminding yourself that *profit* is the sole reason you're spending your weekends painting and not sipping daiquiris by the pool with your friends.

UNLOCKING POTENTIAL IN STRUCTURAL RENOVATIONS

Make no mistake, structural renovations can be intense. Of course it depends on what degree you go to but, generally speaking, the more work that needs to be done, the more profit is up for grabs. It goes both ways, though. Not knowing what you're doing with structural renovations can cause you to burn money faster than a socialite on a shopping spree.

Unlike cosmetic renovations, structural renovations give you the ability to substantially change, reconfigure and add new space to an existing property. Buying under-utilised dumps and maximising their value allows you to create phenomenal financial gains between the price you buy the property for and its resale price. The tricky part is being able to control your costs so you pull a profit at the end of it all.

Another one of my structural renovations. This small two-bedroom workman's cottage was transformed into a four-bedroom family home with a study. It retained the original character of the cottage but now has a modern new rear wing. I netted a $560,000 profit margin via a four-month structural renovation.

With structural renovations, your ability to identify true potential is slightly more difficult. You may need to enlist some help for your first few projects (such as an architect or town planner) until you start to figure out how far you can go with alterations and additions to older style properties in your area. Local councils control the extent of development in your area so a basic knowledge of controls – such as floor to space ratios, building setbacks and height limits – will help you quickly identify which properties have the potential for additional rooms and floor space.

With structural renovations, the best ways to add significant value are by:

- relocating rooms to improve functionality within the property;
- adding rooms to make the property larger in size;
- adding rooms that meet a need, such as a garage;
- opening up areas to create open plan living;
- making rooms larger to better accommodate the occupants of the home.

Always design with the end buyer in mind, not to your own taste. Aim to appeal to the majority of the market, not the minority. Choose neutral colours with simple clean lines to make the most of the space and resist the urge to paint rooms in different colours. You want your renovated property to look like there's been thought put into it to give it an integrated look throughout. Select materials that are timeless and won't date, ones that will add positively to the value rather than detract from it.

TOP VALUE ADDS

Always remember that the basic premise of renovating is to make a property look new again and, in doing this, add more in perceived value than actual cost. But what does this mean exactly? Put quite simply, it's all about return on investment. As a general rule of thumb, aim as a minimum to at least double, ideally triple, your investment for every dollar you spend. This means for every dollar you spend on your renovation, it must return you two dollars at a minimum and ideally three dollars or more for that change to be worthwhile.

PERCEIVED VALUE

FORMULA	PERCEIVED VALUE = ACTUAL COST x3

In renovating terms, perceived value means the dollar worth that a physical property change has in the mind of the property owner or buyer. Actual cost is the physical amount of money spent making the change. The amount of perceived value that you add to a property will also depend on a number of other factors including the actual value of the property to begin with (low, medium or high-value property), the location of the property, the demographic requirements of the owner or buyer in a suburb, the type of changes made and the quality of the workmanship alike.

I hear you saying: "Well, all of this sounds great but what are some of the big changes I can make to a property that add the most value and what should I spend, where?" In my Renovating For Profit workshops, I have and teach 100-plus ways to add value to a property and the general formulas of what to spend in each area. In this chapter, I'll share 10 strategies you can use to manufacture price growth in a property that continue to deliver a high rate of return, time after time.

STRATEGY ONE: PAINTING

Nothing transforms a home like a lick of paint in fresh modern colours. Paint is my number one way to add value to a property of any budget and continues to be one of the easiest, fastest and highest value drivers of a property today. According to 3D Inspiration paint stores, the average cost to have a standard three-bedroom family home professionally painted is $3,500 internally and $4,500 for the external works. If your budget doesn't extend that far, you can do it yourself for approximately $1,600 for the internal and external works. This investment alone can net you a return in the tens of thousands of dollars provided you choose the right colours that are modern and won't date quickly. Get the colour scheme wrong and your return on investment can drop significantly. Most of the big brand paint companies offer colour consultant services and, for the small fee involved, is a worthwhile investment for many people to get it right.

3 BONUS LIVE EVENT TICKETS AT www.TGRProperty.com.au/NEWPROP

STRATEGY TWO: CEMENT RENDER YOUR PROPERTY

One of the easiest and fastest ways to boost your equity in a property is through the application of cement render (a mix of sand and cement applied to the external brick façade and walls of a property). Property owners dealing with older style red or blond brick houses can instantly modernise their property within days through cement render alone. With average render costs between \$35 m² to \$50 m² for a single level home, the investment in this simple cosmetic change can net you phenomenal returns in the league of up to a \$10 return for every \$1 invested. Cement render is also ideal for timber or plastic clad homes where the cladding is removed, blue board is installed and render applied straight over the top. This enables a property owner to have a property perceived to be of a brick-like, more solid construction than traditional cladding and therefore perceived to be of a substantially higher property value.

STRATEGY THREE: ADD A BEDROOM

If space allows, adding an extra bedroom is a significant way to boost a property's value. Adding an extra bedroom can cost on average \$50,000 to \$80,000 (depending on other variables such as location, site topography etc.) but can have massive financial upside. In my target suburb of Balmain (Sydney's inner city west area), the price difference between a three to four-bedroom home is in the range of two to four hundred thousand dollars. Properties are typically valued by two primary means - land size and the number of bedrooms. As a renovator, you can't change the land size but you do have the ability to increase the number of bedrooms in a property for massive financial gain. The price jump difference and the market appeal of a property with more bedrooms is therefore significant. Saying that, never compromise the quality of other important rooms such as your living rooms in order to squeeze that extra bedroom in. A property that was formerly a three-bedroom home with an average sized loungeroom will not have significant value added to it once it becomes a four-bedroom, small loungeroom home.

STRATEGY FOUR: UPDATE YOUR KITCHEN

In terms of adding value, no other room in your property compares to that of your kitchen. This area is the engine room, the pivotal hub of a property, and will single handily add the biggest value to your property. Your kitchen can make or break a sale so don't be afraid to invest money in this area to ensure a high return on investment but do so in a way that your new kitchen meets the expectations of your local market and not go significantly beyond that. As a general rule of thumb, two per cent of your current property value is your total kitchen budget and that includes everything, all of your materials, fixtures and trade labour to see this room transformed from start to finish. Therefore, a property with a current day value of $500,000, should have a kitchen renovation budget of $10,000. Any dollar you spend over this amount means one thing – you're at risk of overcapitalising and diminishing your return on investment.

The key to adding value through the installation of a new kitchen or remodelling an existing one is to increase the bulk and scale of the kitchen so it appears larger and of more substantial quality. Opt for a modern style that appeals to the majority not the minority of people and won't date quickly, and install decent fixtures and fittings relevant to your local market. It's easy to get carried away with all the latest bells and whistles (especially appliances) for kitchens today so exercise common sense and keep your underlying focus on your return on investment. The average cost of installing a fully finished kitchen today is in the range of $7,500 to $20,000 depending on a number of variables (size of the kitchen, type of surfaces chosen, brand of appliances used etc.) but the investment should pay handsome dividends to the effect of at least a three dollar return for every dollar invested.

Before   *After*

STRATEGY FIVE: UPDATE YOUR BATHROOM

Bathrooms are the second most important room in a property and, renovated well, significantly improve the value of a property. A tired, outdated bathroom negatively detracts from your property value. Always aspire to have a bathroom located on the same level and in close proximity to your bedrooms. Aim to spend 1.5 per cent of your current property value to completely upgrade an existing bathroom. A property valued at $500,000, should technically have a bathroom renovation budget of $7,500 per bathroom to cover all material and labour costs associated with renovating this area.

Simple, cost-effective changes that continue to yield massive value include respraying all the tiles and fixtures and fittings within a bathroom which can be done in a day or less for under $3,000 typically. This is a great low-cost option if you're dealing with a bathroom that structurally has great bones but is in dire need of a cosmetic facelift. If tile respraying is not an option, other affordable value adds include updating the fixtures such as bathtub, vanity, basins, toilet, taps and shower screen. Changing the tiles on your walls and floor also delivers massive bang for your buck. Low cost, modern tiles are readily available these days from $20 m^2 and instantly modernise bathrooms for instant financial gain. And here's a hot tip for you: large format tiles (300mm x 600mm or greater) look more expensive than smaller tiles too. They don't cost any extra to buy but have the perceived value of being of higher quality.

One of my low budget bathroom renos. This was a cosmetic renovation on a $320,000 property in Sydney's outer west with the total bathroom budget being $5,250 all inclusive.

STRATEGY SIX: UPDATE THE FRONT FAÇADE

Your front façade is often the first thing buyers see on your property. The saying "first impressions count" is a significant quotation for any property owner. Improvements made to this area of a property can yield massive returns in more ways than one - higher property value, buyer confidence in the property and the ability to sell or rent your property quicker.

Take great comfort knowing that improvements made to your front façade can be done at low cost and relatively low skill level with many tasks within the capability of budding DIY-ers. Have your house washed, clean or recolour your roof, paving paint driveways and pathways, paint your front façade, improve the gardens, fix wonky gates, install a new front door, add a letterbox and dress up a property through low-cost decorative features such as timber finials and fretwork to add bulk and scale to your property. These are big value adds at relatively low expense. An external makeover can cost anywhere from $2,000 to tens of thousands of dollars depending on the extent of work done but will net you far more than that if done correctly and in a way that the property contributes positively to the overall streetscape.

Aim to buy property that has (or has the potential to) contribute positively to your streetscape.

STRATEGY SEVEN: REMOVE INTERNAL WALLS TO CREATE OPEN PLAN LIVING

Architectural planning over the last 50 years saw a lot of older style homes have segregated areas. Renovated homes that have open plan communal areas (kitchen, dining and living rooms) continue to attract widespread demand that positively lifts property values. Removing walls of a non-load bearing nature can be done with very little cost involved. Structural walls that support the roof (load bearing walls) will cost significantly more to take out (average range $3,000 to $10,000 depending on the length of the walls to be removed) but will return a proportionally larger increase in value. Removing walls within a property achieves one thing – it opens up smaller rooms and makes these areas look and feel bigger than before and that is perceived to really add a lot of value to a property.

STRATEGY EIGHT: CREATE AN OUTDOOR ENTERTAINING AREA

Australians love entertaining (think BBQs and pool parties) so it shouldn't surprise you that outdoor entertaining areas that can be used all year round add real value to a property. Gone are the days of the awful, ill-planned extension on the back of a home. Today, outdoor entertaining areas lead off the indoor living areas and have become social hubs that foster relationships with family and friends, and help people relax. They're an area of a property that adds real value simply because of the emotional connection associated with these rooms.

The key is to match your new outdoor entertaining area in with the existing style of your property. Consider how you will use the area (i.e. casual dining or more formal do's) and the flow of traffic between rooms to ensure a seamless transition from the indoors to the outdoors. Try and also work with what you've already got to minimise costs and what items you want included in this area. The addition of an outdoor entertaining area can range from $10,000 to $50,000 depending on the extent of work done but can make a big difference to the value of a property simply by extending the square footage of a property seamlessly from the indoors to the outdoors.

*Australians love outdoor entertaining and don't mind
paying for it when buying a property.*

STRATEGY NINE: ADD A GRANNY FLAT

Phenomenal value can be added to a property (regardless of
where the property is located) simply through the addition of a
stand-alone granny flat strategically positioned in the rear yard
of a property. Granny flats add a unique point of difference to a
property and can be installed to suit a wide range of needs. Today
they are used as dedicated areas for the ever growing needs of a
home office where more people work from the office three days
a week and from home the other two. The separation from this
space away from the main family residence means that personal
privacy is not comprised and a professional working image is
upheld. Granny flats are also the answer for many couples who
rely on relatives or the in-laws to mind their kids while both
holding full-time jobs to combat the growing expenses of living.
Most working couples want their own personal privacy so look
for ways to keep the minders at a convenient arms reach when

needed yet far enough to not intrude on their own personal privacy. The addition of a granny flat solves that dilemma. And let's not forget the ability to convert this space into a separate retreat for older kids to keep them at home within eyesight of parents, or as a guest retreat which technically increases the number of bedrooms in a property and therefore adds significant value or the ability to rent this space out as an income producing asset which can pay for itself within the first few years.

One thing is for sure: granny flats are back in fashion and an endless array of modern, low budget flat pack options right through to premium, snazzy designer versions can be found on the market today. Flat packs start from as low as $30,000 to buy and require council approval and the services of a builder or licenced carpenter to erect within a week or two. Fully finished, the costs are likely to be in the range of $50,000 to $100,000 depending on the size and style chosen but can result in hundreds of thousands of dollars being added to a property depending on the location. The addition of a granny flat can be the one thing that sets your property out against the rest and will result in a more saleable product that sells quicker than other conventional properties on the market.

Granny flats are back in fashion and add phenomenal value to a property depending on what suburb you're in.
Image courtesy of www.grannyflatsaustralia.com.au

STRATEGY TEN: IMPROVE THE LANDSCAPING

The great Australian dream is to have a big backyard yet it is often the most neglected area of a property. Landscaping is really important and frames a property front and back. For the front of a property, simple, low budget cosmetic changes such as installing garden beds, adding plants, bark, pebbles or mulch, installing grass and paving painting tired old driveways can radically improve the visual kerb appeal of a property and hence add value to a property. A well maintained garden shows pride in a property and that speaks volumes alone. At the rear, it's about creating larger open span lawn spaces that allow adults and kids to move freely around, and to provide privacy and shading wherever possible. Works to a rear yard should be to cut back and reduce unruly trees and foliage, install perimeter garden beds and plants, relocate the iconic Hills Hoist to a visually less obvious position and correct irregular fencing where needed.

Adding value to a property through a cosmetic or structural renovation is a real way to rapidly boost your equity in a property. There are a plethora of other changes that positively lift the value of a property to suit all budgets, large and small. Use some of my simple formulas and general rules of thumb to keep your budget in check and remember that changes that emotionally appeal to your intended audience/ultimate buyer will net you a high return on investment. Changes that miss this mark will deliver a negative return that results in overcapitalisation. No matter how much or how little you change a property, changes must be highly visible in order for someone to see a real difference in the before and after status of the property. Always remember your aim when renovating is to get the biggest bang for your buck at the least cost possible.

YOUR FINANCIAL FEASIBILITY

So you've found a property that you think may have great renovation potential. But how do you really know, beyond your own gut instinct, if a great profit can be made? It all comes down to your financial feasibility.

A financial feasibility is your ability to estimate costs, as close to reality as possible, so you can determine whether a project is justified from an economic point of view. It's a process that gives renovators the ability to make clear business-based decisions as to whether they should commit funds, resources, time and effort to potential renovation projects. Using this, renovators are able to see the total cost of not only buying the property but also holding and renovating it as well.

Estimating costs is a fine art and, speaking frankly, your first financial feasibility may not be worth the paper it's written on. Rest assured, though, the more projects you do, the more your financial feasibilities will become increasingly accurate. If you're unsure of costs you should use sensible guestimates (a cross between a guess and an estimate) or, better still, get real quotes if time allows or engage a quantity surveyor to do it for you. Even to this day, I still walk from room to room with a clipboard in hand to visually inspect a property and record everything that needs work done to it. I then make allowances for all of these things in my financial feasibility. Remember, all of this happens *before* you buy.

Always resist the urge to buy a property for which you haven't done a financial feasibility. It's the only true test to determine if you can turn a profit from the project. Don't be in a position where you renovate for months on end, only to find out you haven't made a profit or, worse still, have lost money. Constant number crunching is a habit that's shared by all successful renovators and property investors.

Renovators can easily produce their own financial feasibilities. Microsoft Excel is great for creating your own financial spreadsheets quickly and easily or you can buy renovation feasibility software from me. Smart renovators do a preliminary feasibility either in their head or on a piece of paper, using quick calculations. This is often called a "back of the envelope" calculation. If the preliminary calculations look good, a more detailed feasibility, generally using software, will follow.

When I look back on the financial feasibilities I did for my first few renovations, it seems a miracle I made any profit at all. My initial feasibilities were just 20 vague lines, with broad assumptions as to the costs. Oh, how I have evolved. The financial feasibility I use today is almost 3,000 lines long which I've personally developed over the last 12 years. It's impossible for me to ever forget a cost again. Now when I sit down to crunch numbers on any new deal I'm considering, it's a fairly easy task, without the risk of me forgetting anything.

The good news is that there is no right or wrong way of actually doing a financial feasibility. Generally speaking, renovators use a cost versus profit formula to calculate their anticipated selling price, or else they work back from that sales price and use what is called the Residual Land Value Method to determine what they can afford to pay for the property. Either way, the key pieces of information you need in your financial feasibility are revenue details (income you expect to receive from the sale of the property) less the expense details (acquisition, finance, holding, professional, construction, resale, miscellaneous and tax costs). The financial summary section of your feasibility will tell you if the project is considered financially viable, which will allow you to decide whether or not to buy the property. Remember, it's all about the profit. Never get emotional about the deal. If the numbers stack up, do the deal. If they don't, stay at home and watch Oprah.

Saying all of this, keep in mind though, that your financial feasibility is only as good as the accuracy of the information contained within it. If you're unsure of costs, check the cost assumptions with appropriately qualified people such as a quantity surveyor, your suppliers or tradespeople. Also, don't forget to factor in any taxes that may be applicable to your renovation project (GST, Capital Gains Tax and so on). Taxes can be significant and can wipe out your renovation profit in one fell swoop, so be aware of these costs before you buy.

CONCLUSION

Phew! Profitable renovating may be a little more involved than what you may have first thought. Like anything, your first renovation project will be a huge learning experience. Just remember, there are always solutions to your renovating problems. And rest assured, the more renovation projects you do, the easier it all becomes. Practice truly does make perfect. Learn from each project by reflecting on what you did well and what you could have done better, then take that knowledge and use it to make your next renovation project even better.

I'm honest enough to admit that renovating can be hard work, depending on how much or how little you want to be involved in your projects. I now choose to do only two structural renovations per year. I work eight to ten months of the year and take a month or two off at the end of every project. In effect, I'm on holiday for a significantly longer period than most people in salaried jobs. I'm working less hours and earning an exponentially higher income than salaried employees. Working smarter not harder, right? The reality is that my hard work is rewarded with huge renovation profits, the ability to be my own boss, extended holiday periods and free holidays overseas (from all the credit card points earned during my renovations). Renovating can give you a fabulous lifestyle but it's certainly not a free road to wealth. It requires effort.

I am so grateful and blessed to be a professional renovator. My profession alone improved every aspect of my life. I get to choose when I work and for how long. I get to be involved in something I truly love, rather than trudging every day into a job that I hate. I have the ability to share my wealth with family, friends and other random people who I feel compelled to help. I can jet off to my favourite city in the world (New York) wherever I want to or I can keep it real and simply take the day off work to play Lego® with my small daughter. Very few other jobs will ever give you the ability to do that.

Additionally, for me, there is nothing more fulfilling than standing on the street in front of your completed project, in awe of the amazing transformation that's just taken place. I've bought someone's ugly old house and created a beautiful home for a family to enjoy for years to come. It's a level of personal satisfaction that can't be described. And remember, as a renovator, it's important to create properties that make a positive contribution to the street and community you're in. Always try and do the right thing and don't negatively impact the lives of others in favour of greed. Be proud of your renovation projects and how you build your wealth. Others will notice and have more respect for you. They'll be keener to be involved with you on your next project.

Finally, to recap, my renovating success has come down to my precise ability to:

1) Know what types of homes are in short supply

2) Buy properties that can satisfy the market need

3) Renovate the property beyond buyers' emotional expectations.

Truly, anyone can be successful in property renovations. You don't need to be super intelligent or great on the tools. Renovation doesn't discriminate between male or female. In fact, more and more smart women are jumping on the renovation band wagon these days and capitalising on the male-dominated construction industry. Women have natural skills that men just can't match, which work perfectly with renovations. Regardless of whether you have a lot of money or none at all, renovating can build wealth for you – fast.

Make sure you celebrate your successes and reward yourself appropriately. Good luck, may the force – trade force that is – be with you!

Chapter 3

WEALTH-BUILDING PROPERTIES

"Profits are better than wages."

SAM SAGGERS

SAM SAGGERS

Sam Saggers is the CEO of Positive Real Estate, a leading buyer's agency and property education company. A licensed real estate agent in every state of Australia, Sam has personally brokered more than 2,000 property deals in his 19-year career.

Sam and fellow co-founder, Jason Whitton, established Positive Real Estate in 2003 to provide services for the thousands of Australian investors who lacked either the time or the expertise to locate, negotiate and purchase residential investment property. In 2010 alone, the company negotiated more than $250 million in properties on behalf of clients.

Positive Real Estate now employs more than 50 staff and has offices in Sydney, Brisbane, Melbourne, Perth, Adelaide and the Gold Coast as part of its growing franchise network.

Sam is often featured in *Your Investment Property* and *Australian Property Investor* magazines and many of Australia's top CEO's, as listed in *Business Review Weekly's* Rich 200, often seek out his investment advice. Sam is also the author of two books.

Sam and his team have a strong focus on giving back to their selected charity, Room to Read, whose mission is to educate the world's poorest children. In 2011, Positive Real Estate raised $82,000 to build schools in Sri Lanka, Nepal and Laos.

WEALTH-BUILDING PROPERTIES

THE KEY FUNDAMENTALS TO MAKE EVERY PROPERTY IN YOUR PORTFOLIO ALWAYS PROFITABLE

Buying an investment property is a business decision, so it's important you treat real estate with the respect it requires. To maximise your profits it's wise to understand the fundamentals that will help you reach your goal.

At some stage every buyer is likely to suffer what is known as buyer's remorse. Questions pop into every investor's head when they ponder a property purchase. Have I bought well? Did I choose the best location? Will the property perform?

Psychologists would call this "uncertainty" but in property I think of it as a form of "illiteracy".

If more people took the time to understand the answers to these questions and actually schooled themselves in the art of buying property, wealth-creation would be available for everyone to participate in.

In this chapter, I'll share with you some of my guides and checklists for buying cycles, property finance, town planning, house and land packages, mining markets, self-managed super funds and property management.

A LITTLE ABOUT ME

I bought my first property in 1998 at age 23 in an area in which I lived and worked. Having scrupulously saved $30,000, I purchased a two-bedroom unit in Putney, Sydney, for $250,000. At that stage, I had worked in real estate for five years and wanted to make money via investing.

Looking back, that purchase was a dud – and it was all due to my naivety. I obtained the property well after the growth cycle had hit its ceiling and I failed to negotiate well. I got caught up in my own emotions and neglected to conduct research on cashflow and growth potential. I soon discovered I was out of my depth and that I certainly wasn't the "unit area expert" I had built myself up to be.

Although I suffered a huge loss it did not dampen my passion for future investing. I did not see this experience as negative and it did not cause me to refrain out of fear. In fact, it triggered the opposite response. I now had the benefit of a personal investing experience – and it has impacted every investing decision I have made since.

I grew up at the lower end of the middle classes but was exposed to very rich people who had made money through real estate. My family worked seven days a week at Paddy's Market so I could attend a private school with very wealthy kids.

I owed it to my parents to adapt and learn from the rich. The rich kids and their parents influenced me to invest. They knew I was from a poorer background and would teach me and show me what they had done; they would take me to properties they had bought and talk about investment around me.

My wealthy friends became my mentors and I was like a sponge

- thirsty to learn from those willing to teach. Now I hope to do the same for you.

"PROFITS ARE BETTER THAN WAGES"

One of my key phrases is: "Profits are better than wages." The moment I understood this piece of philosophy I became rich within the first seven years of my economic life. Here's the other key phrase that goes with it: "Anyone can buy a piece of real estate, but not everyone can buy a piece of real estate and make a profit."

If you fully accept that profits are better than wages it will serve you well for a life time. I wish somebody had taught it to me at school but I went for 12 years without hearing it once. It wasn't even mentioned at the real estate college I went to for a year and a half.

The goal of property investors in the market is to target optimistic returns. Understand that companies, banks and institutions are all hunting profits and that they're all hunting in the same safari park as you, called the Australian property market.

Of course, to learn how to create your own profits comes with time and experience. I can give you the benefit of my experience but you'll have to put your own time into it.

THE EIGHT FUNDAMENTALS OF PROPERTY INVESTMENT

1) **Understand emotions** - The market place is made up of many emotions. The moment you let them enter your thought process when buying investment property, you spoil the deal. Don't taint the art of deal-making with your own personal tastes. Property should be bought on the numbers and nothing more. If it "stacks up" and is feasible then

it should be considered. If you truly start to understand the market and comprehend its psychology you can make fabulous money. Most people buy when the market is "thrilled" or "euphoric", when the market has risen as much as it's going to and the chance to make massive profits has already passed. You can make more money in "panicking" or "capitulated" markets, where there are a lot of cheap properties for sale. This is a good spot for another key phrase, this one from Warren Buffet: "Show fear when everyone else shows courage and show courage when everyone else shows fear."

2) **Cash on cash returns** - When buying real estate, you need to find a deposit, which usually isn't provided by a bank or lender and generally has to come from your own savings. The deposit, anywhere between five and 30 per cent, is, essentially, your capital. The formula that's used to measure the likely performance of your deposit is known as cash on cash return. Seasoned investors measure cash on cash returns in 12-month increments. For example, if you were to put $30,000 into a property and achieve growth over 12 months to gain a further $30,000, this is considered to be 100 per cent cash on cash return. It allows you to secure and retain your asset but still have a readily available deposit to fund a new investment. Never buy a property as an investment if you cannot get 100 per cent of your capital returned within 12 to 18 months.

3) **Where to invest** - The words location, location, location seem to echo throughout the Australian property market. Beachside and waterside real estate, as well as those within a 10-kilometre radius of the CBD or major business centre, tend to be considered blue chip choices and over time have outperformed most other types of property within the

market. Not everybody can afford a waterfront investment, though, so you need to learn about secondary markets as well. For years I've made money in secondary markets and transferred the profits to more qualified localities. Within any market, primary or secondary, there are indicators of the market's ability to perform. Understand the market drivers, become familiar with them and you will be able to forecast which areas will grow or trough. Whether it's from a suburb to a town or a city to a state, the same key market drivers exist. The drivers are: population growth, economics, demographics, infrastructure, yield variation and supply and demand.

4) **When to invest** - "After expansion comes contraction but after contraction comes expansion." This is a simple thought but it can have a huge impact on what you do and a massive influence on when you should buy. Understand that 80 per cent of the market buys when the market is more than halfway through expansion, which is when I would sell rather than buy. You can make money no matter what the market is doing but investors will always make more by running counter to the cycle. Aim to buy at a discount when the property market is contracting and revalue the property when the market is expanding. Remember, profits are better than wages so buy low and sell high.

5) **The strategies** – The five residential strategies are: discount, renovation, strata subdivision, subdivision and off-the-plan. I'll discuss these in more detail later when I discuss property strategies and buying cycles.

6) **Patience is a virtue** - Creating a deal that, as we say in the industry, "stacks up" takes endurance and commitments so don't rush into anything. Most real estate is sold in the

market to illiterate buyers who are impatient, emotional and who consider themselves too time-poor to show persistence. The average buyer sees 10 properties and then purchases one based on their personal tastes. I, on the other hand, will make offers on over 30 properties subject to further and better due diligence. I'll then consider counter-offers, make counter-offers of my own and then put a target property under contract with the pre-negotiated due diligence terms and conditions. The more offers you have out there, the higher your chance of finding a better deal.

7) **Due diligence** - It amazes me how many purchasers buy a property after inspecting it themselves, without performing proper due diligence such as employing the services of a valuer, building inspector, pest inspector and surveyor. It's pretty simple: unless you are qualified in these trades, you should not buy property until you have had experts analyse it. Think of it as buying intelligence, as it can tell you things you would otherwise never suspect. For me this is the final step; if all the boxes are ticked, I opt to purchase.

8) **Assemble a team** - Investment, if done alone, is a very tough struggle for success. Striking out on your own is a selfish and antiquated way to do business. Instead surround yourself with family and close friends who can support you as you move through your journey to financial success, as well as a team of professionals who can guide your feet as you take each step. Among the people whose services you will need are conveyances, finance brokers, buyer's advocates, solicitors, accountants and depreciation experts, to name but a few.

Now that you know the eight property investing fundamentals, let's look at some of my specific guides for sourcing profitable property opportunities.

GUIDE TO PROPERTY STRATEGIES AND BUYING CYCLES

To succeed as a property investor you need the right materials, tools and most importantly, a plan. The following quote often comes to mind when considering different plans:

"If you fail to plan, you plan to fail."
Unknown

As an investor you have to have a plan that leaves no bases uncovered that would potentially cause issues in the future. I often meet people who have done just about every education seminar that's been offered in Australia. They will explain that they have continuously researched many groups and philosophies yet when questioned whether they have taken action or followed any new steps following these seminars, the answer is a resounding "No!" In real estate it's called analysis paralysis. Creating a plan will be the first step that helps you move forward because it will serve as a road map. You can be the most educated individual on real estate, but without action, that education is futile.

A solid plan will allow you to go through the three phases of investing successfully. Managing real estate risk can be simple once you follow these phases: acquisition, consolidation and legacy, and then buy the appropriate style of property dependent upon which phase you are currently in. The first phase we enter is known as acquisition, during which we accumulate a property. After getting this property it becomes a little bit easier to pick the next one and then the one after that. If you have less than five properties right now, you are in the acquisition phase of your investment journey!

PHASE ONE: ACQUISITION

The first step is creating what I call an "automatic acquisition plan". When I first started in real estate, my acquisition plan focused on acquiring one property per year, with the aim of having 10 properties in 10 years. It's like going to the dentist - you create a reminder in your calendar to call your dentist for a check-up, but this time you do it for property! This will allow you to be consistent and consistency allows us to ensure our goals become a reality.

So what happens when you buy one property a year for the next 10 years? You end up with a multi-million dollar portfolio. That doesn't sound too bad, does it? Let's work with the numbers. The median investment property price Australia-wide is $250,000 and the average yield is seven per cent. We are searching for an average of 10 per cent per annum growth, which is the one hundred year average according to the Australian Bureau of Statistics. In 10 years, you have $3.6 million worth of property, $1.6 million worth of equity at a 60 per cent loan-to-value ratio (LVR) and a solid cashflow position. The graph below shows how the process above works.

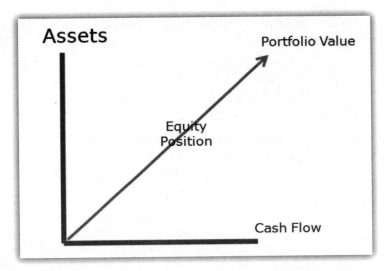

The automatic acquisition plan creates wealth and I endorse three main strategies in this phase of an investor's career: off-the-plan, renovation and growth property/discount property.

Off-the-plan – This strategy involves entering into a contract to buy a property that is not yet built. It exists because of a need to eliminate a debt risk to those involved. Developers and builders are required to provide their bank with pre-sales in their development prior to receiving funding; only then will the bank provide the developer with money for construction. Therefore, off-the-plan purchases provide a guarantee to the bank, ensuring that the market will buy out their risk, making their transaction less of a gamble.

Investors then utilise this strategy to create equity by using the market and time to add value. I stand firmly behind off-the-plan deals because they can give you great leverage for a small amount of money as a deposit.

Below is a checklist for purchasing off-the-plan and to ensure that the transition from plan to product is a smooth one:

- understand the market cycle for future growth. Do this by considering the six market drivers (population, economics, demographics, infrastructure, yield variation and supply and demand);

- choose low-density, boutique properties. Banks often don't like high-density buildings, making it harder to receive a loan. You can also see greater profits in buildings with less than 40 units;

- always buy in stage one of a development because it will be at the best price. Never consider any other stage. Developers withhold further stage releases in order to make additional profits and sell the properties at a high rate of return;

- buy a property at least 18 months off-the-plan, which will allow the property price to increase and, with just a deposit down, you should secure 100 per cent cash on cash return;

- always have the "plan" valued at the commencement of the contract process. You need to buy at the plan's value at the beginning and not the value at the end. Valuers call this method "valuation summation," which involves the cost of land and the building;

- don't get in over your head. Buy properties under $600,000 as they appeal to the entire market should you be required to sell;

- always plan to settle. Never buy to sell midway through the project's construction. You should always confirm your borrowing capacity first before entering into an off-the-plan contract.

Renovations - Adding value to a property by carrying out some basic renovations can help many investors increase their profits on a shoestring budget. Painting a feature wall, replacing carpet, adding new blinds and manicuring lawns should be considered as initial renovations. The unwritten rule for renovations states the following: if your property manager, project manager or you cannot co-ordinate the renovation within three months, then it's possible you may overcapitalise. I'm not a fan of massive renovations because they can often turn into a form of developing and I like strategies that I can handle remotely or quickly.

Below is a renovation checklist and some ideas to consider when renovating a property:

- understand the market cycle for future growth by considering the six market drivers;

- buy well and secure property at a discount;

- invest in rentable suburbs and towns where rents can increase;

- for every $1 you spend, make sure you gain $3 back, so know your costings;

- grasp the cash on cash principle and forecast a deposit recycle timeline.

TOP 10 RENOVATION IDEAS

1) Replace front door and make sure the new door has a warm paint colour.

2) Basic landscaping.

3) Replace carpet for polish timber floors.

4) Paint all internal walls and include a feature wall.

5) Resurface the kitchen cupboards and/or replace bench tops and handles.

6) Make windows into external doors and build a small deck for an external living area.

7) Add another wall to divide living spaces and make another bedroom.

8) Make another window into an external door so the property can have a separate entrance to rent separately.

9) Make the laundry into a bathroom, and a linen cupboard into a laundry.

10) Enclose the carport and see if the garage can become a living area.

Growth and discount - Discount properties are often hard to find and require consistent searching. You can generally find a discount property when a seller runs into financial trouble and is willing to sell a property for less than it is worth. Let me give you an example. In late 2009, I brokered a group of townhouse style properties for clients in Roselands, Sydney. Roselands is approximately 11 km from Sydney's CBD and is considered to be an up-and-coming area. The vendor had a few unfavourable dealings and needed a fast sales solution, so rather than offering the properties at $625,000, which was their valuation price, the properties were brokered for $540,000 and were sold quickly. The strategy, discount, offered a potential opportunity of $85,000 in recyclable value to the buyer and $85,000 in losses to the vendor. In September 2010, the properties were revalued at $615,000, a $75,000 gain in 10 months. The market didn't provide this increase; rather, the gain was achieved by buying well and using the discount and growth strategy. Roselands was later featured in St George Bank's Hotspot Area Report and had impressive capital growth rates.

The Roselands Complex – 20 Positive Real Estate mentoring clients made well over $75,000 each!

PHASE TWO: CONSOLIDATION

The second phase of property investing is consolidation. As you create more wealth through acquisitions, you also need to stop and re-evaluate where you are in your life and what has changed since you started investing. The consolidation phase will help you answer whether you should consolidate your position or enter the trading phase of your investment career. Ask yourself these valuable questions:

• What is my current risk profile?

• Is my earning potential at work in any risk of decline?

• How many property cycles can I keep investing for?

SAM SAGGERS

- Do funders see me as high risk because of my age?

- Do I need to risk more capital to reap higher profits?

- If I consolidated today, would that allow me to self-fund my retirement?

If you choose to consolidate or sell your property portfolio, you will create an "automatic consolidation plan". If you still own the 10 properties worth $3.6 million and have $1.6 million in equity, then you can sell them and have over a million dollars for a long and happy self-funded retirement.

If you answer the questions above and you realise that your profile still has some room for growth, then you can start utilising the trading strategies of property investment. This doesn't mean you change the way your portfolio looks; you don't ever remove your buy and hold properties as they are the backbone of your retirement. You will now need to add some properties that you can buy, hold and sell. I endorse two solid and proven strategies that will allow you to trade property; subdivisions and strata titling.

Subdividing - Subdivisions are an add value strategy and involve buying a property with an extra big block of land and dividing that land to either build another house or create a new block of land you can sell.

When looking to purchase a large block of land, the first question you need answered is the minimum size subdivision that the local council requires. If the council requires 400 m² divisions, then look for 1000 m² to subdivide. You may need the extra space for roads and infrastructure such as water, power, phone, gas, etc.

Corner blocks are ideal for subdivisions as two street frontages make the subdivision easier and also prove to be more valuable. Many places in Australia, mainly northern states and country areas, have timber houses built in the middle of big blocks of subdividable land. Investors often move these houses over by 10 metres and then subdivide down the middle. Other subdivisions have a driveway down one side to access the large block of land at the back; this block creation is known as the battleaxe block.

Subdivisions cost more to complete than strata subdivisions as you will have to complete planning requirements, such as driveways, sewers, water, electricity, phone, as well as other council necessities. Only then will you be able to receive a separate title for the land.

Strata titling – This strategy may often be deemed too good to be true and I call it "adding paper value". There are a lot of duplex and triplex blocks of units and townhouses in the market that are still all owned by the one owner and often not strata titled.

Strata titling involves purchasing a property with multiple dwellings that are not yet strata titled and doing the strata title process for oneself. Be sure to check that the council approves strata titling in your chosen investment area. This strategy can produce profits of up to 30 per cent or more.

Let me give you an example of a property where I was able to do a strata title. I found two blocks of six units all on one title in a western Sydney suburb. That's 12 units on one title! The units were on the market for $2,850,000 and I was able to negotiate a discount and secure the property on a six-month settlement with a five per cent deposit at an agreed value of $2,555,000. The purchase price meant that the individual price of the units would be around $208,000 per unit. I thought this was a good buy and my opinion was reaffirmed considering that the units were renting for $320 a week each. I sent in a valuer to conduct a "gross realisation valuation (GRV)", which advises a purchaser of the total value of the property if the strata was approved and one title became 12 titles. The valuer reported the GVR to be $3,585,000.

I then sent a surveyor out to the site to give me a quote on arranging the strata title or development application. The surveyor returned with a figure of $50,000 to complete the strata and informed me that the development application would take about three months to complete. I also decided to renovate the property, which added about $370,000 to my costs. After paying the loan costs and sale fees, I was left with a fair profit from the strata title in less than nine months!

Ultimately I was able to help 12 buyers who, themselves, are going through their acquisition phase of buying real estate in a solid Sydney suburb.

Before renovation and strata titling   *After renovation and strata titling*

PHASE THREE: LEGACY

The final phase of property investing is called legacy and it is vital to leave one. After you become a millionaire, it's not always the money that's important, but rather the person you have become in the process and the legacy you leave thereafter. Your legacy may be to support your children or support a foundation or an institution that is important to you and become a real philanthropist.

At Positive Real Estate our highest purpose is helping underprivileged people worldwide get an education and we do this through a great charity that we are very fond of called Room to Read. So as you acquire wealth, be sure to share it with those that have not had the same opportunities that we have. Consider giving to a program like Room to Read and you will see some of the rewards may be even greater than those you achieved in your real estate career.

Room to Read has already benefited 5.1 million children

GUIDE TO FINANCING PROPERTY

This chapter wouldn't be complete without some educational tips on finance. As we know, property and finance go hand in hand. Here we explore the best type of structures for investment loans.

The major banks control lending for most real estate purchases. This often complicates investing situations and acts as a repellent to investors as a few banks control the liquidity of the market and hence, the amounts that investors will be able to receive through loan to value ratios.

Most banks will lend investors 80 per cent of the value of the property. To receive more funds, investors need to arrange what is known as Lenders Mortgage Insurance (LMI). This paid premium allows investors to gear their proposed loan higher, often up to 95 per cent of the value of the property.

> **LVR** (loan-to-value ratio) – To calculate it, divide the loan amount by the value of the property then multiply by 100 to get a percentage. Banks and financial institutions use this as a measure of whether you can afford the loan.
>
> **LMI** (Lenders Mortgage Insurance) – Usually required by lenders when you're borrowing more that 80 per cent of the property's value. It provides insurance to the lender in case the borrower defaults on the loan.

Banks and mortgage insurers assess risk using the following checklist:

- population of postcode (rule is 10,000 people or more);
- LVR percentage and type of property:
    - house - 80% lend plus LMI = 90%
    - unit - 80% lend plus LMI = 90%
    - commercial - 70% LVR
    - residential vacant land - 80% lend plus LMI = 90%
    - rural vacant land - 70% LVR
    - serviced apartments - 70% LVR
    - seniors lots - 60% LVR
    - hotel rooms - no lending probably
    - student accommodation - no lending probably;

- size of dwelling - must be bigger than 45 m^2;

- density of complex - under 32 in a unit block allows for more flexible lending;

- banks have exposure limits in areas and even complexes. In other words, if they have lent too much in a postcode, they will restrict further involvement;

- lenders' mortgage insurers have exposure limits in areas and even complexes. In other words, if they have lent too much in a postcode, they will restrict further involvement;

- valuation - the valuer's job is to assess risk for the bank.

VALUATIONS CARRY RISK

It is important to note the distinction between the way lenders and the borrowers view valuations. Lenders have effectively outsourced their risk to valuers. If banks are not able to recover their costs on a bad loan, then valuers risk getting sued. When arriving at a valuation, the valuer must take into consideration the terms of their professional indemnity insurance, which is usually valid only when the lender provides finance using a conservative loan to valuation ratio. Bank valuations are not generally based on true market value of a property, but are rather based on the level of risk to the bank.

PERSONAL RISK

Lastly, your lender has to assess your risk and your ability to afford the repayments. As a rule, lenders will look at 30 per cent of your gross income to assess loan repayments. They use a formula known as "debt service repayments (DSR)". Other criteria the banks consider include:

- Age

- Proof of savings

- Stability of employment
- Other securities
- Net worth
- Employed or self-employed
- Rental incomes.

FIVE RULES OF LENDING

1) **Leveraging with someone else's money** - When we purchase a property we generally use around 90 per cent of a bank's money and a small amount of our own. If we look at the market over the past 100 years, the growth per annum has been around 10.40 per cent. If we purchased a property for $350,000, the potential capital growth could be $36,400 per year. What's the average Australian income? $57,000. When we go to work, we exchange time for money, but your property will be generating another income for you as you work elsewhere. There is nothing better than making money as you sleep.

2) **Interest-only loans** - When choosing a loan structure, interest-only loans are the most advisable. The logic behind this is that your interest-only repayment is always going to be lower than a principal and interest repayment and, with the vast majority of home loans, you have the option of making additional repayments at any time without penalty. So with an interest-only loan, you could choose to make the same repayment as if the loan was principal and interest, but you have the option of making a lower repayment should you ever go through a cash shortage. One of the main reasons I choose interest-only loans is that YOU own the additional repayments you have made. In principal and interest loans,

the bank owns all of your money and you are not able to take it back if you ever experience a rainy day.

3) **All monies clause** - Most banks have clauses in their home loan documents that entitle them to review any one of your home loans with them at any time and ask for additional funds. This can happen if the bank believes that the valuation has decreased or that your debt has climbed too high. This clause also entitles them to force you to use any other of your properties as security in order to provide the bank with the additional funds to resecure the loan in question. In other words, all properties are security for all loans. This can severely limit your investing future. The alternative is to use "securitised lenders" because they only use each individual property as security for each home loan. They give your mortgage to a trustee (Perpetual Trust) to uphold the terms of the mortgage and cannot review your LVR or income position at any time and force you to put in additional funds or sell your property if they think you have become a greater risk.

4) **Say no to cross securitisation** - Sophisticated investors who want to grow their portfolio without the risk of the bank reviewing their position every time they buy another property do not cross securitise. This means that you should have a different loan with different lenders for each security that you purchase. It is absolutely necessary that you read your terms and conditions carefully before entering into a contract with your bank. Watch out for the "all securities" clause, which will allow the bank to use one or more of your properties as security. If you don't read the terms and conditions, then you may really be limiting your investment life and you ability to make investments in the future. I met with clients with extensive portfolios who were then unable to refinance as

their current lender refused to release the securities because they felt the client carried too much risk.

5) **Never be negative again** - Why do only three per cent of Australians purchase more than three properties? The answer is cashflow. Most Australians want to generate wealth through property, but their greatest fear is paying for the shortfall. The first thing I say to a client is to create a buffer in case things go awry; say, a financial buffer that would last for at least two years. Don't confuse the buffer for your property as losing money; capital growth should always outweigh what it's costing you to keep the property every year out of your buffer.

GUIDE TO TOWN PLANNING

72-76 Bayswater Road in Potts Point, Sydney, is now a luxury apartment complex. The combined property value is $25 million. My family had owned this piece of land for over 40 years where we operated a bed and breakfast. In 1982, we sold the property for $200,000 and my parents spent the profit! Five years later, it sold for millions of dollars and has since resold again; now the land alone is worth over $9 million.

So what did those first buyers understand about the property and the area that my parents didn't? At the time, Potts Point was a very different landscape to what is today. Being the neighbouring suburb to Kings Cross it was the underbelly of undesirable activity. However, at the top of Bayswater Road you have amazing city views, including a view of Sydney Harbour. Buying, holding and selling real estate requires some understanding of the suburb where you find the property *and* the suburb's ability to change. In real estate, we call this change to a suburb gentrification. This involves being able to consider the possibilities that might arise in the future and determine how they can change the area. It doesn't require you to be a psychic, but rather a critical thinker.

A great pathway to find capital growth is to follow the spending habits of government and the consumer habits of people and learn about the places they will soon inhabit. It is the social media of the real world, not the Internet! Though real estate embraces the social media revolution, information and power in real estate comes with understanding one key tool – the "town plan".

In the end, it was my family's naivety to the "highest and best use" of the suburb that robbed them of an achievable small fortune. If my parents had looked at the town plan and understood the pending alterations that would allow zoning and infrastructure changes, they would have known that gentrification would soon follow.

The one that got away – existing buildings on Bayswater Road, Potts Point.

TOWN PLANNING ELEMENTS

Town planning reveals the thousands of moving parts to a city, town or suburb and how these parts relate to one another. When factoring in real estate and the town plan, it's best to breakdown town planning into just a few sections:

- People

- Places

- Infrastructure

- State town plan

- Local Environment Plan or LEP (NSW terminology) and Development Control Plan or DCP (NSW terminology).

The principle behind examining the town plan is that investors can find a better property in more sustainable areas if the locality is progressive and well-planned. Extracting value through real estate is most easily done when the market does that for you. Ultimately, you want to control assets, add as much value to them, or have the market add value to ensure that the yields remain high for as long as possible. A town plan will allow you to find this kind of area through easily accessible research. Let's examine some of the variables.

People – Demographics are a huge driver in real estate and it's important to know that people and their migration have a huge impact on property prices. At the moment, there are a number of subcultures present throughout Australia and these subcultures can be further divided when you focus on smaller areas. Generationally speaking, we have the baby boomers and generations X and Y. Each particular generation is having an impact on the property market right now! The keys are working out where they want to live next and what they are likely to spend their money on. For example, there is a theory that the average person/couple buys their most expensive property between the ages of 40 and 44. This timing is due to expanding family numbers and higher incomes that justify spending more on property.

Below are some new subcultures that have been on the rise in the past couple of years.

- TWITS: Thirty-something women who act like teenagers

- NETTELS: Not enough time to enjoy life

- DOWNAGES: 60-plus who act younger than their age.

These changes in household structure mean that Australians have an evolving desire to reshape what property looks like and what it means to them. Australians are becoming less interested in the quarter acre block and, within 15 years, 30 per cent of all homes in Australia will be single-person households.

By studying demographic shifts, you will understand where people are considering moving next and you will find an emerging suburb to purchase property in. This is where the town plan comes in. The area's town plan may have already begun to accommodate the needs of the emerging community and will act as a gauge as to whether to invest there or not. In the 1900s, there were five people to a house in Australia, now it's around two. Everything we do affects housing, such as divorce, which might explain the rise in single-person households! One out of three couples gets divorced, which puts pressure on the property market.

Places - The town plan will show you the future initiatives that will be occurring in a certain place. It's important to look at places that were previously not on your radar as good investments. There are so many examples of grungy, cheap areas that we thought were undesirable, but have quickly become fashionable and spectacular investments. Some examples are Collingwood in Melbourne, Redfern or Marrickville in Sydney, or Fortitude Valley in Brisbane. These areas show the extensive impact of urban renewal and gentrification.

If an area is slowly starting to change, but hasn't been fully transformed, it is a good time to get into the market and see what opportunities are available. Bowen Hills in Brisbane is a classic example of gentrification and getting into a location early.

Infrastructure - Developers and governments spend billions of dollars on infrastructure each year. They provide roads, schools, hospitals, transport and commercial and office infrastructure to address the needs of the community. In doing so, the government and developers reshape and redefine the planning requirements for both the state and local government areas. You will find growth if you can locate where infrastructure spending will be allocated to next. Be sure the infrastructure is real and forthcoming rather than a just a government promise. Check the town plan and government reports to validate your position.

Purchasing an investment property in close proximity to infrastructure projects is a sensible way to gauge future growth and have a higher likelihood of a better return. I also always look at the places where publicly listed property companies are choosing to invest as these people have the best town planners and researchers working for them. I follow their investments with great interest and work out how to buy for less in the same area. Governments and listed companies will spend a fortune, literally billions and billions of dollars influencing areas. Capturing that influence is a very smart way of buying property for the long term.

State town plan - Each state puts out a plan or vision for the future. It is usually a 25-year agenda of what the city will look like. The state town plan focuses on the following elements in order to create better towns and areas. Understanding these elements can help you determine whether there will be enough growth drivers to make the area a good investment.

- Develop standards
- Protect bushland
- Ensure traffic flows
- Develop surplus land
- Promote a higher density
- Rezone areas
- Arrange aged care.

These factors are all about improvement, but remember that governments tend to over promise and under deliver. At 18, I was a real estate agent in North Ryde, Sydney. During that time, a government planning initiative focused on linking Chatswood to Epping via a new rail link that was to unfold over a three-year period. As a result, numerous investors purchased property in the area; however, it took about six years before a track was laid and 10 years for the infrastructure to be wholly delivered. So the lesson is to buy just at the start of construction.

LEP – Each local government area puts out a plan or vision for the future, which can be accessed by visiting that area's council or their website. The biggest changes that can occur in the local environmental plan are height and density changes. These form the backbone of subdivisions and extensions and adding value to real estate.

The photo below is an example of air space changes in an LEP. The property, located at 444 Marine Parade in Biggara Waters, Queensland, was built 20 years ago. At the time, the height restriction was two storeys; today it's seven. Understanding such changes by looking at the LEP can ensure that you stay ahead of the trend and plan accordingly to get the best use out of your real estate.

444 Marine Parade, Biggara Waters

DCP - Each council area also has a plan that details specific elements for consideration including:

- Car parking requirements
- Height limits
- Building lines, such as distance shadows
- Laundry facilities
- Water, sewerage, drainage and electricity
- Beautification of unused land (landscaping)

- Minimum frontage and depth
- Minimum block size
- Plot ratio (number of floors)
- Density ratio (number of 1, 2 and 3-bedrooms)
- Ingress and egress, (in and out) driveways, right of way, walk way
- Fire ratings
- Covenants, caveats and encumbrances.

Town planning is a key education requirement for your journey through investing. It can be the difference between selling a property for hundreds of thousands or millions of dollars. By carefully researching attributes of people, a suburb and having explored an area's ability to change (all information found in the town plan), you can diligently find great investment opportunities.

GUIDE TO HOUSE AND LAND PACKAGES

A popular method for securing an investment property is to buy in a new housing estate; this strategy is known as purchasing a house and land package. At the time of writing, we are now in the middle of the biggest residential undersupply Australia has ever seen—some 180,000 dwellings short across the country. The majority of the shortage is on the east coast of Queensland, New South Wales and Victoria.

Although a house and land package is an excellent way to acquire a residence as well as a plot of land, not all of these packages are ideal investments and as with every piece of real estate you're interested in, these also need to be heavily researched. The principle behind examining a house and land community is that investors need to find the best property and estate from which to extract value. Let's examine some of the variables we need to consider when looking at these packages.

NEW ESTABLISHED BENCHMARK (NEB)

The real estate market often exposes investors to a mixture of new and old property, leaving some investors perplexed as to whether to buy new or old. For example, if an old property in a micro market (suburb or town) is worth $200,000 and a comparable new property is worth $300,000, then the old property would be the better buy because the New Established Benchmark (NEB) variation is $100,000. One could add value to the old property through renovation and extract a profit because of the high NEB variation. If the old property was $280,000 and a similar new property in the micro market was worth $300,000, then the NEB variation is low at $20,000. The new property is the better buy, as the investor would not be able to add value through renovation to the old property to compete with the new property.

BLUE CHIP ZONES

When considering a house and land package, look at investing in premium localities and estates often known as blue chip areas. If you do not locate a house and land package in one of these areas, do NOT enter the cheaper estates of the area. A new house and land neighbourhood or suburb may be made up of several estates. As the state government releases land, major developers, who have been waiting for the rezoning changes, dominate the landscape. These big time developers then allow smaller developers and builders to control land in their estate and sell the properties accordingly. To minimise their risk, some major land owners will sell to developers who sell only to investors, which then creates a neighbourhood of tenants rather than a house-proud neighbourhood of owner-occupiers. This often creates a poor-looking and non-family environment, which can minimise your profit potential. You should buy in areas where land owners and developers are targeting owner-occupiers and will only sell limited positions in their estate to investors, in some cases less than 10 per cent. These are great estates to buy in because of the upside of a house-proud neighbourhood that will take better care of the area than tenants.

RESALE

Purchasing a property with less investor activity in a house-proud neighbourhood will also be helpful when reselling your property. New purchasers prefer to buy in areas where there are more owner-occupiers than tenants.

SUPPLY AND DEMAND

As is the case with off-the-plans, house and land packages are often released in stages so that the developer can attain higher profits. The first release will generally have the lowest entry point price whereas the last release will most likely have the highest price. The major difference when purchasing house and land packages with developers that are catering to owner-occupiers is that land is only released when the developers know they have more interested purchasers. This suggests that investors flooding the market do not artificially drive up the stages and prices. So there really is never a huge oversupply problem and prices do go up. Further, more established stages become more valuable than new sections drip released.

RENTAL RETURNS

Rental returns are a significant factor in the success of many areas. If yields are high, growth usually follows. Owner-occupied estates, with limited investor stock, have yields that are up to one per cent above close neighbourhoods that have a greater investor influence. Yield variation is an instrument to gauge future growth of markets because as the yields expand, growth will follow and compress closer to already expanded yields. The further the yield advances, the more likely that a growth expansion phase will follow. Simply remember that **growth follows yields**.

INFRASTRUCTURE
In housing estates, well-planned infrastructure focuses on underground power, lots of green space, community supermarkets and day care centres. They all add up to explain why one housing estate will be a success and another will not.

ABOUT THE BUILDER
It's important to use a proven builder with a successful track record. Too often investors engage a less expensive builder only to have their home project delayed, costing them both money and opportunity. Remember your new home will come with a new home warranty for seven years. So you will need to engage a builder with a long-term approach to business, rather than a less expensive alternative.

GUIDE TO MINING MARKETS

The influence that the world's biggest mining companies can have on world markets is profound, let alone what their activities can do for local Australian property markets. Over the next decade, trillions of dollars are expected to be made from mining in Australia.

Mining towns are central to high rental returns in Australia. Huge returns, well over 11 per cent, can be achieved by navigating your capital to small towns controlled by BHP, Rio Tinto and others.

I have brokered around 1,000 positive cashflow properties, from small towns to secondary cities and in particular, in mining markets. Passive cashflow returns are especially available in the market. When negotiating high yielding properties, remember to do the numbers and make sure you are truly buying positive cashflow. Genuine positive cashflow properties should give the benefit before tax and not be reliant on deductions.

The main drivers in mining towns, where positive cashflow investments are available, are socioeconomic factors, also easily represented as average income versus average house price. By way of example, let's use the history of old boom towns to explain these factors. During the early 2000s, the country experienced an impressive and profitable resources boom. This boom slowed during the GFC, but is once again experiencing a renaissance. However, the socioeconomic driver of average income versus average house price is no longer viable in many of the mining market towns. These are what I call old boom towns.

In 2003 I was brokering a property deal in Port Hedland and South Hedland, Western Australia - towns with a combined population of approximately 15,000 and both experiencing high wage increases due to the mining boom. The average wage was well up around $100,000 or $1,400 a week after tax. Conversely, the average home price in 2003 was very affordable at around $200,000 or a weekly repayment of $250.

To fuel socioeconomic growth, a market needs to be bearable, equitable and sustainable in order for both investors and owner-occupiers to purchase there. To understand the example mentioned above, let's ask the following questions of the Port Hedland/South Hedland market in 2003.

SAM SAGGERS

Was the market:

- **Bearable?** Yes. The average income of $1,400 could afford the average debt of the average house price of $250 per week.

- **Sustainable?** Yes. The market could sustain fluctuations in house price growth. Let's take the 120-year Australian average of house growth of approximately 10.4 per cent and compound the growth for three years. A house initially costing $200,000 would be worth $220,000 in one year and $266,000 by the third year. Could $1,400 income a week afford the house price of $266,000? Yes! In 2003, the Port Hedland/South Hedland was very sustainable and the future looked good!

- **Equitable?** Yes. Assuming the owner of the property wanted to take the gain made in property growth in the form of equity, could the average income afford it? Yes. The Port Hedland/South Hedland markets in 2003 and the pursuant years were very equitable markets.

- **Viable?** Being bearable, equitable and sustainable in 2003, the Port Hedland/South Hedland was extremely viable to buy within.

The towns of Port Hedland/South Hedland went on to outperform the market and posted huge profits for those property investors who understood the socioeconomic factors driving the market. Much has changed since 2003, including major global economic fallout and although the Port Hedland/South Hedland market is bearable, it is no longer sustainable, equitable, or viable.

I am personally not a fan of single market economies unless

the entry-level price is very low. The new mining markets of this decade, the "new boom towns", have high return and low entry points, but many of them are also not solely dependent on commodities and international commodity prices. The GFC proved that single market economies are not sustainable if there is a monumental economic shift and I have seen single mining markets shut down and vibrant communities turn to dust.

The current wage of individuals working in mines is still around $100,000 per annum due to the limited supply of people interested in working in the mines. The old boom towns saw an undersupply of housing that increased property prices and hence, put pressure on wages. Mines in old boom towns are attempting to provide "dongas," which are portable shacks that are available to miners. These shacks minimise the undersupply of housing and also decrease wage pressures. If considering investing in mining towns, you need to ensure that your rentable property will not be replaced by a donga.

Further, remember that real estate is an investment that will help you retire comfortably. With that in mind, you need to ask yourself these final questions: will the mine be yielding and operating the day I retire? Or will that be the year they close or slow down production of that commodity and my valuable asset becomes significantly less valuable?

MINING CHECKLIST

1) **Single market economies are towns that have one resource, for example, copper.** The fate of the township therefore fluctuates with the price of world supply and demand and, in this case, copper prices. The new mining markets of this decade have high returns and low entry points, but many of them are also not solely dependent on commodities and international commodity prices.

2) **Was there a purpose to the township prior to the boom?**
Take Gladstone, Queensland, for example. Prior to the
$90 billion announcements and the LNG plant occurring,
Gladstone was seen as a port; a bauxite refinery to aluminium.
It had a purpose. Conversely, there was not much in
Middlemount, Queensland, prior to coal being needed by
China.

3) **Is there more than one company in the township?** If there
are multiple heavyweights collaborating it means there will
be huge capital injections, accommodation will be needed
and jobs will be created which forces rental and house prices
up. Additionally, if one company has an unexpected share
market dip, there are other companies still operating.

4) **Are the mining companies planning to provide housing
to miners in the form of dongas?** Some mining companies
provide on-site accommodation for fly-in-fly-out (FIFO)
employees to ensure they keep costs down. One reason miners
earn such high incomes is their need for accommodation,
often due to the housing shortage. Some mining companies
have started camps and roped that into their salary which
reduces wages and ultimately affects the growth of property.
The more dongas, the lower the wages of the workers are
and therefore house prices will stay the same in that town.

5) **Is there a local property manager in town?** Having a
good rapport with your property manager means you are
protecting your investment. If there are no real estate agents
in the township, you can just imagine the nightmare of trying
to look after your property, especially if you are located in
Sydney.

GUIDE TO PROPERTY AND SELF-MANAGED SUPER FUNDS

The purpose of your superannuation is to provide you with money for your retirement. Today, $1.18 trillion dollars sit in the accumulated super funds of Australians. For a long time the responsibility over these funds and ultimate control over investment decisions was left to investment banks and companies, whose goal it was to invest the monies and provide direct dividends and returns to the beneficiaries in retirement. It was long believed that these institutions had the knowledge and expertise to make financial and investing decisions over everyone's retirement money.

For the most part, superannuation became a pooled savings plan with fund managers using the money in attempts to outperform the share and property market. The evolution of the self-managed super fund (SMSF) has given Australians the ability to challenge the idea of institutions and gain more control over their retirement funds, prior to reaching retirement.

The greatest fault with managed superannuation is the fact that regardless of results, the industry is still remunerated. Fees and charges can often cause super funds to stagnate. For example, a salary of $100,000 with nine per cent compulsory super payments (known as the "superannuation guarantee" or SG) from your employer would see your fund rise by $9,000 during a 12-month period. However, institution fees can often eradicate up to 100% of the contributions, leaving the beneficiary barely better off.

SMSFs aren't necessarily complex, but it is advisable to arrange an accountant to set them up as their core structure and anatomy needs a professional touch. Only recently has new legislation been introduced that provides the SMSF the ability to borrow and leverage further funds to increase your wealth. This simple opportunity creates two major benefits:

1) Investors can buy property via a SMSF

2) Investors can further borrow money on behalf of their SMSF to leverage into bigger deals and generate greater returns for their SMSF.

Funding a SMSF is just like borrowing to buy a property outside of your super. You will need security in order for the bank to lend you money. You can choose to borrow using the assets held within the super security (non-recourse loan) or using your personal assets. Non-recourse loans are leveraged from 50 to 70 per cent LVR.

Look at leveraging your super as an exposure prospect because purchasing property and using the LVR percentage of a SMSF will allow you sizable exposure limits. On average, SMSFs can borrow on a 70 per cent LVR or up to 95 per cent LVR with a line of credit.

Let's use some simple mathematics and two examples:

$100,000 of superannuation is invested in the share market or an international property fund; the market performs at 10 per cent and your investment is now worth $110,000

or

$100,000 of your superannuation is invested into direct property, which would allow you to buy a property for the approximate value of $320,000; the market performs at 10 per cent and, hypothetically, your investment is now worth $132,000. The difference is that by starting with bigger assets, the asset is working for you, not you working to build up the asset.

Setting up a SMSF takes between 60 and 90 days. Once operational, banks will lend on the structure and you can choose a property investment. There are a few elements to consider when talking to your accountant or financial adviser about investing in direct property. These include the following:

- purchasing the property outright or leveraging other funds;

- joint venturing into a pooled superannuation fund;

- adding employer super payments to the property to further pay down borrowings;

- salary sacrifice or employee contributions to the property to further pay down borrowings;

- reinvesting gains from the investment;

- using rental returns from the investment;

- understanding instalment warrants;

- understanding bare/simple trusts.

THE BENEFITS OF THE STRATEGY

- Use leverage to create wealth and generate income.

- Fund an investment property without affecting your personal cashflow or lifestyle.

- Interest deduction on the loan.

- Pay off your loan sooner, using tax-free rental income, SG contributions and tax return, payments and salary sacrifice contributions.

SPECIFIC TAX BENEFITS OF INVESTING THROUGH YOUR SUPER

- Property purchased through a super fund will not attract any Capital Gains Tax (CGT) when sold after age 60 and if sold before 60, you pay tax at the 10 per cent tax rate, compared to the average individual rate of 37 per cent.

- Rental income is taxed at 15 per cent as compared to the average income tax rate of 37 per cent, if you owned a property in your name.

- There is no Stamp Duty payable if you fund a property entirely with your super savings.

FOUR WAYS TO FUND YOUR PROPERTY THROUGH YOUR SUPER

1) You can fund a property in super using your employer's SG contributions.

2) Rental income is taxed at 15 per cent in your super, which means you have more after tax (net) dollars to pay off your loan, when compared with owning a property outside of your super.

3) You can make additional salary sacrifice contributions or use PAYG variations (speak to your accountant or one of our property experts about this option).

4) Using these methods, you will be able to halve the term of your loan.

Interest deductions/Terms of loan: Just like the benefits of negative-gearing, you can deduct the loan interest in the name of the highest tax paying entity (personal, trust or company). Further, the average loan term is 30 years, but by using the above ways to fund your super, you can pay off the average super property loan in 13-15 years, saving you thousands of dollars in interest.

FIVE DIFFERENT PROPERTY STRATEGIES WHEN INVESTING THROUGH YOUR SUPER

Now that we are aware of the tax and funding benefits of investing in property through your super, let's look at how you can apply these savings to real life scenarios.

Investment property scenario - Investing through your super will ensure that you can still enjoy the things you love and not sacrifice your lifestyle. Purchasing a property in your super fund ensures that you will not need to use the income generated from employment to fund the interest and cost of your super property. This is because your SG contributions, rental income and one other payment method will simply allow you to pay off the loan a lot sooner. Further, the funds in your super can be used as a deposit for your property, so you don't have to use any other savings that you may have accumulated.

Income property scenario - You may have seen your industry fund super savings dwindle over the last three years, but you were impressed with the returns you received with your mortgage income fund investments. You want less exposure to debt and you are in your mid-fifties. Well, have you thought about buying a high yielding unit to fund part of your retirement income needs? It works like this. If you are 55 – 60 years old and over and have some good savings in your super, you can purchase a unit with minimal debt and convert part of the fund into a pension phase. This will allow you to receive the rental income annually, totally tax-free. This strategy can be a great diversification and income retirement strategy and it will help fund your retirement lifestyle, while exposing you to the robust Australian property market and increasing annual yields, without the worry of a fluctuating share market.

Commercial property scenario - So you own your own business and you've heard that you can buy your business property in your super fund and you want to know what the benefits are? What if I told you that you could buy the suite or unit you are currently renting and use your rent to pay off your business property loan and deduct all your contributions made to your super fund? It's fair to say that you would be interested. Business property in a super fund is a very popular strategy to create wealth for your retirement. It is without doubt one of the most beneficial property strategies in super, given the generous tax concessions offered to business owners.

Retire your debt and fund your lifestyle in retirement - Many middle-aged, affluent, Australian couples find themselves on great incomes, but with a sizeable property debt that they use most of their income to support. Whilst it is great to live in an exclusive suburb with great views and neighbours, the reality is that high-end property is both overvalued and hard to sell at the best of times. The far greater issue is how these people will fund their retirement income needs given that most of their income is funding this debt, with little of it saved or invested for the future. Well, the fact is with an ever-increasing aging population and less money to depend on from the government, investing in lifestyle property using your super could lead to a more comfortable retirement. The way to solve this problem is to purchase a cheaper retirement lifestyle property well before you retire, in a suitable coastal or suburban area, well before urban sprawl and population changes increase capital values significantly. This is achievable by buying your selected property in your super fund, where the cost of funding and managing it is not a concern, nor will it have any impact on your current lifestyle. The second step is to timeline the sale of your expensive residential property, so as to pay off the debt and use the surplus funds to purchase the property you bought in your super fund in your own name. By doing this, the capital will be contributed into your super account to be used to generate a retirement cashflow stream.

Property syndicates - You like the idea of property investing, but you don't have enough savings and you don't earn a whole lot, so you don't think the bank will lend you money to fund a property. Well, what if we told you that by pooling your resources with other similarly young or old interested investors, you could create wealth, buy your first property and create an enviable borrowing history to enable you to buy your own property at some stage in the future? This is how it works. Pooling two, three or five investors' funds in a property syndicate that purchases one property (unitised), owned equally or divided between these investors, is the simplest way for people to spread their risk when investing in property, create a credit history with banks and start your journey to property wealth-creation.

GUIDE TO WHAT TO BUY - NEW OR OLD?

By adding both new and old properties to your portfolio, you will have more diversified investments that will reap rewards for years to come. You will pay less tax by buying new property and you'll have a multiplier of value in your portfolio when you buy older property.

NEW PROPERTY

As a guide, depreciation allowances are a great way to minimise your tax. The newer the property, the better allowances you can claim both on the building value (if the property is built after 1984) and the fixtures and fittings or chattels. The average Australian can claim back 70-80 per cent of their tax for providing rental housing to the market. To put it more simply, the average Australian could actually claim back the money they earn by adding new housing to their portfolio.

According to the company, Depreciator, who are depreciation experts, 85 per cent of people who own property investments do not claim all the tax deductions they are entitled to. You need to get a professional depreciation schedule, performed by a depreciation company, otherwise you're throwing money away by not claiming it all properly. The ATO will often refund between $1,400 and $12,000, even if your property is cashflow positive. So provide this schedule to your accountant, because without it, they will inaccurately estimate your claim because they will not be familiar with the costing of your property's fixtures, fittings, furniture, common areas, etc.

New properties come with structural building guarantees and are often seen as a low risk way for people with limited cash or equity to enter the property market, as reserves for unexpected repairs are usually not needed.

OLD PROPERTY

The major advantage of older property is that it has the scope for potential improvements. The older the property, the more funds for repairs and maintenance are needed to service the property. Buying an old property is sensible if you wish to reap the rewards of achieving greater profits and multiplying the property's return through add-value strategies.

The age of the building is also relevant because of rental returns. Tenants often prefer more modern housing and if your property is too old, you will find that that property suffers from high vacancy rates and ongoing high cost of repairs and maintenance bills. Hence, these properties are great to renovate, but they are not a good source of cashflow.

In order to buy an old property well, focus on the suburb and find benchmark sales, then purchase next to the newly created benchmark. In real estate, there is a phrase known as "worst house, best street". In other words, find a property that is literally a blank canvas and in need of work (worst house), close to properties that have recently been purchased at higher prices (best street), and the money entering the best street creates the new high Owners Established Benchmark (OEB).

The following table is a buying matrix for new, renovated and old properties:

	Old	Renovation	Off the Plan
Tax Deductions	Low	Medium	Maximum
Occupancy	Low	Good	Over Supply Then Good
Rent $	Low	Good	Low then good
Maintenance	High	Low	Low
Tenant Quality	Low	Good	Good
Marketability	Low	Excellent	Good
Stamp Duty	Medium	Medium	Low
Valuation Challenges	Medium	Low	Medium
Sqm Rate	Low	Medium	Medium to High

GUIDE TO PROPERTY MANAGEMENT

Understanding the basics of property management is a key element to buying a profitable property. I don't recommend self-managing property because the work involved can far outweigh the expense of hiring a solid property manager. Further, many tenants get turned away from the idea of dealing with an owner-landlord as opposed to a professional property manager.

There are many elements to consider when choosing a reliable property manager. One of the most important elements should be ensuring that the property manager is relationship-based. The relationship building with different parties and tenants is the basis of successful property management, while the collection of rent, disbursements and bill paying, etc, are the mechanics.

Most investors do not have a sound understanding of the different types of property management that exist in the market today. The choices typically are on-site property management, residential property management and investment property management. Property management is not about rent collection, bill paying and trying to negotiate agent fees. I have found that the agent fees are well worth the trouble and stress that a property manager has saved me in the long run. Property management fees are relatively inexpensive for the work that they do and cheaper fees are a sign of an agent that will not work as hard for you because the incentive to do so is not there.

The most important relationship is between the landlord and the tenant. The agent is the conduit between the two. While this relationship is at arm's length, both parties should enter into it with the right frame of mind and a firm understanding of each other's goals. For example, the owner should understand that the tenant wants to live in a clean, safe environment with all aspects of the property in good working condition and in turn, the tenant must realise that the property they live in is a valuable commodity for the owner and they have spent a lot of time and money investing in this property.

There is a saying I often use in my career that goes: "Build the relationship and the conditions become negotiable." This saying is especially relevant in property management. The agent must have a good working relationship with the tenant, otherwise major problems can arise such as non-payment of rent, theft and worst of all, vandalism.

Having a good relationship with the tenant doesn't just help with keeping the tenant on side for the reasons above, but it also works when the tenant's situation becomes dire and you need to get the tenant out of the property as quickly as possible, often using channels such as the Tenancy Tribunal System.

Choosing a property manager is important and just like when buying real estate, there are different tenancy laws in every state of Australia. Here are some general tips that can help investors assess a good property management agency.

- Does the agency specialise in provision of property management services or is the agency a general sales and property management business?

- Is the agency's principal or one of the principals actively involved in property management activities?

- Check on the reputation of the principal(s). Speak with those who have had business dealings with them, assess their ethics, integrity and experience.

- Will you be provided with a dedicated property manager or do you have to liaise with several staff about your requirements?

- Will you be supplied with the direct contact details for your property manager– phone, mobile and email?

- How many websites will be used to promote your property?

- Are prospective tenants given keys to inspect properties without supervision or are they personally shown the property by the property manager?

- Are prospective tenants required to provide sufficient levels of identification (100 points) when applying to rent your property?

- Does the agency utilise national tenancy databases to check the renting credentials of applicants?

- Are reference checks completed comprehensively from applicant's employers, referees and previous and current managing agents?

THREE TYPES OF PROPERTY MANAGERS

Residential property manager - They tend to look after family homes or older established housing, such as a residential house or units. The benefit of using this type of agent for this kind of property is that their proceedings are fairly routine and there aren't many moving parts other than rent collection, repairs and maintenance requests.

On-site property manager – They look after larger complexes and often are costly as their fees are frequently also a component of the strata levy. Typically, on-site managers buy a business that allows them to run and manage the portfolio of real estate that is sold by a developer as part of a new development. There is no legally binding agreement that says a buyer has to use their services. The success of an on-site manager is very dependent on the competency of the manager and their business abilities. Some are not real estate agents by trade and have actively invested in management rights as a retirement income. Results can be mixed. Queensland properties often have an on-site manager.

Investment property manager - Investors of new real estate should consider an investment property manager. Buying new property has its advantages, but many of these advantages, such as defect clauses and warranties need to be enforced and this is often not done by residential property managers whose skill set is based on other types of real estate. Property investors buying new or near new investments should choose a manager who is focused on being able to keep builders accountable under the terms of warranties and defects. Investment property managers also understand the needs of investors in servicing debt and are conscious of keeping rents high to ensure an investor is able to increase his serviceability.

Tenants do have requirements and I think it prudent that investors study what is important to them. Property managers who understand the consumer habits of tenants have a better chance of getting you a better return on your investment. Apart from the property's features, there are a number of factors that tenants consider when choosing a home to reside in. These include:

- **Security** - It is important to provide a tenant proper locks for windows and doors, as well as lighting.

- **Reverse cycle air-conditioning** - This goes a long way in providing comfort to tenants.

- **Lock-up garage** - Your tenant will have greater level of comfort knowing they have both storage and a place to put their car.

- **Dishwasher** - This simple object is often a deal breaker for many people.

- **Light** - There is nothing worse than a property that is dark. Provide ample lighting.

- **Location** - Tenants love living near transport.

- **Privacy** - It is very important to provide blinds and/or curtains to property.

These considerations will ensure that you maintain low vacancy rates for your property.

PROPERTY MANAGEMENT MATRIX

Property manger	Residential	On-site	Investment
Dwelling type	Old, established	Large complexes	New property or up to seven years old
Expected jobs	Repairs, maintenance, leasing and rent collection	Repairs, maintenance, rent collection, understands defects and warranties (but is questionable as they bought business from developer/builder)	Repairs, maintenance, leasing and rent collection, legal direction, strata savvy, understands defects and warranties, understands yield variation and serviceability
Typical cost	5.5% to 8.8%	5.5% to 11%	5.5% to 8.8%

CONCLUSION

Our goal as property investors has always been to create an automated vehicle through the power of property to generate cashflow without consuming time. All the cashflow strategies in this chapter are proven and work. Learn the purpose of each style and adapt the style of your choice to make it work for you.

You now have the foundation and fundamentals, as well as some ways and means that will allow you to take action. Real estate wealth is available to everyone. Learn the currency that is real estate and you will soon be enriched with its power, able to provide certainty and enjoyment for yourself and your loved ones.

Your lifestyle will change accordingly but there's one thing you must always keep in mind as you find success: the more your wealth grows, the more you will face the temptation for more and more and more. It can easily distract you from your purpose. You have to make sure you never exceed your limits. Be always productive but never greedy.

Your goal should be to create a passive business that is the architect of wealth-creation but you must never lose sight of what is real and what is just real estate. One final thought to leave you with: happier is the man who lives in a tent with the person he loves, than a man who lives in a mansion all by himself.

So get ready. Decide to create your dream, become rich along the way and in doing so always remain happy.

Chapter 4

SUCCESSFUL PROPERTY DEVELOPMENT

"Does the idea of making over $2,000 per hour in your spare time appeal to you?"

BOB ANDERSEN

BOB ANDERSEN

Bob Andersen is the founder and CEO of Positive Property Strategies (PPS), a property development company at the cutting edge of the industry.

He has 30 years' experience in the property development and investment sectors and has held both state and national management positions with some of Australia's major development companies.

Known in the industry as the "Dealmaker", Bob has developed high-rise buildings, commercial buildings, shopping centres, retirement complexes, student accommodation complexes, land subdivisions, townhouses and apartments.

Bob is a member of a select group of property developers with over one billion dollars' worth of projects under his belt and through his development company PPS he typically has between $50 million and $80 million worth of projects in the pipeline at any one time.

These days he splits his time between his development company and educating up-and-coming developers (dealmakers) through his Property Mastermind property development course and a limited amount of private mentoring.

Applying the principle of "working smarter, not harder" Bob is the king of leveraging the time and expertise of other property professionals. This is the system he employs in his business and which he teaches to empower his students to make maximum profits from minimum effort.

Bob is also a specialist in structuring little or no money down deals within the property development arena. In fact the first two deals he ever did were made possible using OPM (other peoples' money) since he had very little of his own. The profit from these deals enabled him to "sack the boss", take control of his life and pursue his passion for property.

When not formulating his next deal he can be found on *Site* (his boat), travelling or involved in his various philanthropic pursuits in Australia and overseas.

SUCCESSFUL PROPERTY DEVELOPMENT

IF YOU COULD EARN FIVE TIMES THE AVERAGE FULL-TIME WAGE AND WORK THREE HOURS A WEEK, WOULD YOU WANT TO LEARN HOW?

If being a successful property developer was a result of being born with the right genes – I would be a top shelf panel beater and spray painter. That's what my dad was, and he never did a deal or had an entrepreneurial bone in his body.

That's one of the things I love about being a dealmaker and property developer. Anyone can do it with the right training, application and will to succeed. It doesn't matter if you are six foot four or four foot six, fifty kilos or one hundred and fifty kilos, fifth generation or new citizen, high school dropout or with double degrees, independently wealthy or just independent – you can learn to be a successful dealmaker and developer.

I appreciate the time and effort you have taken in reading this life-changing book Stuart Zadel has put together and in particular for reading this particular strategy that has given me the life I once only dared to dream.

Be reassured – successful property development deals will create great chunks of cash. That's important – and it happens as a matter of course. But for me it's all about the excitement in crunching a deal and the freedom that comes as a by-product of the cash. Freedom to jet to the other side of the world on a whim, freedom to take time off when I decide to go fishing or watch my son's mid-week soccer game, freedom NOT to buy a

Ferrari and Lamborghini but knowing I could buy one of each for cash if I ever felt like it.

So join me now as I take you on a journey through the exciting world of residential property development as I peel back the layers, bust a few myths and divulge some insider secrets.

HOW I GOT STARTED

Nobody is born to be a property developer, but if you have a passion for property and an understanding of what it can do to turbo-charge your wealth-creation, you are off to a good start.

In my case I had an early inbuilt love of land and an interest in watching things get built. After a few years of tyre spinning in jobs that bored me crazy I kicked off by getting a job in a real estate office which primarily marketed land estates and builder's spec houses. I did well making sales but I got my real buzz watching scrapers, excavators and graders building the estates. I wanted to learn more about the development side and approached the consulting surveyor and engineer who worked together on a number of estates.

I wanted to learn the "front end" – the due diligence and number crunching. My idea was to package up land subdivisions for developers or investors and get a project management fee and maybe even some of the marketing. In return for teaching me "the ropes" I offered to refer all work to the surveyor and engineer.

And so started my apprenticeship. They taught me how to calculate the yield, issues to look out for and all the costs involved and how to do a feasibility. That was the beginning of a lifelong passion with all things property.

It was hard work and a steep learning curve and I managed to get a couple of deals away. But it didn't take long before I wanted to get my own deals set. The only element missing was a big enough wad of cash. At this point I had been a year at the agency but my heart and mind were locked into a higher vision.

My first personal deal was a potential four-lot subdivision that had been listed by one of the other salesmen in the office.

Soon after, the owner dropped by the office and I got talking to him, saying how I liked his site and wished I had the money to develop it. It turned out he was in the property industry himself and made his fortune by amalgamating and packaging high-rise apartment sites for developers on the Gold Coast.

He went on to say that if I was really serious he would help by leaving half the purchase price in the deal on a second mortgage when I settled and he would take the other half when I developed and sold the lots and I would pay him interest on the half of the purchase price I owed him. He obviously didn't need all the money immediately. The irony is that in my ignorance I had a seller (much smarter than I) explain to me how to do a vendor finance deal. This of course is the reverse of what should happen.

To this day I believe he did that deal with me because he saw through my naivety to a young man just starting out, full of enthusiasm and questions and a desire to make it in the property world. I think he might have seen himself in me as he was 15 years earlier.

With the agency job now a memory I embarked on my second project – a joint venture with my eldest sister's boyfriend who owned an earth moving business and who supplied the capital; my first joint venture but certainly not my last.

So the spray painter/panel beater's son was away. Not in my wildest daydreams did I imagine where it would take me.

WHAT IS PROPERTY DEVELOPMENT?

If I was to conduct a "word association" test in front of an audience and call "property development", you could guarantee most of the audience would picture in their mind visions of buildings, cranes etc.

But that's only one aspect of property development. In fact you can make a fortune from property development without ever building a thing – or even owning a property. Sounds crazy doesn't it? Look at some of my "Little or No Money Down" strategies later in this chapter to find out how.

Traditional property development is all about value adding to real estate and selling for a profit. Most developments, from pure land estates to townhouses or apartments, include the subdivision of land and/or the subdivision of buildings. This is a form of "multiplication by division". By dividing the land and/or buildings into separate parcels you make the sum of the parts worth more than the whole.

While some developers are builders, most are not. The building part of a development is run by the builder. It is the builder who coordinates the tradespeople and organises the materials. I am currently developing a four-storey building with basement car parking. Hundreds of tradies have worked on that building. One day 40 tilers were on-site. However I deal with only one person – the builder.

At the end of the day all property developments start with a deal being done. The better and more creative the deal the more profitable it is likely to be.

WHY CHOOSE PROPERTY DEVELOPMENT?
While property generally, and specifically property development, is a great passion of mine, there's no diminishing the fact that it is a brilliant way of making great chunks of cash or building a massive portfolio quickly.

Below are eight tremendous benefits – some overlapping – you can receive by becoming involved at the "cost" end of production and not at the "retail" end like most investors.

1) **Profit** - You have the flexibility of either making a cash profit by selling your developed properties or you can keep your profit in the properties and hold as an investment – or a mix of both.

2) **Deposit** - You can use your development profit as the deposit to purchase your completed property as an investment on completion of the project. This profit (not hard cash) might be all you need – with the bank putting in the rest. See the later section "My Wealth Strategy".

3) **Capital gain** - You don't have to wait for the market to rise because you can create your own capital gain (your development profit) up front. This is particularly valuable in periods of low capital growth when you need to be more active in moving your wealth-creation forward.

4) **Rental yield** - Your rental yield (rent as a percentage of purchase price) will automatically be higher because your purchase price (developer's cost) is lower than the market but you still get the normal retail rent.

5) **Tax benefits** - If you hold your developed properties as investments you can claim very favourable depreciation write-offs and providing you are structured correctly you will gain Capital Gains Tax relief should you sell in the future.

6) **High returns on capital** - This is not one we normally concern ourselves with as developers but if you were to calculate the annual percentage return on funds invested (upfront equity required by financier) to create the development profit on an average project you would find it to be in the vicinity of 80 – 100 per cent. That's somewhat higher than a term deposit wouldn't you say?

7) **Rapid portfolio growth** - This is a key benefit. You can acquire investment properties much faster by acquiring them at cost through property development than you otherwise could by paying retail price like the rest of the market.

8) **Special savings** - If you are holding your developed properties on completion you can save on Stamp Duty, marketing costs, agent's commission – and you get to keep the profit. Providing you are structured correctly you will benefit from Capital Gains Tax relief should you sell in the future.

This is just an outline of the technical, quantifiable benefits you can reap as a property developer. The immeasurable benefit is LIFESTYLE – having control over your wealth accumulation - and therefore the quality of your life and those around you.

WHAT TYPE OF PROPERTY DEVELOPER COULD YOU BE?

Another great aspect of property development is the flexibility available in regards to how you approach it. You can be active or passive, part-time or full-time.

You can gain the benefits of property development by being either an active or passive developer. An active developer is one who learns all about property development and gets in "boots and all" in developing their own projects. A passive developer wants to take an "armchair" approach and have someone do everything for them such as becoming involved in a syndicate. I cater for both approaches in my business.

Most novice active developers, making the step up from investor to developer, start developing on a part-time basis. Property development is all about managing people and processes. It is not difficult to manage at least one small project while holding down a full-time job.

This is particularly the case for investor-developers wishing to build their investment portfolio while maintaining their day job. In fact some small developers never leave their day job. They develop one small project at a time, keeping some or all of the completed stock, and build an enviable property investment portfolio in a surprisingly short time.

Even if you're planning to eventually become a full-time developer, it would be wise not to hand in your day job until your project is about to produce its profit. This might mean you sell part of your project to give you ongoing income until your next project produces a profit.

If you developed a three-townhouse development you might decide to sell two units and hold one for your investment portfolio. The two sold might produce a taxable income of $180,000. This would give you the equivalent of an annual income of $90,000 for two years while you get your next project completed.

BOB ANDERSEN

MY WEALTH STRATEGY

My philosophy is very simple. Residential (and a little commercial) real estate is my chosen asset class to build wealth. Why? Because it is a proven, tax effective, long-term strategy that works. Property development is the vehicle that turbo charges that asset class because it allows for a much faster and easier accumulation of that asset.

The Auchenflower project two weeks before completion

Let's go through the numbers on a recent apartment project I did in the Brisbane suburb of Auchenflower (see the table below). This is a great example of the difference between creating investments at developer's cost compared to buying them at retail price. For simplicity sake the numbers relate to a per apartment basis.

	Developer cost price $	Investor retail price $
Market value	590,000	590,000
Less development profit	132,000	0
Purchase price	458,000	590,000
Plus Stamp Duty	0	21,000
Total acquisition cost	458,000	611,000
Net equity	132,000	-21,000
Difference	153,000	

As you can see, if you were the property developer you would have acquired your own investment property $132,000 cheaper than a retail investor and $153,000 cheaper after taking acquisition costs into account.

Now let's take a look at how the money flows. We will look at how the development finance works and how the "takeout" finance works when you finance your investment on completion of the project. Both types of finance might be from different financiers.

Development finance	$
Acquisition cost	458,000
Developer contributes 25%	114,500
Bank contributes 75%	343,500
Takeout finance	
Market value	590,000
Bank contributes 80%	472,000
Payout to development financier	343,500
You receive	128,500

The total development cost is $458,000. The financier will lend 75 per cent of that amount ($343,500) and you have to put in 25 per cent ($114,500) up front. On completion a retail financier will lend 80 per cent of market value ($472,000). Your 20 per cent deposit is your development profit ($132,000) which is more than 20 per cent. From the $472,000 you pay out the development financier ($343,500) and you get the balance ($128,500). This reimburses you initial equity input of $114,500 plus you have $14,000 left over.

In summary, the equity you put in at the beginning you get back at the end so you can start again on another project. You also own an investment property with good equity and the bank has put in all the cash.

This is the simple strategy I and my investors have used to build substantial wealth fast.

THE SECRET TO MY SUCCESS

I won't hold you in suspense – here it is. I leverage the TIME and the EXPERTISE of the experts.

I have a hand-picked team of key experts (professional consultants) and they do all the heavy lifting on my behalf.

Property development is all about managing people and managing processes. The processes I will explain soon in my nine steps to property development success. The people are the team of experts you draw around you.

On a land subdivision the primary expert is a consulting surveyor. On townhouse and apartment projects the primary expert is the architect sometimes assisted by a town planner.

A good architect will have access to a group of other downline experts (professional consultants) such as a surveyor, various engineers etc. with whom he regularly does business. The right architect can organise these consultants on your behalf when obtaining a development approval or building permit/construction certificate.

You (including me) will never know as much about design as an architect or as much about town planning as a town planner etc. But that doesn't matter – you simply need to know what they do, when you need them and then engage them.

I'm not saying you should enter the property development arena knowing nothing, and expect the experts to do everything and carry you along. You will need to educate yourself first so you know how things operate and what the expected outcomes should be.

I personally put about 10 hours of my time into obtaining a development approval and about the same amount of time into obtaining a building permit (construction certificate). My architect drives the process and coordinates the other eight or so consultants. They're the guys with the university degrees and decades of experience in their chosen fields. I just deal with the architect. This is similar during construction when I just deal with the builder, and of course the financier once a month to make sure the builder gets paid.

But it gets better. I recently worked out the amount of time spent at university by the experts used in a recent four-townhouse project and their approximate years of experience. I was amazed – 34 years at university and 165 years of experience.

Then I worked out who made the money. Collectively all the experts made $42,000 and I made $340,000.

Can you grasp the significance of this? Remember what I said earlier:

> *"It doesn't matter if you are six foot four or four foot six, fifty kilos or one hundred and fifty kilos, fifth generation or new citizen, high school dropout or with double degrees, independently wealthy or just independent."*

You can be any of the above, yet still grasp hold of 34 years of university learning and 165 years of practical experience from the experts and make **eight times** as much money as all of them put together. Why? Because you are the dealmaker!

DOES EARNING $2,000 AN HOUR IN YOUR SPARE TIME APPEAL TO YOU?

Does that sound better than working overtime or stacking shelves or telemarketing at night?

Now that you know about the power of leveraging the time and expertise of the experts I want to let you in on an analysis I did recently of the time spent on a four-townhouse project. I did this same analysis on another project three years ago and the numbers this time were consistent with the previous result. We log our time on projects so it is not hard to work out.

Below is a breakdown in hours spent on the different stages of the process.

Stage	Hours
Site location	18
Due diligence	14
Finance	12
Acquisition	3
Development approval	14
Building permit	11
Construction	56
Sales and settlement	17
Total	**145**

Based on the profit of $340,000 and the time spent of 145 hours the amount earned per hour is $340,000/145 = **$2,344.**

All this is made possible by the power of leveraging the experts. But imagine if I were to super leverage this deal by paying an experienced development manager to handle the process and pay him $80,000. Let's say I put in 20 hours of my time dealing with the project manager.

My profit would now be $260,000 ($340,000 - $80,000) for 20 hours work and my hourly rate would rise to a staggering **$13,000.**

Such is the result of harnessing two powerful commodities – property development and leveraging the experts.

SWEET LITTLE DEAL

Have you ever heard the saying "small fish are sweet"? Normally the deals I do these days are much larger than this one but I just wanted to show you how you can still make a great return from minimum effort from small deals. In fact, this one only showed a return on cost of 15 per cent (profit as a percentage of total cost) – less than I would normally accept – but the hourly rate was fantastic.

I acquired an investment property that consisted of a "pretty ordinary" house on an 809 m² lot. The intention was to gain approval to subdivide into two lots and build a new house on each lot.

The survey and town planning approval to produce the two lots were handled by my town planner. They offer town planning and surveying services under the one roof. The two houses were built by a project builder I had used previously using two of their "off-the-shelf" plans for small lot houses.

I spent three hours dealing with my planner to get the subdivision approval, three hours organising the extra service connections, one hour with my lawyer to arrange the separate titles, five hours with the builder to finalise the plans and specifications, three hours on-site and two hours post construction. That's a total of 17 hours.

The profit was $158,900 and the whole process took eight months from subdivision application to building completion. That's $158,900 for 17 hours' work on my part. You can do the maths.

YOUR NINE STEPS TO PROPERTY DEVELOPMENT SUCCESS

Remember how I described property development as managing people and managing processes? Well these are the nine processes you manage. If I asked what the first step in the process might be most people would say "find a site". But what would be the point of that if you did not know if you could afford it, if you did not know what structure you should buy it in? As a result you will see that locating a site is step four in my nine-step process. So let's start at the beginning.

STEP ONE:
ASCERTAIN YOUR FINANCIAL CAPACITY

If you don't have any financial capacity it's pretty simple – you will have to be creative in structuring the type of deals you are going to get involved in. That's how I got my leg in the property development door. Later in this chapter I have included an overview of seven types of creative deals.

If you have equity or cash you need to find out what sized project you can afford to develop. One of the best ways of doing this is to consult a commercial finance broker who understands development finance. A commercial broker is quite different from a retail broker who sources finance for individual houses and apartments for owner-occupiers and investors.

Based on your financials the broker can ascertain your borrowing capacity and therefore the scale of project you can afford to do. Always allow a buffer rather than borrow to your absolute limit.

STEP TWO:
GET YOURSELF STRUCTURED

Would you rather *legitimately* pay no tax this year or a million dollars in tax? You might be tempted to jump in and say "stupid question - no tax of course". Now I hate paying tax as much as the next person but if I had to pay a million dollars in tax I must have had a good year, right? To pay no tax I would assume I had a terrible year or I'm catching up on previous years' losses.

So the name of the game is to not pay one cent more than we legally have to and to be structured in such a way as to derive the maximum benefit (minimum tax) from our endeavours.

The reason I have this as step two is because you need to get your structure sorted out before you find a site. It is critical to purchase your site in the correct entity as it can be very expensive to change it at a later date.

There is no "off-the-shelf", "one structure suits all circumstances" type of structure. It can vary depending on such circumstances as whether you are selling your completed stock, holding or a combination of both. Also whether you are developing alone, in a joint venture or part of a syndicate. Even if you are single or married, young or moving into retirement.

So how do you work out the appropriate structure? You don't! You ask an accountant experienced in business structures and with property experience. In most cases this may not be the person who does your tax returns. The right (or wrong) choice here could cost you big dollars – and the Australian Tax Office will love you for it. As an example the accountant I use for structures has about 20 developers as clients and recently completed a 32-lot subdivision with his business partner.

An experienced accountant like this will decide whether a company, unit trust, discretionary trust or other entity or combination is appropriate to your particular circumstances. Taxation, asset protection and possible future transfer of assets need to be considered. Your intentions will also impact on such issues as income tax, Capital Gains Tax, GST and Stamp Duty.

Once again the power of leveraging from the experts comes into play. You don't have to know much at all about these issues, you just need to find yourself a good business/property accountant.

STEP THREE:
DECIDE ON PROJECT TYPE, SIZE AND LOCATION

This is where the importance of step one comes in. Based on how much you can afford you can decide on your project type and at this point let's assume it will be a residential development.

So what are our choices? Here are some examples.

- Splitter (two-lot subdivision).

- Slider (moving a house if possible to make room for a second lot).

- Dual occupancy (second dwelling on a lot).

- Duplex (two attached dwellings).

- Townhouses (more than two dwellings usually attached vertically).

- Apartments (dwellings attached horizontally and vertically).

- Specialised residential (student accommodation, retirement etc.).

Most people start off with a small subdivision, sometimes building on the newly created lot – sometimes not – or a small townhouse development (three to four townhouses).

Remember, it doesn't matter where you start it's where you finish up that counts. But at least get a start. And you start exactly from where you are today.

If your first deal is one of the more creative strategies I refer to later in this chapter you might be able to start off with a larger project.

So where should you start to look for your first deal? I usually recommend that you look around the area where you live first. This makes sense because you will have knowledge of where the shops, transport, schools etc. are located and you should be knowledgeable about the state of the local market and what properties are selling for.

It will need to be an area where development is occurring. Look for houses on larger lots where second dwellings are being built or where vacant lots are being sliced off. Look for medium density projects like townhouses and apartments being developed. If this is not happening in your area or the price demographic doesn't suit your budget you might have to look further afield.

My recommendation is to choose an appropriate area with these characteristics which might cover two or three suburbs and to become an expert in that area. There's no point looking at every opportunity from Narrabeen to Penrith to Cambelltown if you're in Sydney or from Geelong to Sunbury to Mornington if you're in Melbourne etc. You need to choose a containable area and "farm" it.

That means you need to know where infrastructure is. You need to know what houses, new townhouses and apartments are selling for. You need to know what sites are selling for and what the local zonings are and what can be developed on those zonings.

Zoning and town planning knowledge can be gained by looking at the planning scheme and zoning maps on the council website. Another quick and easy way is once again to leverage the experts and buy an hour's sit-down with a local town planner. This might cost at most $150 - $180 (or even free) and could be the best investment you've made in a long time.

To accumulate this knowledge you need to locate which real estate agents in the area specialise in selling sites and new projects. For sale signs and the various Internet real estate portals are good sources for locating them. Check what is for sale and, particularly, what is selling.

One great method is to attend "open houses" for townhouse and apartment projects. Tell the agent you are not there to buy but you are in the market for a deal on a site. Hopefully that will disarm him from "sales speak" and you can then have a meaningful conversation. Ask about foot-traffic numbers through the display, what offers have been made, what he likes and dislikes about the project and plans and what the public has been saying. Look at the design, features, standard of finish - particularly in the kitchen and bathrooms - and take photos for your file.

This will propel you on your way to becoming a "local expert" so that when an opportunity pops up you will be in a position to pounce.

STEP FOUR:
LOCATE A SITE

If you haven't got a site you haven't got a deal. That's not to say you have to own it – but you do need to control it.

There are basically two categories of sites that may be located, one being "on market" and the other being "off market".

On market sites
On market sites are those sites that are publicly advertised and are officially for sale. On market sites are generally sourced using one of the following methods.

Buyer's agents - As the name suggests, buyer's agents represent the buyer, unlike a normal real estate agent who represents the seller. They charge the buyer a fee, normally around two per cent of the purchase price, for finding a suitable property.

A good buyer's agent should have an extensive network of contacts and should be a good negotiator. In theory at least they should be able to negotiate a lower purchase price that more than compensates for their fee.

Some buyer's agents just locate properties for owner-occupiers or investors. You will need to locate one who deals in development sites and who has a reasonable grasp of town planning issues.

Buyer's agents can be particularly useful if you have limited time to track down a suitable site. Being able to leverage their time, network of contacts and negotiating skills can get you off to a good start.

Internet - Internet sites have fast become the medium of choice for connecting real estate to prospective buyers. These portals enable you to search for development sites and the agents who are selling them.

Some sites enable you to "grab" properties that are for sale on a number of portals using specific criteria (e.g. location, size, frontage etc.) and by using key words and phrases such as "development site", "DA approved" etc. This can be a really beneficial tool as it filters unwanted results which saves you time when searching. You can also set up alerts that notify you when sites that meet your specific criteria come on the market.

Another benefit of such Internet sites is that they allow you to identify which real estate agents are active in selling development sites and new projects so that you can make contact with them directly.

Print - Print media (e.g. newspapers and property magazines) provides a relatively good medium from which to find development sites. Most newspapers contain property advertisements on a specific day of the week so it is important to know which day is applicable for the newspaper circulated in the area you have targeted for development.

Usually the Saturday newspaper is preferable and you will need to locate the correct section that lists sites for sale. This will usually be in the commercial section and may have a heading like "Property Investments" or something similar.

I always prefer to deal directly with a seller rather than through an agent. You will often find private sales in newspapers and some Internet sites where sellers are going direct to the market and not through an agent.

Real estate agents - The final and most obvious avenue is finding a site through a real estate agent. Once you have decided on the locality in which you want to develop you will need to find out which agents in the area specialise in selling development sites.

Agents who sell sites often sell new projects so you can locate them by open townhouses, Internet advertisements or cold calling the various real estate offices.

A number of larger real estate offices have certain individuals who specialise in the sale of development sites so be sure to speak with the appropriate person. Most real estate agents specialising in site sales have regular mail outs of development sites so be sure to receive them also.

Off market sites

Off market sites are those sites that are not publicly advertised and are generally considered to be not for sale. Off market sites generally provide the best conditions under which to purchase a site. This is largely due to the fact that there is often no real urgency as the owner generally does not need to immediately sell the property. There is also a lack of competition from other buyers which gives you time to investigate the site prior to signing a contract. Off market sites are generally sourced using one of the following methods.

Advertising - It pays to be proactive and not just rely on those sites that are advertised but to take the initiative and advertise your interest in purchasing a site. This may simply be in the form of a newspaper advertisement in the appropriate section of the newspaper distributed in the area you have targeted for development.

While your primary intention is to prompt contact from a landowner willing to sell a site you might also pick up a contact in the form of a real estate agent who might have a suitable site for sale.

A typical small "run on" classified advertisement in the appropriate section of the newspaper might only take up three or four lines and cost less than 50 dollars.

Consultants - Quite often consultants work on behalf of individuals to obtain development approvals where the individual does not intend to develop the site or is undecided on whether or not to develop. Such consultants typically include architects, building designers, town planners, surveyors and civil engineers. My architects know to contact me should one of their other clients decide to sell their site after obtaining a development approval.

Also, some larger town planning and surveying firms have staff that search for sites and buyers. They match sites to their existing client base as well as using it as a method of attracting new clients. It is a way for them to proactively source more work.

As is the case with real estate agents, it pays to regularly contact the consultant to ensure you remain in the front of their mind for when an opportunity arises. Also make sure they are aware that subject to their fees being industry standard you will use them in any deal they refer.

Site flickers - "Site flickers" is a term I like to use for individuals who purchase sites with development potential and go on to obtain the necessary local authority permits and then sell the site. Some site flickers perform this activity as a full-time occupation and are generally not interested in going on to develop the site. Site flickers are therefore an ideal supplier of development sites, particularly if you are in the market for an approved site.

You will find them placing private ads in the newspaper and they like to build a pool of potential buyers for their sites.

RESEARCH TOOLS

The Internet heralded the age of information technology and what a huge help this has been for investors, developers and dealmakers.

Council websites offer a huge amount of information such as planning schemes, zoning maps, services locations, how to prepare and lodge applications etc.

There are also private companies who provide information on the status of various development permit applications. Such companies provide regular reports which include a lot of useful information including the subject property's details, the status of the local authority application, and the details of the consultants used in the application e.g. architect, surveyor, various engineers etc. – some for free, some for a fee.

On my computer I also have access to the local authority's planning scheme, zoning maps, contours and service locations (available for a monthly fee). So in effect I can pull up outside a potential site, fire up my laptop on wireless Internet, and using a combination of the above information sources, tell the zoning, what can be done under the planning scheme (densities, heights, setbacks), the lot size, contours, where the storm water drainage, sewer and water reticulation services are, if it is affected by flooding, who owns it, when they bought it and for how much, previous owners and purchase prices, if it has been marketed, by which agent and at what price(s), an aerial view, proximity of major roads, schools, shopping centres etc., if there are any current development applications, a copy of the title deed, if the owner has a mortgage and to which bank, a copy of the registered plan and more – all from the comfort of my car seat.

WHAT TO LOOK FOR

Generally when looking for sites I look to the areas that have a history of good capital growth. These areas tend to have supplies of suitably zoned land for increasing the density by subdividing into smaller lots or increasing the density by building townhouses alongside or behind an existing house or demolishing the house and building.

I also look for proximity to transport and other infrastructure. With the cost of fuel and traffic congestion becoming such big issues, proximity to transport such as a train station, bus stop or bus interchange is a big plus.

I also look at proximity to shops, particularly regional shopping centres that supply retail shops plus bulky goods and service industries. This is particularly important when developing further out in fringe areas. Areas close to "coffee precincts" have proven popular in recent times.

Proximity to large scale employment such as the CBD, hospitals, shopping centres and industrial areas (near but not in) can also be a big plus.

When looking for owner-occupier sites I do look at the above criteria but also lifestyle aspects. These could include areas with less investment product, consistent high growth, and physical characteristics such as views or proximity to the beach.

In securing your site you might use an option or contract. We would typically look for a due diligence period followed by a finance approval period. On small sites you might simply be purchasing a house as an investment property with development potential. On large sites you might buy subject to obtaining a satisfactory development approval.

STEP FIVE:
DUE DILIGENCE AND FINANCIAL FEASIBILITY

This is a very important step because it decides if the deal you are investigating is THE deal – the deal that shows the required profit.

The due diligence phase encompasses three areas – town planning, design and engineering. The financial feasibility is simply the number crunching.

The town planning aspect covers such issues as zoning, and what can be developed and how many and what are the constraints (limiting factors). For land subdivisions the required expert is a consulting surveyor. For townhouses the expert is a town planner or in smaller projects an architect familiar with lodging development applications could suffice.

You need to become familiar with town planning matters in the location of your choice. These days many councils have the town plan, zoning maps, current and recent development applications etc. on their website. This is a great source of self-education.

As I mentioned earlier, another great way of increasing your town planning knowledge is to buy an hour of a town planner's time for about $180. S/he can tell you all about zonings, what can be subdivided or built, how many (yield) and what constraints might exist.

The design phase has to do with the layout of the project. For a land subdivision that is a plan of the lots and can be done by a consulting surveyor. For a townhouse/apartment project that is a site plan showing how the building(s) are situated on the site, driveways etc. and can be done by an architect. At this stage floor plans are not so important – just the size, number and layout of dwellings are sufficient.

The engineering phase has to do with slope and the availability and location of services such as water, sewerage and storm water and can be done by a civil engineer. Once again, on small projects, an experienced architect can advise.

If the site already has a development approval (DA) much of the work has been done. The main issues are seeing if the plans suit market requirements and if the conditions are reasonable.

An experienced architect can be of great assistance with the whole due diligence process.

The financial feasibility produces the moment of truth – is the deal really a deal? There are a few good feasibility software programs on the market that will make life easy but I recommend you become proficient in doing manual feasibilities before moving to software programs.

A typical manual feasibility is like a profit and loss statement for a business. It has three columns. The left hand column has the item name, the middle column has the expenditure (project costs) and the third column has the income (sales). At the bottom is the profit – the sales minus the costs. You also need to calculate the return (margin) on costs (ROC) which is the profit as a percentage of total development costs. Financiers like to see a minimum of 18 per cent but I look for 20 per cent or better.

I have set out below a very simplified version of a manual four-townhouse feasibility.

	Item	Costs	Income
	Sales	2,000,000	
Less	Land	660,000	
	Consultants	50,000	
	Construction	680,000	
	Council	88,000	
	Finance	90,000	
	Selling	66,000	1,634,000
	Profit		**366,000**
	ROC		**22.4%**

If a deal doesn't stack up it is often a good idea to work out why. In a typical project the combined cost of land and construction can be around 80 per cent of the total costs. When a deal doesn't stack up it will be one of these two items that is wrong – providing you have your sale prices right.

If you are confident with your construction price, the problem will be the land price. Armed with the correct information you might be able to renegotiate a better land price. If not, walk away. The deal of the year is only ever a week or two away for a diligent dealmaker.

STEP SIX:
OBTAIN FINANCE

Unless you have an uncle named Bill Gates or Warren Buffet it is most likely you are going to need the assistance of a financier to develop your project.

For those starting out in property development I strongly recommend the use of a commercial finance broker. Notice the word "commercial". This individual is quite different from the "retail" finance broker you might use to arrange finance for the purchase of a house or townhouse. A commercial broker will be knowledgeable about the development process, feasibilities etc. and will have the right contacts in banks and other organisations that lend on development projects. I have seen too many deals unravel when retail brokers have tried unsuccessfully to put together commercial finance packages.

It might be a good time for me to explain the difference between "retail finance" and "commercial finance". Retail finance is for the purchase of existing houses, apartments, townhouses etc. Small projects up to say three dwellings might be able to be financed with a retail loan. The project and the serviceability (ability to meet monthly interest payments) of the borrower are considered carefully.

Funding for a project falls under the "commercial" area of lending because developing a project is a bit like a business and the end product has yet to be produced. Normally commercial finance would be used if developing three or more dwellings. One big difference between retail and commercial finance is that the interest is capitalised in a commercial loan. That means that the financier works out the expected interest payable on the project funding and adds that into the loan. Therefore the borrower does not have to make interest payments on the way through. It forms part of the loan that is paid out on completion from sales proceeds.

So how much can you expect to borrow? Banks tend to lend a percentage of the total development costs (TDC). This can vary a bit with the state of the property and financial markets. Typically it would be in the range of 70 – 75 per cent of TDC and up to 80 per cent in the good times. That leaves 25 – 30 per cent for you to put in and it goes in first and the bank's money follows.

Sometimes it is possible to arrange "mezzanine finance" which can supply part of your 25 – 30 per cent requirement leaving even less for you to tip in.

There are alternate lenders other than the banks. Called non-banks, private equity lenders and/or gross realisation value (GRV) lenders, they look at deals a bit differently from the more conservative institutional banks. They tend to lend a percentage of the end value of the developed product called the gross realization value. They tend to lend in the range of 65 – 75 per cent of GRV and up to 80 per cent in the good times. They value risk differently from the banks. They tend to look at the project but less at the borrower. Often they will not ask for pre-sales. To offset these "concessions" they charge a higher interest rate and higher application fees than the banks.

So as you can see there are many different aspects and options to structuring development finance – and I have only scraped the surface of the subject. That is why I recommend the use of an experienced commercial finance broker when you are starting out.

STEP SEVEN:
OBTAIN APPROVALS

In order to get permission to subdivide land you will need to obtain a development approval (DA) from the local council. To build townhouses you will firstly need to obtain a development approval followed by a building permit.

A DA for a subdivision can be managed by a consulting surveyor and for townhouses a town planner or experienced architect can fill the role.

The development approval has to do mainly with town planning issues. This would include such things as how many lots/dwellings, heights, boundary setbacks, turning circles for vehicles, garbage collection, car parking etc.

Certain engineering matters will also need to be dealt with including how storm water and sewerage connections can be made. Some councils will also ask for a concept landscape plan.

Plans form a critical component of the development application – a survey plan for a subdivision and architectural plans for townhouses. The detail of the plans at the DA stage is not sufficient for a builder to use but it would typically include a site plan showing the layout of the townhouses on the site, the floor plans showing a layout of the rooms and side elevations in four directions.

Most councils offer a service whereby once you have an initial concept plan you can have a "pre DA lodgement'" meeting with council to discuss the proposal and both parties can discuss any issues. This way you will have a pretty good idea what council wants and can finalise your application accordingly.

Some councils offer a fast-track system of gaining a development approval where certain approved private town planners can process the application. In my part of the world this process is called RiskSmart. Although slightly more expensive than the council path it is much quicker. Usually it is restricted to smaller projects with no engineering issues.

Usually the council will want some minor amendments along the way before granting approval. If council refuses the application there exists in each state a higher authority to hear an appeal.

STEP EIGHT:
CONSTRUCTION

When most people think of property development they often picture a building under construction. Guess what? Construction is step eight of nine steps. By this stage you will have gained the required approvals and have the finance in place or already flowing.

This stage, along with crunching the initial deal, is where I derive the most satisfaction. I love to watch a building come out of the ground and take shape. The thought that the big pay day is coming closer is also enticing.

If you have gained a development approval and a building permit it is quite possible that the construction time is around half of the total project time. The great thing is that during this time you are only dealing with one person – the builder.

The builder on the other hand will be dealing with dozens of tradespersons. That's his job. Your job is to communicate with the builder and be the intermediary between the builder and the financier. On most projects of three townhouses or more the builder gets paid once a month.

You might visit the site once a week to meet with the builder and inspect progress, and check if he is on track with timing. If the builder ever has questions of a technical nature he would immediately refer them to the architect or engineer.

If you wanted to forego some profit and go for an easy ride you could appoint a project manager to operate between you and the builder.

One thing many people don't realise is that you can rightfully pay yourself a project management fee. Financiers are okay with this because if you didn't do it someone would have to get paid to do it. The monthly cashflow is handy to keep the wheels moving while you steam towards the big pay day.

There will be a building contract between the developer and the builder. This will usually be what we call a "lump sum fixed price and time" contract. It will have a set building price and minimum opportunity for variations – which is a good thing - and a start and completion date. You can get advice on building contracts from a quantity surveyor (QS). In fact the financier will usually insist on a QS inspecting the building contract before advancing funds for construction.

Builders can be sourced by tendering the construction, by referrals from say a reputable architect and even by building brokers. A good builder is worth gold. As a result I have a small band of builders to suit different construction types and rarely go outside of that group.

STEP NINE:
SELL OR HOLD

One of the great things about property development is the flexibility to sell or hold the developed product – or a mix of both. You can sell and make an immediate cash profit or hold as an investment for long-term capital growth.

It is always best to work out in advance if you are selling or holding (or a mix) as this will be relevant in choosing the most tax effective structure.

While you can derive plenty of satisfaction along the way by crunching a deal and watching the building take shape you will find a special satisfaction watching big chunks of cash appear in your bank account as your developed product settles.

Depending on the size of the project some banks might insist on a certain level of pre-sales. You can legally sign up a buyer on a contract long before it is built. The contract is known as an off-plan contract and is prepared by a property lawyer. I like to wait until I have a DA first so that there are no further variations to the plans.

So who can sell your developer product?

You - Developers can sell their own product although there may be state legislation as to how many you can sell each year. Nobody knows your project as well as you or has the same passion for it.

While you will be saving on commission you will need to be confident and able to negotiate. You will also need to be able to prepare marketing material and place advertising.

Local agents - Local real estate agents will know the location and surrounds well and hopefully be experienced in selling your type of product. In most states commission varies between two and three per cent plus marketing costs. I have found that many real estate agents aren't all that good or enthusiastic at selling property off-plan. Some aren't good at selling investment stock and having to wait 12 months for their commission can weaken their enthusiasm. A good, active agent who understands investments and can sell off-plan is worth gold.

Project marketing agents - These are agents who specialise in selling new projects. You will see them advertising on the real estate portals and see their signs at the front of new projects. They will market properties to owner-occupiers, investors or a mix.

They usually have a database of potential buyers and generally charge in the vicinity of four per cent which often includes a one per cent budget to cover basic marketing costs. They are used to selling off-plan and will use a range of strategies in marketing properties.

Investment marketers - I usually refer to this group as hard marketers. While some of them have received a bad name there are a number of reputable groups.

They tend to specialise in investment product not owner-occupier product. They generally have a large database of potential buyers and often use intermediaries such as finance brokers, accountants and financial planners to refer buyers. They gain many of their purchasers by running investment seminars. Hence their fees are often in the range of six to seven per cent and they prefer to market larger projects.

SUMMARY

So there are my nine steps to property development success. The sequence may be altered a little depending on how you are structuring the deal. You might decide to take an early profit and exit the deal at an earlier stage – leaving some profit at the backend for the next dealmaker.

For those readers who are starting out like I did – with very little capital – I have set out some opportunities that can get you a good "leg into" this exciting industry.

MY SEVEN LITTLE OR NO MONEY DOWN STRATEGIES

1) **Packaging a deal and flicking** - This can be a great way to generate some cash once you have learned how to put a deal together. You need to become conversant with steps four and five in the property development process.

   To make this strategy really work you need to do some reverse-engineering by starting with your takeout buyer – in this case a developer. You need to approach developers, find out what type of deals they are interested in and come to a financial arrangement whereby they will pay you a spotter's fee if they purchase the deal you put up to them.

By packaging a deal I mean locating a potential site using the methodologies explained in step four and carrying out the initial due diligence and preliminary feasibility explained in step five. This is necessary because you should only put up deals that you think stack up. The takeout buyer will do their own due diligence also but you will lose a good contact and potential buyer if you keep putting up unqualified deals.

This is quite different from being a buyer's agent where in some states you will need a real estate agent's licence. All you are doing is introducing them to a potential deal where they can then deal direct with the landowner or seller's agent.

2) **Creating free equity through a development approval** - Obtaining a development approval for a site will add to the value of the site – for example getting an approval for townhouses on land zoned for townhouses but currently holding a single house. The biggest uplift in value occurs when the development approval includes a change in the zoning from a lower use to a higher use – for example changing a rural zoning to residential use.

A few years ago I was involved in changing the zoning of a site from rural to residential and simultaneously getting an approval for a mid-sized retirement village. The cost of the land and the development approval was $1.15 million. Upon approval it was valued by the bank's valuer at $2.6 million. After spending a further $100,000 on the construction permit the site was revalued at $3.1 million. That's a big uplift in value of $1.85 million created by the approvals – from $1.25 million to $3.1 million.

Recently I worked on a development approval with one of my mentoring students. We managed seven three-level townhouses where most people were expecting four two-level townhouses. That extra yield added $500,000 of free equity to the land value and the student was able to fund it with $200,000 of his own money and $500,000 of free equity. The financier wanted $700,000 from the developer and they put in the rest. Not all financiers have the same opinion on the use of free equity so you might need to shop around or get a good commercial broker.

3) **Vendor finance deal** - The very first development deal I ever did was a vendor finance deal. The irony is that the seller was more experienced than I was and showed me how to purchase the four-lot subdivision site on vendor terms.

The key to this type of deal is getting the seller to accept part of the purchase price at settlement and the balance at a later date – preferably when you sell the developed stock. It works best when the seller is not in a hurry for the money and has debt level of 50 per cent or less. It also works well in a soft market although offering a bit above the asking price can be advantageous in any market.

The mechanics are simple. A sale price and conditions are negotiated. Upon settlement the seller is paid his first payment (say 50 per cent) with the balance (50 per cent) being payable at a later date. Funds are borrowed from the financier to the maximum loan-to-value ratio (LVR) (say 80 per cent). That leaves the 30 per cent surplus to cover part or all of the development costs. The seller secures his position with a second mortgage and receives interest on the outstanding 50 per cent debt until paid out (preferably from the settlement of the developed stock). Because of the lower development costs this type of deal works well with land subdivisions. If the seller will take less than 50 per cent at settlement, all the better.

Recently I worked on a vendor finance deal with one of my students in buying a house on acreage and subdividing it into five lots. The cost of the house was $1,720,000 of which the financier lent $1,290,000 (75 per cent). On settlement the seller was paid $800,000, leaving $490,000 to cover acquisition and development costs of $355,000. Upon sale of the house plus four lots for $2,450,000 the owner was paid the balance of $800,000 plus interest. The profit from this deal was $345,000. Although not a high profit margin, it was a good deal because the student made $345,000 without putting in any of his own money.

4) **Joint ventures (JVs)** - There are more types and variations of joint ventures than any other structure. I have done JVs with individuals, public companies, financiers and even governments. The second deal I ever did, after the vendor finance deal, was a JV with a money partner. This partner was the boyfriend of my eldest sister who had an earth moving business.

There are many ways to structure joint ventures. Two common types are joint ventures with a money partner and joint ventures with a landowner. I would say that a majority of developers starting out with insufficient capital use joint ventures to get started.

The key to any successful deal is to create a win/win for both parties. The best joint ventures are done when each party has something to bring to the table that the other party does not possess.

A joint venture with a money partner is a great way to get started. What I have found is that there are a lot more people with money looking for great return than there are people who can produce that great return. That's a perfect opportunity for a dealmaker. The dealmaker can find the deal and project manage it to a successful conclusion while the money partner supplies the finance. The profit share split is subject to negotiation and there are no set rules but many are done on a 50:50 basis.

Joint ventures with landowners are a favourite of mine. More correctly it is a profit share and project management deal. Usually the owner of a site with development potential sells it to a developer who goes on to get approvals and develops it and makes the big profit. Many landowners would like to develop their own site but lack knowledge, courage and contacts to do so. Enter the dealmaker!

The key to success here is to have a seller wanting more out of the deal than just selling the site. They want profit share and must be willing to become part of the deal and get paid for their land and profit at the end. Ideally the site needs to be financially unencumbered or carrying low debt.

These are the simplified mechanics of the deal. The landowner puts up the land as security for the developer to borrow against for the development finance. The developer obtains the required finance, approvals, develops and sells the completed product. On completion, as the sales settle, the bank is paid out. Next the land owner gets the pre-agreed land value. The final sales hold the profit which is distributed 50:50 between the land owner and developer.

The win/win outcome is that the landowner gets his land value plus 50 per cent of the profit. The developer gets a project management fee plus 50 per cent of the profit. The developer may have put in none of his own money or at least a greatly reduced amount.

I recently helped one of my mentoring students do this type of deal on a 20-lot subdivision. He pocketed $450,000 and didn't put in one cent of his own money.

5) **Call option deals** - There are many types of property-related options. The type of option I am referring to here could best be described as a real estate option deed – more specifically – a call option deed.

A call option deed is a legally enforceable agreement between the holder of the option (optionee) and the granter of the option (optionor) which grants to the optionee the exclusive and irrevocable *right* to purchase a property for a specified amount during a specified time period and on specified terms.

The twist which gives the flexibility and power to the option is the word *right*. It is a right to purchase – not an obligation to purchase.

Often referred to as being able to put a property on lay-by, options create for the user a great way to gain control of and profit from a property s/he could not possibly afford to purchase while at the same time reducing risk, creating huge leverage and saving capital.

For a buyer looking to value add to a property and on-sell it for a profit, call options are a very powerful instrument. By entering into a call option the buyer in effect takes control of the property without having to own it. The owner continues to maintain the property, pay rates, pay the mortgage etc. For a small fee (option fee) the buyer (optionee) has the exclusive and irrevocable right (via the option) to control the property for a period of time (option term) and on or before that time may sell (assign) that option to a third party, exercise the option and settle at a pre-agreed price (strike price) thereby making a substantial profit or walk away from the deal.

The leverage power of a call option can be enormous. For the expenditure of a small option fee the buyer can potentially control a property worth hundreds or even thousands of times the option fee value. A smart operator can control and profit from dealing with properties way beyond their ability to purchase outright with minimum downside risk.

6) **Syndicates** - Syndicates differ from joint ventures in that they usually consist of more parties and those parties are often unrelated and don't know each other. The dealmaker who puts one together is called a syndicator.

Syndicate structures vary but are usually either trusts or companies although unincorporated structures on small projects using tenants in common are sometimes used.

Structures will vary depending on the intent e.g. selling on completion or holding. Correct structure is critical in determining the best way of dealing with issues such as income tax, Capital Gains Tax, GST and Stamp Duty. A top shelf "property" accountant with access to a tax lawyer will come up with the right solution. This will almost inevitably not be the accountant who does your tax returns.

I like to have $30 - $40 million of syndicates on the go at any one time. They are a great source of cashflow and building equity from acquiring investment stock at absolute cost – not retail price like the rest of the market. The passive investors in the syndicate do very well also obtaining investments way below valuation.

There are many ways of structuring syndicates so here is a simple example of how you might profit by forming a syndicate for say a six-townhouse project.

You will need five syndicate members (investors) or less if an investor takes more than one townhouse, plus yourself making a total of six. You create the advised structure (development entity). The development entity signs a project management agreement to pay you for forming the syndicate and managing the project. The development entity will purchase the site, borrow the balance of development funds after putting in the upfront equity required by the bank, sign a contract with a builder and hold or sell on completion.

Let's say the bank wants $600,000 in upfront equity to finance the project and they will supply the balance. If you raise $120,000 from each of the other five members you can go for a "free ride". This gets sorted out at the other end from settlement funds if sold or takeout finance if held. The five investors get their $600,000 back and in effect you get the profit of one townhouse at cost without putting in any money plus a project management fee.

However, a word of warning. These types of deals, particularly when you are in the business of doing them, fall under some heavy legislation administered by the Australian Securities and Investments Commission (ASIC). You should consult with a corporate lawyer familiar with such legislation to keep on the right side of the law.

7) **Capital raising** - As the name suggests, this type of deal involves the collection of money from investors to be used in a specified fashion in the funding of a project. I'll keep this section simple because there are other types of capital – for

example seed capital that can be used specifically in the due diligence and approval stage.

In simple terms there are two types of capital that could be raised to fully or part fund a project – loan capital and equity capital.

Loan capital: Let's assume you will be borrowing most of the funds from a financier – say 75 per cent of total development costs. You will therefore need to put in the first 25 per cent yourself. You could raise part or all of this 25 per cent from investors.

In this case the loan would be between the investors (via a fund raising entity) and the developer. The investors might secure their position by way of a second mortgage behind the first mortgagee (financier) and possible other guarantees. The key point is that the investors are not involved in the project. They take no project risk and regardless of the outcome of the project they are owed their capital investment plus interest.

Technically you could raise 100 per cent of the required funds via a capital raising and replace the financier. With first mortgage security on offer to the investors, a lower interest rate would be payable by the developer.

Equity capital: The primary difference between loan capital and equity capital is that the investors supplying equity capital take "equity" in the project and share somewhat in the project risk. As well as a high interest rate they usually want a profit share. In many instances they might supply all of the upfront equity required by the bank.

*Doing the "hard yards" on the Gold Coast Broadwater with a
bunch of my deal-making mentoring students.*

WHERE TO FROM HERE?

You've read quite a bit now about property development and
you might be feeling excited about the possibilities. You've seen
a few myths busted like "you have to have heaps of money to
get started" or "it takes a huge amount of time" or "you have
to know a lot about construction".

So where do you go from here? Let me say: "It's not where you
start but where you finish that counts." In other words start from
exactly where you are today – but at least start. Don't pick up
this book in five years time, dust it off, read this chapter again
and wonder how much better your life could have been if you
had kicked off the first time you read it.

Remember how I started out with no money. Be bold, get
creative if you need to. I shudder to imagine what my life might
have been like if I hadn't taken that first step. And remember,
I had no one to show me the way. There were no property
magazines, books, courses, mentors – nothing – and I still
made it. If I could, you can. Everything I have done, you can

do – only faster because of the abundance of knowledge that is available today.

That reminds me – if there's one tip I want to leave you with it is the statement below, old and often used because it is so true:

The greatest investment you will ever make is in yourself.

Hunger for knowledge. Seek to leverage from those with great knowledge in your chosen field of wealth-creation. If they teach – be taught. You will knock years off your learning curve, reduce the risks and maximise the profit and reach your personal goals and a dream lifestyle so much sooner.

Chapter 5

CREATING CASHFLOW FROM SCRATCH

"Positive cashflow gives you choice."

RICK OTTON

RICK OTTON

Rick Otton is a self-made multi-millionaire, author, speaker, property investor and coach.

He is the founder and director of We Buy Houses Pty Ltd, a leading property enterprise which has successfully expanded into the international markets of Australia, the United Kingdom, New Zealand, and the United States.

In 1991, Rick uncovered an innovative strategy of buying and selling real estate and went on to amass a portfolio of 76 properties in his first 12 months of active investing. Since then, Rick has been buying, selling and trading property, using little or none of his own money, and structuring transactions to create positive cashflow.

Since 2001, he has taught more than 35,000 national and international students how to buy, sell and trade residential property without getting bank loans or acquiring debt, using little cash and minimising risk.

Rick's mission is to transform the way people buy and sell property – to empower others with the knowledge that there is another way. He regularly meets with leading government officials who seek his advice on solving the housing affordability crisis.

Rick is the host of a weekly podcast, Creative Real Estate, which ranks in the top 100 in the business category of iTunes.

His philosophy has been highlighted in various Australian TV shows. He appeared in the ABC documentary Reality Bites as well as on *Today Tonight* and *Hot Property*.

Rick has also been profiled in numerous national and international magazines and has been featured in the following books: *The Secrets of Property Millionaires Exposed!*, *Ideas: Original Perspectives On Life and Business from Leading Thinkers*, *Walking with The Wise*, and he has authored *How To Buy A House For A Dollar*.

CREATING CASHFLOW FROM SCRATCH

HOW TO BECOME A PROPERTY ENTREPRENEUR USING LITTLE OF YOUR OWN MONEY AND WITHOUT ACQUIRING A BANK LOAN

If you could buy your next house without qualifying for a bank loan and your deposit was small, as little as one per cent, would you buy one?

I've discovered that most people would prefer to buy their house or unit this way, given the opportunity. And up until now, most people didn't know it was possible or how to put it together.

In this chapter, I'll show you how it's possible to buy property using little or none of your own money. And how it's possible for both the buyer and the seller to get what they want at the same time. And how it's possible to turn a negatively-geared investment property into cashflow neutral or positive. I'll take you through transactions my students and I have done using a variety of cashflow strategies that, once you know how, can be duplicated over and over again.

You'll discover why this is the new way forward - to capture the benefits of property - even if you've never invested before. And if you're an experienced investor or you currently own your own home, you may be surprised by how quickly and easily you can apply your newly found knowledge. As success author Napoleon Hill said:

"Your big opportunity may be right where you are now."

We're in a crisis that most people haven't ever had to face in their lifetimes. Since banks have pulled back on lending money due to the Global Financial Crisis, it's become more difficult to qualify for and receive a bank loan. But I'll show you why you don't need a bank loan to create cashflow.

In many ways, what's happening today mirrors the Savings and Loans Crisis in the USA of the late 1980s and early 1990s, when I first started buying property using these strategies to create cashflow.

What I learned from that experience was while the media spreads gloom and doom, opportunity can come from times such as these. In my opinion, some of the best times to buy are in a falling market, when fewer people are buying or selling. One of the earliest lessons I learned was:

The profit is in the terms, not the price.

In traditional negotiations, sellers want the price high and buyers want the price low; nobody wins except for agents, banks and lawyers. My strategies take the focus off the price, and onto flexible and convenient payment terms which, for me, are a key ingredient for successful property transactions. I believe in structuring transactions where both the buyer and seller get what they want first, and I'm looked after as a result. My philosophy is similar to Napoleon Hill's belief:

"You give before you get."

While most people buy and sell property one way only, there are actually many strategies that enable buyers and sellers to both get what they want, without the usual hassles that can occur when you buy or sell property.

IT'S ALL ABOUT CHANGING PROCESSES

People say that I'm a property guy, or that I'm the creative finance guy. But really I'm a processes guy. I look at processes that have been accepted and unchanged for a long time, and I ask these questions:

> **"Is this the best way? Or is it just a**
> **hand-me-down process that no one ever changed?"**
> **"Is this the most efficient process?"**
> **"Just suppose we did it this way…"**

I apply this way of thinking and changing process to everything, and I recommend that my students do too, as soon as possible. But I'm most passionate about changing processes with property because property affects everyone. It's such a big part of our lives. Whenever I change part of the process of buying and selling property, it unlocks hidden opportunities for people, solves problems that old processes simply couldn't, and has a positive outward ripple effect that can help many people and improve so many lives.

WHAT STOPS YOU FROM MOVING FORWARD?

Here are common roadblocks that occur when selling property. The good news is they can be avoided if you are open to a new way of thinking and transacting property:

- agent commissions and advertising fees
- having the house on the market for months on end
- nobody showing up to open houses
- agents unable to sell so they drop the price
- market fluctuations make it harder to sell
- Stamp Duty and legal fees
- saving up a 10 or 20 per cent deposit
- qualifying for a bank loan
- dealing with real estate agents.

Many of these problems can be solved and the key is using some strategies that may be unknown to you yet proven and tested in Australia for over the last 100 years. In fact, among my students, the following situations are much more likely to occur:

- sell a house in an hour, a day, or a week
- no agent commissions or advertising fees
- little or no deposit, just move in and start making payments
- get the price you want fast, even in a flat or down market
- Stamp Duty is paid but not by you.

When the profit is in the terms not the price, everything's possible, and everything's flexible. Once you really take that on as a guiding principle and fact of life, things will change.

Questioning convention and creating new processes is a valuable skill. The current traditional processes can often create problems. I'm into solving problems and creating processes that solve problems with ease. I'm always finding easier ways and more efficient ways to do things. Why does it have to be hard? It doesn't.

Most of us unconsciously make things difficult for ourselves because along the way we've been trained to believe that good things require hard work. So when good things come along, even if they're really simple, we tend to unconsciously overcomplicate processes and make them harder than they really need to be.

Let's say two people meet at the side of the road. One person has a coffee, and the other person has an ice cream. And they start talking and decide between themselves that they want to swap the ice cream for the coffee. Nobody thinks anything of it. They agree, they swap, they're both happy and it's no big deal. It's simple and it's easy.

But if you change that same simple swap from food and drink to houses, all of a sudden we generally think it's different. It's no different at all, but we've all learned to make it more difficult – for ourselves and everyone else. If houses are involved there are all these extra rules in people's heads.

Most of the time we're not told the most efficient way, and it's definitely not the only way to do things. It's just the most commonly accepted way, which usually hasn't been improved or made any more efficient for a few hundred years or more. The conventional processes usually make things easier for the solicitors (because they don't have to think, they just photocopy the same form that was used in the 1800s) while making things unnecessarily complicated and expensive for the buyers and sellers.

Here's what I believe, and I've seen it work in practice thousands of times: if two people want to transfer an item or two between them, those two people should be able to agree and come to a simple arrangement that works for them both.

Before banks got involved, farmers swapped sheep and grain for pieces of land, paying instalments over a number of years instead of paying the full amount up front. They were flexible. They were open to different ideas. When the usual process wasn't going to solve their problems, or before a "standard process" had been invented and accepted far and wide, they thought things through, talked and created a process that worked.

This process is called seller financing and it's about creating processes that solve problems. If we talk to each other like the farmers, the buyer talking directly to the seller, it is part of making these strategies work. When you are talking to a real estate agent, you aren't getting the whole story. If we're going to

RICK OTTON

solve someone's problems in the terms of a deal, we need to talk directly to that person so we can find out exactly what problems need to be solved.

Here's something I've always found fascinating:

**The majority of self-made millionaires
in any country are new immigrants.**

New immigrants can't go back to the old country, so their backs are really against the wall and they have to deliver results to survive. They have ideas, perspectives and habits from the old country, not the new country, so they automatically think differently to everyone else around them. They don't have a group of "that'll-never-work" friends influencing them or holding them back or trying to get them to *stop* thinking differently. They don't have anyone to lose face in front of. They didn't grow up being told the same version of "that's-just-the-way-things-are" as all the people around them.

As a result, they ask obvious questions that others don't; they challenge unquestioned processes and accepted conventions. They find a better more efficient way. They think differently and do things differently. They've got nothing to lose – not money, friends, reputation, status… not anything. And usually, they *do* have themselves and their family to take care of, and everything to gain. With no fallback plans, they have to make it or die trying.

It's never too late to think like a new immigrant.

You see, it's not actually *being* a new immigrant that makes the difference. It's *thinking* like one. And anyone can do that. Anyone. Anytime.

It was thinking like a new immigrant that helped me get started in property in the first place.

As an Australian living with my American wife in the USA during the early 1990s, I didn't have much money. But I noticed that the real estate in Dallas, Texas, was really cheap. After doing some research I found out that the whole Savings and Loans Crisis was unravelling before my eyes.

I originally started in property because I hated my job. Everything in my life seemed to take money out of my pocket, and nothing except my job brought money in. I was looking for something else to bring money in so I could escape from my job. I read in a book that only five things increase in value over time, and property was one of them.

So I went out and bought a bunch of books and how-to tapes and learnt how to make money in real estate. Because I didn't have any friends in Dallas, there was nobody to tell me all the reasons that those books and tapes don't work. I didn't have any friends or support system to show me the old ways and talk me out of it. I didn't know any better. My ways simply made more sense. So I started doing as the books and tapes said.

In fact, I'd already bought a dozen houses from banks before I'd made enough friends who tried to convince me that the banks didn't have anything to sell. The property was being sold at ten cents on the dollar, but the locals wouldn't touch it because they would say, "We've seen values drop 80 per cent, what makes you think it won't drop further?" I discovered that this was a great opportunity for a new immigrant like me who was familiar and comfortable with real estate and who thought differently from the locals. We invited some of our Australian friends over for our wedding, and they too saw the opportunity and made the most of it.

Looking back now, I can see the new immigrant thinking in action.

**Friends are great to talk to
but can be terrible to take advice from.**

I didn't listen to my new American friends, instead I saw an opportunity where everyone else saw a problem, and I changed what needed to be changed to make it financially viable. From then on I could see that houses were like a money machine giving me more money than I put in each week. So I kept getting more houses.

The more deals I did, the more "problems" (aka opportunities) I saw, the more ways I found to do things a little differently. Without friends around to tell me all the reasons it wouldn't work, I looked at each problem and said "What if we did it this way?"

I discovered that if you ask this powerful question, it can change the results you're getting in your life:

**Is this the best way, or simply the hand-me-down way that
no one has ever changed?**

Here is why. There are generally two kinds of people in this world: those who say "you can't do that" and those who say "let's find a way." I've always been someone who "finds a way". I'm often inspired to find a way when I hear "you can't do that".

If someone says, "It'll never work", is that based on the process that they know, or is it based on the process I'm about to create? You see, there's no such thing as "we can't do that". I believe we can do anything, it's just that there are some things we haven't figured out the new process for yet.

I have a friend called Geoff. We've been friends since we were kids. Geoff owns over a dozen real estate offices, is a private lender, and has over a hundred of his own buy-and-hold properties. If there was anyone in the world that I would want to impress with my new property skills, it was Geoff.

When I came back from the USA, after I'd done many transactions there, I told Geoff that I wanted to do the same thing in Australia. Geoff said, "It might work in the States, but that won't work in Australia." That just inspired me to prove that it *would* work in Australia. So I started doing property transactions in the western suburbs of Sydney, such as Blacktown and St Marys. I did the transactions the same way I had been doing them in the USA. I brought my results back to Geoff to prove to him that it worked in Australia. It should have been obvious. He had to admit that it worked because I'd already done it. But Geoff said, "It might work out in the west, but that won't work in the rest of Sydney." Which inspired me to prove that it would work *anywhere* in Australia no matter what – regional, suburban, or mid-city.

Geoff was very specific about which suburbs he thought it wouldn't work in. So I did deals in those suburbs. He was specific about which kinds of houses and units and price points it wouldn't work for. So I did deals with those kinds of houses and units and price points. Everything he said wouldn't work, I did it. And it worked. So then Geoff said, "It might work for you, but it wouldn't work for anyone else." I knew from the start that if I could do it, anyone could do it. But that last piece of "you can't" inspiration from Geoff was what got me to start teaching these strategies to other people.

My first home study course was about just one strategy, and other people used it and started getting results. I have since created several other home study courses and run live training events and mentor students all around Australia and around the world. The strategies and principles keep working for everyone who uses them.

HOW TO CREATE CASHFLOW

There are a few keys to growing wealth, but the one that seems to be most important (and often overlooked) is cashflow. To grow wealth you need to own something that grows in value, like property, and to hold it while it grows.

Buy-and-hold investments will make you wealthy eventually, but "buy-and-fold" is much more common. Many people don't get what they want or lose money when they invest in property. According to the Australian Bureau of Statistics, 70 per cent of Australians who buy an investment property sell it within five years because it's not giving them what they want. And 47 per cent of those who sell will either lose money or barely break even.

Before the property grows in value enough for you to live off it, buy-and-hold investments will usually take money out of your pocket every month. This can cause problems. Cashflow solves this problem.

Life takes money out of your pocket. Family commitments take money out. Investments take money out. Health challenges take money out. I didn't have any money to put into property when I started. I needed property to bring in money, not take it out. So from the beginning, all my strategies had to create more ways to bring money in. And that's exactly what they do.

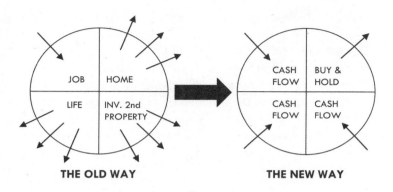

THE OLD WAY **THE NEW WAY**

Here's what I learned to do early on:

Use some properties to generate cashflow, and use other properties to grow wealth.

This is why all the strategies I teach in my live trainings enable people to generate cashflow from property. Cashflow solves lots of problems. Instead of traditional price-led negotiations, with the strategies I use we get a bit more flexible with how we swap property for money. And both the buyer and seller end up better off.

Some retailers understand that to create cashflow, it's about convenience, not price. I buy and sell houses with flexible finance terms, the same way major brand retailers sell over 60 per cent of their home theatre systems – some now, some later, no interest, easy terms. When you get creative around the way a transaction is financed, there's no need to haggle over price. As a buyer, you can pay some of the price now and pay the rest later. As a seller, you provide convenience at a premium, so you don't need to drop your price.

Let's take a look at the main strategies I use to create cashflow.

SELLER FINANCING = CASHFLOW

You can only have so many negatively-geared properties taking money out of your pocket before you send yourself broke. Even just one negatively-geared property can cause enormous problems and stress. The solution is cashflow. So the main strategies that I show my students (and I'm about to show you) are strategies that enable you to generate cashflow from all of your property transactions.

All three of these cashflow strategies are various forms of vendor finance, which is also known as seller finance. With seller finance, the seller provides more convenient ways for the buyer to purchase the property than conventional bank finance. Every situation is different, and it's also referred to as creative financing because you can get creative with whatever specific terms best suit the buyer and seller.

Legal experts believe seller financing has been in Australia since settlement in 1788. The banking system in Australia developed quickly in the 1850s when the banks had some gold due to the gold rush. Prior to that, finance was only accessible to merchants, not everyday people. As the economy expanded, people making money wanted to buy property so the owners would offer the property on payment terms.

For example, standard instalment terms for a house block of land in the 1880s involved paying the purchase price over four payments: 25 per cent up front, 25 per cent after six months, 25 per cent after 12 months and the final 25 per cent after 18 months. The purchaser had to pay six per cent per annum interest on the outstanding amount. That way the vendor could get the price they wanted. The vendor was able to get 12 pounds per block of land instead of the three pounds the buyer might have had in his pocket at the time. Also the buyers were able to purchase the land immediately instead of waiting and losing the opportunity to purchase because they were able to pay the purchase price off over time out of their earnings.

That system continued to work well through the 1960s. People would first buy the house block on vendor terms and once they had paid off the land, the bank would then provide finance to build their house. This was the start of the "Great Australian Dream" to own your own home.

Seller finance decreased from the mid-1960s because the banks made home loan finance much more readily available. Prior to that time, banks gave loans for houses but not for land. In the mid-1960s banks began to offer loans on land and home packages for the first time. In the past, seller finance would go in and out of fashion based on the banks' availability to lend. Now seller finance is becoming a mainstream method for buying and selling.

When you use any of the seller finance strategies to on-sell a property, you make it easier for buyers to buy. You basically make it possible for buyers to buy now and pay later. And when you make a property easier to buy, it will sell faster. My students often buy houses for a dollar, then on-sell them in under a day, and without dropping the price.

This is great news if you have a property you want or need to sell, because when you want to sell, you usually want three things: to sell fast, to get the price you want, and to pay as little in fees as possible.

I hear you say, "That's great, Rick, but I don't have a property to sell, I can't even buy one." That's fine. All these strategies are designed to solve buyers' problems by making your property easier and more convenient to buy. This automatically solves sellers' problems by selling fast without dropping the price. You can use the same strategies as a buyer and a seller. Once you have the skills to sell a property fast for a good price, you will find countless properties out there waiting for you to buy. Just like my students, you can keep some and on-sell the rest - fast!

SELLER FINANCE = EASY TO BUY = EASY AND FAST TO SELL

Legal professionals use technical terms to describe these strategies. We prefer to use what I call "mum's and dad's language" instead of professional jargon. So, in the explanations that follow, I'll define the jargon for you, but I'll be using mum's and dad's language most of the time. Now let's take a look at some of the most common cashflow strategies in detail.

DEPOSIT FINANCE

The professional jargon name for this strategy, and the paperwork that supports it, is a Second-Mortgage Carry Back. But Deposit Finance is a much simpler name that perfectly describes what's actually happening. The seller simply finances the deposit for the buyer, so the buyer doesn't need to pay the full deposit up front.

Three trends in today's market make deposit finance not only appealing, but often necessary in more and more cases:

- rising property prices
- tough economic times
- poor saving habits.

People simply don't save the way they used to. Nobody uses lay-by anymore. Whenever we buy furniture and electrical goods we all use the buy now, pay later option. And retailers have had to provide these easy finance terms to compete. They provide convenient finance terms that enable their customers to have a big-screen high-definition movie experience in the comfort of their own home today, without saving up the money first. And if they didn't (i.e. if they had to wait for people to save now, buy later), they would lose more than half their sales.

Obviously, if people aren't saving for the small things, then coming up with a deposit for a house is going to be a big challenge. Many people have great incomes, but they just don't save. These same people can and do, however, reliably pay things off over time.

House prices have been rising for quite some time, so much so that the price of an average house has become out-of-reach for the average buyers in some cities. Prices in Sydney are often over one million dollars for a quite average house. Because banks will only loan 80 to 90 per cent of the value, the higher the price of the house, the bigger the deposit.

Let me ask you something: how many people have a lazy $250,000 sitting around in a cheque account to cover deposit, Stamp Duty and legal costs of buying a house? It's fewer than one per cent of Australians, which means that even if they can qualify for finance with a traditional lender, fewer than one per cent of Australians would be able to buy an average house in Sydney.

House prices may not continue rising in tough economic times, and interest rates might drop and ease the mortgage burden a little. But other constraints come into play at such times. Banks have been known to reduce the amount they will lend on property. So instead of getting a loan for 90 per cent of the property value, you can only get 70 per cent or less. In the USA Savings and Loans Crisis of the late 1980s, banks wouldn't lend money on property at all. We had to get very creative in those times. We even organised finance on a car and threw in the house for free.

Things may not be that extreme, but you can see how helpful providing deposit finance can be. The biggest benefit is that it will enable you to access many more buyers, and sell your house fast without dropping your price.

DELAYED DEPOSIT

Let's say you're selling a property worth $400,000. The property has been on the market for six months and it hasn't sold. The agent has already dropped the price by $10,000 every month, but it still doesn't entice buyers. And with the price down below $350,000, you're not sure if you want to take an offer that low.

You know a couple that would love to buy a house like yours, have got their finance ready to go for $320,000 (80 per cent of the $400,000 value), but they just don't have $80,000 in cash for a deposit.

Based on getting your $400,000 price, would you be willing to allow this couple to pay 80 per cent now and pay off the deposit over the next 10 years at the same interest rate as their bank loan? Of course you would: $320,000 in the hand now is better than the possibility of $350,000 maybe someday. And based on the agent's track record, the price will probably be dropped to $320,000 in the next three months anyway.

If you finance the deposit, you'd get $320,000 now, and the $80,000 "deposit" paid back in instalments over the next 10 years (or however many years you and the buyer agree upon). By being willing to accept delayed gratification with the deposit, not only would you sell your house faster, you'd receive about $950 per month for the next ten years, or until the buyer refinances and pays you the rest of the $80,000 in full.

By putting paperwork in place by which you finance the deposit, you can get the price you want now, and you're creating an opportunity for the buyer. When buyers compare all the properties they've seen, and yours is the only one that says "No deposit required, move in now, pay later," they'll naturally find your house more attractive than any of the others they've seen because of the payment terms.

If you make these terms available in the first place, you won't have to wait months to find a buyer. They'll find you and you'll usually be able to sell within a week or two. For each of our financing strategies we provide for our students a step-by-step sales process that makes it easy for ideal qualified buyers to find you – fast.

HONEYMOON PERIOD

When you make something easy to buy, it becomes easy to sell. The key is to differentiate your property from the other properties that your buyers are looking at. This is especially important if there are a lot of very similar properties for sale at the same time – such as in an apartment block or housing estate.

If all the houses are the same, only the terms will set you apart and make yours sell faster than the rest.

Put yourself in the buyer's shoes. If they can get into a house without paying a big deposit, that would make their life easier. In most cases they'd be grateful to you for the opportunity that no one else offered them, they'd pay full price for the house, and they'd never miss a payment.

You can also make your house more appealing and easier to buy by offering a "honeymoon period" of some sort. When everyone else is trying to discount to make their property more attractive than the one beside it, your honeymoon period would actually be more attractive to buyers. Based on getting your full price, there are many creative variations on the honeymoon idea. You've probably heard a few from retail chains. Anything the electrical and furniture stores can do, you can do too.

You can offer a reduced interest rate, two per cent less in the first year, and one per cent less in the second year. You can offer three per cent interest for the first 12 months. You can offer whatever you like. Just work through the numbers to make sure it works, and make sure your offer will be enticing to buyers.

The paperwork for the honeymoon period interest rate simply states that the buyer pays the first three per cent and you make a payment to offset the rest. This is all processed at settlement; the offset amount is either paid to the bank up front or sits in an account to be drawn down on each month. Let's look at an example.

If you're selling a property for $600,000, and you offer two per cent reduced interest rate for the first 12 months, here's how it would work:

If the buyer has a 25-year bank loan for $540,000 with an interest rate of 7.25 per cent, their full monthly payment would be $3,903.16.

If they were to pay only 5.25 per cent, their reduced monthly payment would be $3,235.94, making the offset amount $667.22 per month that you would pay for them.

$667.22 per month x 12 = $8,006.64 for the first 12 months.

So, you can see from this example that the real cash out of your pocket is only $8,006.67. But the appeal of a two per cent reduction in the interest rate would mean that you wouldn't need to drop the price of your property, resulting in a faster sale and a far better price. If you must discount, discount the interest rate. By selling faster and getting the price you want, a strategy that discounts the interest rate would leave you much better off than any strategy based on discounting the price.

HANDYMAN SPECIAL

There are many people who would love to renovate a run-down property and make it their home, but they simply don't have the deposit to get started. Renovations invariably improve the value of a property. Just suppose there was a way that the renovation itself could be the deposit.

I call this strategy "Sweat Equity" or the "Handyman Special". The main point of the strategy is that buyers use their elbow grease as the deposit.

There are some ground rules for this strategy, but the big picture is this: it's very important that they cannot live in the property while they're renovating it under any circumstances. They have to have their finance, the renovation must meet certain standards, and they must be motivated to turn my house into their home. Most people redecorate anyway. This way they get to renovate and redecorate before they move in.

Here's how the numbers work:

A run-down property in Penrith, NSW, was valued at $278,000. With a renovation it would be valued at $340,000. So if the property was already renovated, the sale price would be $340,000. A 10 per cent deposit on that property would be $34,000, so I offered to accept a deposit of a renovation worth $34,000. We agreed on the price of $340,000. The buyers qualified for a loan for the other $306,000 and got to work renovating.

When the renovation was complete, it was better than I had imagined. They bought the house, paid me the $306,000, and moved in. The new owners then got the house valued at $395,000, so their hard work actually enabled them to grow $89,000 in equity. Let's look at a couple of examples from my students:

Deposit Finance Examples

Seller got a new Winnebago and I received $23,000 cash

Student Ben

I call this the Winnebago Deal, because this guy was selling his house in Craigmore, South Australia, to buy a Winnebago. I didn't know this at first. We were negotiating how much money he'll take now and how much he'll take later. He was definitely open to flexible terms, but the whole time I was struggling to figure out what he really wanted. As soon as I found out that he wanted a Winnebago, we got the catalogues and looked them up online. He was so excited! He was in his mid-60s, and he'd decided it was time to drive around the country and live off his pension. And he also wanted a little extra cash to help for maintenance and repairs to his Winnebago.

When I started doing property transactions, I connected with a few accountants and finance brokers. Interest rates were on the rise at the time, and the only people buying properties were investors. So each time I got a house, I'd send a few photos, and they'd broadcast it to their clients. They helped source investors interested in buying the houses I found, and they never had any problems getting finance.

So, I on-sold this house to an investor. The house was valued at $290,000, and he owed $110,000. The Winnebago cost $75,000, so he took $203,000 up front, leaving him with $18,000 in the bank to cover repairs and maintenance. We even got the cheques made out directly to the Winnebago dealer. The investors then rented the house back to the guy on a three-year lease.

He was happy to wait three years for his "deposit" - the $87,000 balance, that's how happy he was with the deal.

Ben made $23,000 up front.

$8,000 cash and $47,200 backend profit

Student Rob

Knowing what I do, a couple asked if I could buy them a house. They had no deposit, but they said they could get this house really cheap. It was an unadvertised mortgagee in possession property on the Central Coast, NSW. It was selling for $160,000 plus Stamp Duty, so I borrowed the money short-term for a week for a fee of $5,000.

I on-sold the property to the new owner (the guy who had asked me to buy it for him) for $213,000 plus Stamp Duty. It was valued at$215,000 at that time. He gave me an upfront deposit of $8,000. He got a bank loan for $160,000. He owes me a deposit of $47,200, which he's paying back over a 30-year term with interest. He'll probably refinance and pay me out in a couple of years.

Up front: $8,000 cash deposit.

Monthly: Instalment payments of $363/month.

Backend: If the buyer refinances before 30 years, I'll get the rest of the $47,200 deposit that has not yet been paid off.

One way to create long-term cashflow

Student Ben

A few years earlier I had sold another house in Craigmore to a family of four on a rent-to-own. They paid me $5,000 to move in, and then paid me $300/week. At the end of the lease term, they went ahead and got their bank loan approved, and had the rest of the deposit saved up to buy the house. The solicitor rang them two days before the settlement to ask for the rest of the funds to cover the Stamp Duty. They asked, "What's that?" True story, they had everything ready, but they didn't know they needed to pay Stamp Duty. It was going to cost another $15,000. They called and asked me what they should do.

I had made a profit of $29,000 on this house, so I said I could loan them the money for the Stamp Duty. We drew up some paperwork for a loan, I charged them 8.5 per cent interest, and they were able to buy their own home.

SELLER FINANCE

When people talk about vendor finance, they're most commonly referring to this one particular strategy. The modern professional jargon name is an Instalment Contract, or I.C. for short. In years gone by this strategy has also been known as a Terms Contract, Vendor Terms or Seller Finance. The slang term is a Wrap-around Mortgage, or a Wrap. Simply put, the seller finances the whole purchase price, and the buyer pays instalments to the seller instead of the bank.

Just as the seller was able to creatively finance the deposit in the previous examples, you can also creatively finance the full price of the property. This is helpful for people who may have a deposit, but have trouble qualifying for a loan from a bank.

Fewer than 54 per cent of people can qualify for a bank loan today in Australia. I'm not talking about people who shouldn't get approved for finance because they genuinely can't afford it. I'm talking about good reliable people, with reliable money coming in every month that just don't fit the criteria for the computer modelling approval process, and hence can't get finance. These people might be self-employed, new immigrants, or have moved houses or jobs too many times in the past three years. One bill that got forgotten years ago while you were in the middle of a relationship breakdown can ruin your credit history. Someone who owns 17 fruit shops, or who has too many properties, usually can't qualify for finance for the next one.

Any of these things can prevent a perfectly good potential buyer from getting a loan from a bank. But before there were banks we figured out how to transact between ourselves. And we can do that again.

WHAT ARE THE BENEFITS OF SELLER FINANCING?

As a seller using seller financing, you nearly double the number of people who can qualify to buy your property. Your property would appeal to 100 per cent of the potential buyers out there because the financing is already in place. You've made it easy for everyone to buy.

You can get the price you want and receive the full retail value for your property. You make money three ways: the upfront deposit, ongoing monthly payments, and a big chunk of money at the end when the buyer either sells or refinances the property. You pay no agent's commissions or large advertising expenses. You also pay no running costs associated with the property.

You will also reduce your property holding costs, because finding a buyer for a seller financed property is much quicker than a conventional real estate sale.

As a buyer, it is easier to qualify for seller finance than a bank loan. The buyer can buy a house with a reduced deposit, and move in more quickly than with bank financing.

The buyer benefits from the house appreciating in value, because the purchase price is written into the Instalment Contract up front. And the buyer has time to pay off the house.

THE BABYSITTER

Let's say someone is trying to sell a house worth $400,000. Different problems arise based on how big their loan is. People only ever sell for one of three reasons:

- to get their hands on the cash bit (equity)

- to stop paying mortgage payments

- to solve a people problem (divorce, inheritance, etc.).

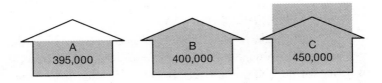

Houses A, B and C are all worth $400,000. But each house has a different loan amount against it. This means each seller has a different motivation, a different reason for selling. When you ask why they're selling, they'll all say "we need the money". But you need to dig deeper than that. Which money they need (cash bit, income or mortgage payments), and why they need it is very different in each case, so they'll each need a different solution.

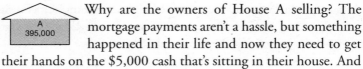 Why are the owners of House A selling? The mortgage payments aren't a hassle, but something happened in their life and now they need to get their hands on the $5,000 cash that's sitting in their house. And they need it as soon as possible.

A traditional real estate agent would charge an advertising fee and maybe get them access to their cash (or less) in four months (or more). If I could write them a cheque for $5,000 in 60 seconds and then have paperwork systems handle the rest of the details, do you think they'd prefer that? Of course, because they just wanted to access the cash bit now. They'd get instant peace of mind, plus their $5,000 cash.

Some people, like the owners of House B, don't even have a cash bit. They just want the debt bit to go away, so it stops killing their marriage and their joy. There's no cash bit in the equation.

So I can go in there with a form, and start to look after the debt bit for them. I don't have to give the seller any money in exchange for their house, I just start to babysit their loan. How much money have I just used to buy my first home? None. I would end up with a payment of about $4,000 a month, and my first home. Or I could use another strategy to turn that payment into positive cashflow for myself (as you'll see in the examples below).

The point is they didn't have to wait four long months while losing money and sleep. I could make the seller's whole problem disappear immediately with the right paperwork system, so they get instant peace of mind and no more mortgage payments.

CREATING CASHFLOW FROM SCRATCH

Why are the owners of House C selling? Obviously it's not about the cash bit, because there isn't one. Even if they sell the house today for market rates, they'll have to find an extra $50,000 to settle their debt. They want the pain and the problem to go away. Just selling the house doesn't make all that disappear. But my systems will.

You can see how this problem is also created when someone in the House A or B situations discounts their price. The lower they drop the price, the worse it gets. But they don't even have to discount it much before there's trouble. This is exactly how the old system creates more problems than it solves.

So, I can babysit the loan with a form, just like I did for Houses A and B, but to solve the $50,000 dilemma we'll have to add another step. This is where I use the phrase:

"I can't transfer the problem from you to me because I didn't create it. But here's what I can do. I can come in as a transaction engineer to create a solution and help you find someone as fast as humanly possible."

Then I'd either find a rent-to-own buyer, or do a handyman special or use one of the other cashflow strategies that work equally well to turn negatively-geared property around.

THE 10.10

Over 38 per cent of homes in Australia are owned outright, with no debt against them. When someone sells one of these houses, it's not usually about getting their hands on the cash bit, or about ending the pain of the mortgage payments. Usually it's about funding a lifestyle instead of being asset-rich and cash-poor.

3 BONUS LIVE EVENT TICKETS AT www.TGRProperty.com.au/NEWPROP   215

Most people think they need to sell their house and put the money in the bank or some managed fund or investment scheme to create an income. But with a 10.10 it's a lot simpler than that. With the 10.10 I just pay 10 per cent more over 10 years. Here's how it works:

ME: "Why are you selling?"

SELLER: "I need the money."

ME: "What do you need the money for?"

SELLER: "I need it to retire, take holidays, have a decent lifestyle."

ME: "You're asking $400,000 for it. I'll give you $440,000."

SELLER: "Sure, what's the catch?"

ME: "If I agree to give you $440,000, that's 10 per cent more than you're asking for, would it be ok if I gave you some now and some later?"

SELLER: "I suppose. How much now? And how much later?"

ME: "Well, I could give you the full $440,000 in monthly instalments over, say, 10 years. How would you feel about that?"

SELLER: "How much would that work out to?"

ME: "Could you punch in the numbers?" *(I give seller the calculator)* "440,000...divided by 10 years...divided by 12 months a year. How much is that?"

SELLER: "3667."

ME: "So that's $3,667 per month. How soon would you like the first cheque? I can give it to you right now. How does that work for you?"

SELLER: "Sure, that's great."

Of course, we'll come to arrangements with a different number of years, and different instalment amounts, but it's the same basic framework. Sometimes they want to calculate how much they'd get if they sold the house and put the money in the bank – my deal's better for them. Sometimes they ask why I'd pay more. I pay more for the flexibility of paying it off in instalments – just like at major retail stores. Everyone knows you pay less for cash.

Here's how it works out for me. At the end of ten years, I've paid $440,000 and I own a house outright. At the end of a normal 30-year mortgage on the same house, I will have paid over $1 million in payments for the same house. I like the 10.10 deal better. I win and the seller wins, and the bank doesn't win for a change.

A student of mine was working with a pensioner who wanted to sell his house. Now, when a pensioner sells a house for $435,000, it's not about selling the house; it's about what it will do for the pensioner. Here's how the dialogue went:

STUDENT: "Why are you selling?"
SELLER: "I need the money."
STUDENT: "What do you need the money for?"
SELLER: "I need money to live on in retirement."
STUDENT: "What will you do with the money from the sale?"
SELLER: "Dunno, probably just put it in the bank."
STUDENT: "So, are you more interested in getting the most money for this house, or do you really want as much income as possible every month when you retire?"
SELLER: "Well, as much income as possible every month."

STUDENT:	"How much interest can you get at the bank?"
SELLER:	"About five or six per cent, I guess."
STUDENT:	"Would you rather get five per cent or eight per cent?"
SELLER:	"Well, eight per cent of course."
STUDENT:	"And if you were getting eight per cent, would you really care which bank it was with?"
SELLER:	"No, of course not."
STUDENT:	"Why don't you let me buy this from you, I'll pay you 50 per cent more than the bank was going to give you every month."
SELLER:	"That'd be great. Why didn't anyone ever offer me this before?"

So the seller wins because he gets income stream that I pay him monthly. As a buyer, my student got to buy the house, no money down, no bank loan forms, just move in, and simply start making monthly payments.

Are you starting to see the possibilities now? How many doors could this open up for you? Understand that I'm just giving you the basics here. These strategies are pretty cool, but they're just the fundamental scaffolding, so you get the idea of what's possible. Like I said before, once you get your head around this, it's amazing what you can do! Here are some transactions that my students have done:

Instalment Contract Examples

Helped a family and made $595 monthly cashflow

Student Steve

I put the normal advertising up, a couple of signs, some flyers, and a line-ad in the local newspaper. I got a phone call on a Thursday from a lady. She said: "I hope you can help me, I'm in real trouble. I have a house in Maryborough, and if I don't sell my house I'll be bankrupt or homeless on Wednesday. Or both."

This lady and her husband had gotten into financial difficulties because they couldn't afford the house they were living in. They were living beyond their means, but they put their heads in the sand and hoped things would just work out. Eventually they realised that it wasn't going to work out unless they did something, so they put the house on the market. But they listed it at a very unrealistic price. As time went on they started to get further in arrears on their bank loan. "The bank's taking us to court, and the court case is on Wednesday." She rang me up only five and a half days before the court case. She said: "I'm either going to get blacklisted, kicked out, or go bankrupt on Wednesday."

I said: "You've really left me no time to do anything creative. I'll make some calls and see what I can do." I called some people I knew, and I put together the funding through private money from two lenders. I let her know that because she had left it so late to call me that I could get her out of trouble, but I couldn't make her any money. With the money from the private lenders, I could clear her out of her debt and her arrears, and leave her some money leftover so she could get re-established in a rental property. The total cost, including the private lenders' fees, was $156,000. I paid her arrears up to date, and settled in 10 days.

Then I re-advertised the property, and within a month I sold it on an instalment contract for $230,000. I took a $5,000 deposit in the hand, and put an instalment contract in place for $225,000. I then took out a bank loan which covered the $156,000, because I had to repay the private lenders in six weeks. So, the new buyer is paying $225,000 to me, I'm paying $156,000 to the bank, and the buyer will finance me out in three years.

Up front: $5,000 cash deposit.

Monthly: The buyer pays me $1,950 and I pay the bank $1,355, so the difference is a monthly positive cashflow of $595/month.

Backend: When the buyer refinances in three years, I'll get $225,000, repay my loan and be left with a backend profit of $69,000.

$65,000 up front cash and $207 weekly cashflow

Students Julie & Dave

A guy had a house in Dandenong, Victoria, on the market, but the agent could not sell it. He'd started at $240,000 and had dropped to $220,000 over time. I said, "I can buy it today, how much do you need?" He needed $200,000 to clear his loan. I bought it for $200,000 with a $40,000 deposit just as a normal purchase.

I sold it four weeks later to a couple who were new to Australia, and had not been in their current jobs long enough to get a loan. They both worked and earned enough. I asked them about the deposit. They had $50,000 of their own, and qualified for the homeowners' grant. So they paid $65,000 deposit which means I got my $45,000 profit up front, and they pay me $402/week, which is $207/week positive. They've been in the house for 18 months so, as well as the profit, that's $16,133.58 in positive cashflow so far.

Up front: $65,000 cash deposit. $45,000 profit + recouped $20,000 of my invested funds.

Weekly: The buyer pays me $402/week and my loan and fees are $195/week, leaving a weekly positive cashflow of $207/week. After 18 months, that's $16,133.58 so far.

Backend: $0, because I got all the profit up front.

$10,000 up front cash and $72,000 backend profit

Student Rob

This guy was going bankrupt in Deception Bay, Queensland, when he found me. I paid $2,500 of his arrears payments, and put joint venture paperwork in place which said I would guarantee to babysit his loan while other people bought the property. The loan debt was $178,000. I on-sold the property on an instalment contract for $250,000 to an air-conditioning guy. He then spent $50,000 on it, did it up and increased the value by $120,000. I got a deposit of $10,000 up front and monthly instalments. After two years he cashed out, and I made a profit of $72,000 on the backend. Now he's got the place on the market for $370,000.

Up front: $10,000 cash deposit.

Monthly: Instalment payments from the buyer.

Backend: When the buyer refinanced in two years, the rest of the $250,000 that was remaining, for a backend profit of $72,000.

$17,000 up front cash and $27,000 backend profit

My wife and I spent a few days in the country town of Taree, looking for a house to buy and then on-sell for a profit. We bought a place for $125,000 with a six-week settlement, and access to the property for four of those weeks to put signage up and show people through.

Student Brett

We used the normal yellow signs that said "no bank qualifying, for sale by owner, low deposit, $325/week". We put ads in the local paper as well.

We put the signs up, started driving back to Sydney, and the phone started ringing before we hit the freeway. We got a lot of inquiries, a lot of people on welfare who didn't qualify as buyers. We on-sold it to a first homebuyer with a $10,000 deposit plus the $7,000 grant up front. They bought it for $152,000 on an instalment contract. They paid us instalments of $325/week and paid out a lump sum of $100,000 12 months later.

Up front: $10,000 cash deposit + $7,000 grant.

Monthly: Instalment payments of $325/week.

Backend: When the buyer refinances, there will be a backend profit of $27,000.

RENT-TO-OWN

A Lease Option or Rental Purchase Agreement is the name of the legal paperwork used with the Rent-to-Own or Rent-to-Buy strategy. There's also another strategy that utilises Lease Options called a Sandwich Lease, which is also known as a Back-to-Back Lease Option.

A lease option is an abbreviation for "lease with an option to purchase" or "lease with an option to buy". If you have an investment property, you can either rent your house to a tenant, or on-sell the house to a new buyer using a lease option. With a lease option, the buyer can choose to buy the property at any time before their lease expires, which is the exact duration as their option period.

At the time of this writing, in NSW you must wait 42 days before exercising the option, and in other states there is no waiting period. It's important to check for the updated ruling in your state or territory.

The paperwork used is a *lease* (Residential Tenancy Agreement) combined with a document called an *option*. In NSW you'll also include a *contract for sale*.

Because of the flexibility of these strategies, the babysitter example shown earlier can be done using either a lease option or seller finance. The main difference between seller finance and a lease option is that the tenant/buyer has the opportunity to "rent before they buy".

With seller finance, the buyer chooses to buy immediately by making instalment payments to the seller. The buyer pays a deposit to the seller, and the seller provides finance. With a lease option, the buyer rents first with the option of buying later. The buyer pays an option fee up front, and makes rent payments to the seller until the end of the lease term or until they decide to buy.

You will most likely get more money up front as a deposit from a buyer using seller finance than you would from an option fee from a tenant/buyer using a lease option. The buyer choosing seller finance is making a 25 or 30-year commitment right now. The tenant/buyer is only signing a one to two year lease with the option to buy later, and is more likely to have a tenant mentality.

A lease option is a very fluid and flexible piece of paperwork that can be written for any length of time. Every rent-to-buy agreement will be different, depending on the needs and desires of the buyer and the seller. The buyer and the seller agree to the terms between them.

The option fee is the "getting started money" that the tenant/buyer pays to get into the rent-to-buy property. You can think of it as upfront money, just like a deposit. The sale price is agreed and fixed at the start of the lease option term.

Some sellers write a long lease option of 25 to 30 years and structure it similarly to seller finance. Other sellers choose a shorter term, and review the sales price and collect another option fee every time the lease is extended. Depending on your circumstances and your reasons, it is important to consider the different benefit when structuring the length of a lease option.

WHAT ARE THE BENEFITS OF LEASE OPTIONS?

As a seller using lease options, you've made it easier for everyone to buy your house. You can get the price you want and receive the full retail value for your property. You make money three ways: the upfront option fee, ongoing monthly rental payments and a big chunk of money at the end when the tenant/buyer buys the property.

You pay no agent's commissions or large advertising expenses. You will also reduce your property holding costs, because finding a tenant/buyer for a property is much quicker than a traditional sale.

As a buyer, it is easier to qualify for a lease option than a bank loan. And the buyer has time to save up a deposit, and try out the house before they buy.

Many tenant/buyers prefer a lease option over a traditional rental arrangement because they have more control over the property and they're able to renovate and change the style to suit themselves. The buyer also benefits from the house appreciating in value, because the purchase price is written into the option contract up front. And if they can sell it for a higher price at the end of their lease option term, they can keep that profit.

Another benefit of using lease options as a buyer is that you can build up a whole portfolio of these rent-to-own properties and it's a hidden asset. Some people like that for various reasons. Also it's a lot quicker and easier than buying the usual way. You can usually move into the property in three days or less, and it costs you a lot less cash to get in.

FIRST HOMEOWNER STEPPING STONE

Many first homeowners have trouble getting over the psychological hurdle of making the transition from renting to buying. They get stuck thinking, "What if it's the wrong house?" It's not only financially a bigger commitment than what they're accustomed to, it's also a bigger step emotionally.

A lease option can help serve as a stepping stone between renting and buying. First homeowners can "try before they buy", and lease the property for a year or two or three before committing to buying it.

Women's shoes are pretty expensive. There's nothing worse than paying a lot of money for a pair of shoes, then learning after a couple of weeks that they hurt your feet. Wouldn't it be great if you could rent the shoes for a while to see if you like them? Then when you've decided that the shoes are right for you, you can come back and buy them.

I once bought a beautiful waterfront property, which was south-facing. What I didn't know when I bought it was that the house didn't get any sun and it was absolutely freezing all through the winter. On a lease option a buyer can try out the house and find out all they need to know, and then commit to buying the house when they're ready.

Another way this strategy works for first homeowners is to help them save up a deposit. Tenant/buyers can pay extra rent that goes towards saving a deposit. It almost works like a forced savings plan. Then after the first year or two, their savings record is proven and they can go to the bank and get a loan to finance the rest of the price and buy the house.

This is how it is possible to get higher than market rent with a lease option. Some transactions result in the seller receiving rental amounts that are more than double what tenants would pay in a conventional rental tenancy.

A lease option is also a great stepping stone from private finance to bank finance. If someone doesn't qualify for traditional bank finance for some reason, this can be a great way to get into their own home straight away. Then a year or two down the track they can refinance and get into the traditional banking system. Take a look at a transaction one of my students has done:

First Homeowner Stepping Stone Example

$63,000 profit in three months

Student Brett

A couple in Lower Beachmont on the Gold Coast, Queensland, had been trying to sell their house for over six months. They had already dropped the price a fair bit. They were motivated to sell, and found me through my website. We met at a local coffee shop on Saturday morning. Instead of keeping the house empty, I suggested: "How about I give you your current asking price. Would you be happy if I can look after the loan payments until I'm in a position to go through with buying it?" They jumped at that idea, because it had been vacant and eating a hole in their pocket for so long. Their asking price was $370,000. I started paying them $575/week straight away on a lease option, with two years to get finances together.

I knew I had a buyer to on-sell this property to. I had someone looking in the area. This couple had even looked at a house in the same street. They were very keen and although they were both on very good incomes, and they had a reasonable deposit, it wasn't good enough for the bank. The lady was self-employed, so they could only go on the husband's income. I knew this house would suit them. I made a phone call and explained that I might have a house for them. They drove by the place on Sunday and got excited. We met on Monday and I gave them the keys.

I on-sold the place to this couple. They paid a $15,000 deposit up front and $855/week, with the option to buy it at $418,000 in two years. Only three months later they refinanced. This was the perfect stepping stone they needed to get into their first home. Houses in their street are easily worth $450,000. After they moved in, they were so grateful they invited us around for dinner. They put on an amazing feast, with a three-tiered platter of seafood, and cut out pineapples and pina coladas. I got a call from them the other day. They still love it!

PROFIT WITHOUT FEES

A normal pattern for people is to buy a house, live in it for five or six years, then move. Then buy another house, live in it for five or six years, then move. They do this over and over again. Every time they sell they get to profit from the increase in the value of the house. But every time they buy and sell they incur all kinds of fees and rates, obligations and liabilities that come with ownership.

Lease options enable you to get all of the profits without the hassles.

With a lease option, you can move into a property within a few days, so it's a lot quicker than waiting for a sale to settle. Also, with a lease option the sale price is set when you sign the paperwork. So if the price goes up, you have already fixed the purchase price and you can sell it for a profit.

With a lease option a buyer can get control of a piece of property and do things with it before incurring all the normal ownership costs. Tradespeople do this a lot. They'll use a lease option to get in, use their skills to renovate and increase the value of the property, and then sell it for a profit without taking on the ownership costs up front.

It's also possible to do a joint venture with the owner of a property. I set the price, pay the owner rent, and I take the full profit when I sell. Here's another way to profit from the property. I could move in rent-free, renovate the owner's property over time, and we can agree to split the profits that are created when I increase the value of the seller's house. The possibilities are endless! See for yourself, here are some transactions my students put together:

Joint Venture With Owner Examples

Helped out single mum and made $7,500 profit

Student Dave

I got a call from a single mum in Singleton, West Australia, with teenage kids. She was a chef, and her work hours had been slashed by two-thirds. Her house was run-down. It needed floor tiles, fresh paint, landscaping, and a new kitchen. Because she was only working one-third of her regular hours, she couldn't do it. And if she had to sell the house as it was, she would take a hefty loss.

She found me through word-of-mouth. She sounded like a serious motivated seller, but I wasn't sure what I could do to fix her situation. Based on my research, if I was going to buy it, I was going to have to offer $250,000, but houses were selling in that area for $310,000 - $330,000. I could fix it up, but there wouldn't be much for her.

This was my first no money deal. I had an idea. Why don't I do a joint venture with her? My dad could do all the work, and we'd pay for materials and labour. We agreed to split the profits over $250,000.

It took dad a month to fix the place up. We put it back on the market, and it sold for $310,000. After the expenses, I made $7,500, dad made $7,500, and the lady got $265,000 instead of $250,000. It was great!

$33,000 profit with $130 weekly cashflow

Student Rob

I just did this deal today. Some of the local real estate agents know to bring me properties that need to move fast. So an agent called me and said that this guy really needs to sell. He first listed at $270,000 and has dropped the price to $225,000. I offered $210,000, which he refused. I said I'll pay $225,000 if the seller pays the $5,000 commission to the agent. I pay $300/week on a two-year lease option.

I on-sold it to a new tenant/buyer on a lease option for $250,000 at $430/week. It's good weekly cashflow, and I've got no loan debt and no fees. The old owner pays for insurances and rates, and the new owner takes care of maintenance.

Up front: $8,000 cash deposit.

Monthly: I pay $300/week and I receive $430/week, so I net $130/week.

Backend: If/when the tenant/buyer buys the property, I'll get $25,000 profit.

NEGATIVE-GEARING TURNAROUND

Based on average rental rates and average loan rates, average investment properties will usually end up being negatively-geared. But we want positive cashflow. If you have a negatively-geared property, getting a tenant/buyer in on a lease option instead of normal lease can turn your cashflow situation positive overnight. A lease option is much faster to put in place than a traditional property sale. On a lease option, the tenant/buyer has bought into the idea of home ownership, so they generally pay much higher rent, and they take care of any maintenance or renovation expenses themselves.

Different sellers use long and short-term lease options depending on their needs and preferences. A longer-term lease option can secure positive cashflow from your property for as long as possible. A shorter-term lease option will encourage your tenant/buyer to refinance sooner. Let's take a look at some transactions where my students have turned negative-gearing problems into positive cashflow in just a few weeks:

Negative-Gearing Turnaround Examples

Helped investor and made $73,000 profit with $170 weekly cashflow

Student Dave

The investor had a negatively-geared property and needed cashflow relief. We agreed to put a rent-to-own buyer in the home and split the positive cashflow and profits if it sold for more than $230,000. The property was in Cairns, I was in Brisbane, and the investor was in country Queensland.

This was a long-distance deal. I put an ad in the local newspaper, and I phoned the local supermarket, faxed a flyer through, and asked them to stick it on the community notice board out the front.

I spoke to the existing tenant, who hated the agent and the owner because of late repairs after a cyclone a while back. I got the tenant a referral and helped them find a new place and get released from this terrible lease. In return they showed people through the property for me, all at one convenient time.

In a couple of weeks we found a suitable buyer, who bought the place for $300,000, and paid a $3,000 option fee and $500/week for two years. Ironically, this buyer had been knocked back as a tenant by the agent six months earlier because they had dogs. I never even saw the house until I flew up for the day to get all the paperwork signed, had a swim and flew home for dinner.

Up front: $3,000 cash deposit.

Weekly: Rent $500/week, minus loan and outgoings of $330/week = Positive $170/week.

Backend: $70,000.

Car plus $140 weekly cashflow and $50,000 backend profit

Another investor found me through word-of-mouth via an investors' group. He had a property and wanted to turn his negative cashflow positive. We agreed to put a rent-to-own buyer in the house and split the profits over $250,000.

Student Rob

The buyers found me in a few days from a newspaper ad for the property. This couple rang up and viewed the home on Saturday morning, then signed the paperwork and had the keys to the house on Saturday afternoon. They bought the place on a two-year lease option for $300,000 and $550/week.

The buyers were talking about selling their second car to get the money for a deposit, so I suggested (for speed and convenience) they just give me the car. They signed the car transfer papers as well as the lease option papers all in one meeting and moved in that day.

Up front: Car (I got $3,000 cash from a wrecker on Monday morning).

Weekly: Rent $550/week, minus loan and outgoings of $410/week = Positive $140/week.

Backend: $50,000.

BACK-TO-BACK LEASE OPTIONS

By using two lease options back-to-back, you can give this opportunity to someone else, and they can rent before they buy. So you buy a property as an investor on a lease option, then you on-sell the property to an end buyer on another lease option at a slightly higher price. You make sure that you're receiving more money than you're paying so the deal generates cashflow each month.

Lease options are the most flexible of all the creative strategies we've talked about, and there are countless ways you can use them. You can use lease options in combination with pretty much every kind of strategy. Back-to-back lease options enable you to build up a portfolio of properties and benefit from positive monthly cashflow capital gain profits, without taking on the usual fees and obligations of ownership. Here are some more examples from my students you may find interesting:

Back-to-Back Lease Option Examples

Big returns on small money

Students Julie & Dave

Dave took the phone call. This lady told us about two investment properties in Berwick, one of the nicest suburbs in Melbourne's outer east, and asked, "Are you interested in buying them?" She and her husband had bought house and land packages a few years before and had them built. But they were not cut out for being landlords and being negatively-geared. That's the plain simple truth of negative-gearing; you lose a dollar to get back 25 cents. So, they were struggling financially because of the burden these properties had put on them.

They actually sold one already at $302,000, but the loan was $318,000. At settlement they had to write a cheque for $24,000 of hard cash out of their own pockets. They simply didn't have enough money to sell the other two the same way.

We did the paperwork to take over the properties on a lease option for 10 years. We paid up their rates, and guaranteed to take care of the loan payments. We advertised the properties just by using the usual handwritten signs and newspaper ads.

We on-sold one to a young couple from Beaconsfield. She had been in a car accident, and they had lost their house when they were down to one income during her recovery. They had plenty of money, and could maintain the payments, but they couldn't make up the arrears that occurred during the accident and recovery time.

They moved in on a rent-to-own basis. They've never missed a payment. They bought it at $350,000 and the house is worth $385,000 now. It's great that they've got all that capital growth out of it.

They just needed somebody to give them a chance when the banks wouldn't. They've paid $600/week since they moved in. If I'd just tried to rent that out on a normal rental I'd only get $300/week. We're cashflow positive because the loan is only $486/week.

We on-sold the other one on a lease option as well to a single mum. She had a lot of money, but life sometimes gets in the way. She told us it wasn't working out and it was too much of a commitment for her, so we released her from the paperwork. We're keeping that property as our own buy-and-hold, and we didn't need any bank loan, or a deposit. We've just taken control via the paperwork. It's perfect for us.

It's not unusual that people get into this situation. They don't get told everything. Real estate agents just want to sell them a house. People get in over their head, and they can't get out. This is a no-fees-no-charges way to fix those problems.

$17,500 cash, $350 weekly cashflow and $30,000 backend profit

This couple needed to move towns for work. They needed $7,500 for moving, and were happy to leave the rest of the money in the house for a few years. We bought the house on a lease option for $285,000, and we pay $350/week.

Students Julie & Dave

We on-sold it on a lease option to a lady who runs a truck company for $345,000. She had $25,000 to put towards her own home, and pays us $700/week. She only needs 15 months before she will refinance and pay us out the rest.

Up front: $25,000 cash deposit – $7,500 for the seller = $17,500 cash in hand.

Weekly: Positive cashflow of $350/week.

Backend: $30,000.

In one hour made $10,000 cash and $45,000 backend profit

Student Brett

The buyer and the seller both found me via referral.

At 11am I met the seller, who was absolutely stuck. He had already moved out, and was renting somewhere else. Then the sale of his property fell over, and he was stuck making payments on two places. He was asking $340,000. I bought it on a lease option at that price and paid $640/week with $50/week credited to the sale price, and I agreed to pay one mortgage payment.

At 12pm I met the buyer. The buyer had a decent income but didn't have enough of a deposit to buy the traditional way. He gave me $10,000 for a deposit. I on-sold the property to him on a lease option for $385,000 at $725/week. Win/win/win!

THE NEXT STEP

I believe these cashflow strategies can be the key to your property future. By looking at things a little differently, you'll start to find opportunities everywhere. You'll even discover that inside every property problem is an opportunity.

If any of these strategies sound interesting to you, you can get started straight away and do this yourself.

There are two ways to do anything in life – the slow way and the fast way. If you are the kind of person who wants to do things the slow way, and go through all the trial and error yourself, I would be surprised that you'd have picked up this book in the first place!

If you want to do things the fast way, my programs are designed to be an accelerator pack. Obviously I have way too much information to put into one chapter. This has been designed to open your eyes to new possibilities, to give you a glimpse of what everyday people like you are doing.

They're transforming people's lives, by structuring transactions so the buyer and seller get what they want first and my students get looked after in return. I've shown you how they receive cash up front, monthly cashflow and backend profits. And it's possible you can do the same.

Every one of my home study courses, my live training events and my coaching programs are designed to accelerate your learning and get you real results fast. You'll also connect with peers and mentors who are doing these transactions and they will hold your hand while you take your first steps. You'll get all the legal paperwork that supports these strategies, specific to your state or territory.

You have read about some of the transactions that my students have done - these are cashflow systems that can be duplicated over and over. They are not reliant on getting bank loans. There is nothing stopping you from getting started. Each of our courses includes a step-by-step process, as well as in-depth coaching, including word-for-word scripts that will help you talk easily with real estate agents, buyers, sellers and investors, and handle every question that arises.

Even if you have never invested in property before, you can start building your property portfolio today, if you want to buy property for a dollar, or you need to sell fast, or turn negative-geared property into positive cashflow, I can show you how to do this in person at live events.

I hope to meet you very soon and remember what Napoleon Hill said:

"Don't wait. The time will never be just right!"

Chapter 6

ASSET PROTECTION

"Those who own nothing
but control everything will
be set for life."

DOMINIQUE GRUBISA

DOMINIQUE GRUBISA

Dominique Grubisa is a property developer and investor, an entrepreneur, published author, speaker and practising barrister with over 20 years' legal experience.

She has become the "go to" guru for all matters legal and commercial in Australia, and has been widely featured in print media, radio and on national television.

Dominique has developed new techniques and strategies which have helped thousands to not just survive but thrive in these unique economic times.

ASSET PROTECTION

BULLETPROOF YOUR WEALTH: HOW TO PREPARE FOR CHANGING FINANCIAL TIMES

Most people think that the world economy will get better soon and that this is just a normal recession. That may not happen. I can tell you what you want to hear, or I can try and help you enormously by showing you how to prepare and to protect yourself while you still can. You may not like what I have to tell you, but it will definitely be information you can use to your advantage. Forewarned is forearmed. Of course, as American statistician and professor, Dr William Edwards Deming, once said: "It is not necessary to change. Survival is not mandatory." But now is the time to get your house in order – if you choose. The economies of the developed world are undergoing major change and you need to change too. The good news is that there is plenty you can do to actively and correctly manage your investments and protect your assets right now. And I can show you.

WHY SHOULD YOU LISTEN TO ME?

I am a practising barrister with over 20 years' legal experience in commercial and debt-related matters. I have acted for both sides, debtor and creditor, over the years and I am probably your worst nightmare if I am chasing you as a debtor. You don't want to come up against someone like me. If need be, I can be ruthless and leave you with nothing!

Unfortunately I had the misfortune to personally be on the receiving end of the legal system a few years ago and I got a taste of my own medicine when some unscrupulous people pursued me personally. It was then that I realised how vulnerable my wealth and everything I had worked so hard for over the years could become in one unexpected instance due to unforeseen circumstances beyond my control.

As human beings we fear change. When we are afraid we become paralysed. I learned a valuable lesson when things changed for me and that was that fear is just your body warning you that a different course of action is required. It is your personal, in-built alarm system saying to you: "Some form of action is required here." You need not freeze or despair; all you have to do is note what your body is telling you and then set about a course of action. The winds will always change and we cannot do anything about that. What we can do is adjust our sails.

So when I listened to my fear telling me that all my wealth was exposed and could be lost because of an unexpected chain of events beyond my control, I quickly readjusted and I set about protecting everything I had to make it bulletproof. I researched the subject thoroughly and reverse-engineered my vast knowledge on how to target debtors' wealth in order to build myself the best possible defence and shore up my worth so that no one could touch it.

Whilst doing research to formulate my system of asset protection I realised that the very wealthy of the world have been protecting their wealth for themselves, their families and their future bloodline for hundreds of years. They are untouchable because they can afford to be. They invest in the very best systems to make sure that what is theirs stays theirs. When a dying J.D. Rockefeller was asked about the secret to amassing his vast fortune, he famously said:

"Own nothing but control everything."

That is what everybody should be doing, and there should be no barriers to access this ultimate protection. Unfortunately it is something that has previously been reserved only for the very wealthy and, in reality, it is something that everybody needs and should be able to access cheaply and easily. Fortunately I have now devised a system to enable this to happen for anyone who wants to protect their wealth and their family's future in these uncertain times.

But firstly let us examine why this is necessary.

WHAT IS HAPPENING WITH THE WORLD?

For the last 40 years the developed world has been on a massive spending spree. Credit was easy to come by, banks lent quite readily and anyone could borrow money to use the power of leverage to grow their wealth. Yes, there were some hiccups along the way and yes, there were some recessions but essentially for the last four decades we have enjoyed strong economies, a lot of growth, and high employment. We have had a great time and everybody has been comfortable. Unfortunately though, many individuals, corporations and governments have lived beyond their means, so that in some countries several bubbles which have been growing exponentially for the last 40 years are now deflating rapidly and simultaneously. Australia remains somewhat buffered by our ongoing resources boom but if the rest of the world continues to cough, Australia may well catch a cold.

So what are these bubbles?

THE HOUSING BUBBLE

As we know house prices have always risen in Australia. Sometimes the rate of price increase has plateaued or slowed but it was unheard of for house prices to fall or go backwards. The experts have always told us that house prices double on average every seven to 10 years. Historically this has been correct yet experts are now divided on whether this trend can continue. Certainly, prices in some Australian markets have softened in recent times – but nowhere near those in the United States which resulted from the subprime mortgage crisis of the late 2000s. So what happened in America? In a nutshell, lenders lent to people who couldn't afford repayments, on property that didn't have – or hold – its mortgage value. Personal debt increased, housing prices dropped and mortgage delinquencies sky-rocketed – and the credit tap was turned off, not just in the US, but around the world.

So why did we have a credit bubble and where did it go?

THE CREDIT BUBBLE

After the deregulation of the banking industry under former Prime Minister, Paul Keating, in the mid-1980s, the Australian credit market was opened up to competition from other lenders around the world. We no longer had a closed shop oligopoly for a banking industry where a few lenders controlled the market; suddenly lenders had to compete for business and the goal was to lend as much money as possible, therefore lending standards slipped until we got to a point in recent years where anyone with a pulse could get a credit card and anyone who owned property could use it as an ATM to draw money out of.

Newfangled loan products - known as low or no doc loans where lenders could legally lend to borrowers with little or no income on the strength of the value of their property - were introduced. Creditors did not care if the borrower had no income to make repayments – they would lend them more money than they needed, secured against the equity in their property, and the borrowers could use this extra "buffer" of loaned monies to make their repayments and when this ran out they could have their home revalued at a higher price and draw out more money to keep on going. Debt is not a problem whilst ever you can get more debt; it is when the credit bubble bursts and you can't borrow any more that the day of reckoning comes. This is what we saw so dramatically in the United States.

In 2009 there was a Joint Parliamentary Commission Inquiry in Australia into the financial services industry as well as the lending practices adopted by banks in relation to the low and no doc style of loan.

The banks have since "recalled" this product in that they no longer offer these loans in the way that they did and the whole process has become much stricter. New laws came into force on 1 July 2010 in the form of a National Consumer Credit Code. This statute was designed to protect consumers from brokers and lenders adopting predatory lending practices to line their own pockets.

To understand how it all started and where it all went wrong, we first have to understand the nature of the product.

WHAT IS A LOW DOC LOAN?
A low doc loan was officially said to have been designed for self-employed people who did not have tax returns to support their earnings.

What lenders required for this style of loan was:

- for the borrower to verify that they were self-employed by providing an Australian Business Number (ABN);

- for the borrower to provide details of income (on the loan application); and

- for the borrower to swear a statutory declaration that the amount stated was what they actually earned.

WHAT IS A NO DOC LOAN?

These loans were initially said to have been created for those who had adequate funds to service a loan but were unable to show any of this information or swear a statutory declaration as to earnings. What lenders required for this product was for the borrower to swear a statutory declaration saying that they could afford to make all loan repayments in respect of the loan.

HOW DID THESE LOANS COME ABOUT?

The cynic in me – who takes a "glass half empty view" when it comes to banks - suspects that the banks didn't so much think, "Let's just help people who can't show income by relaxing our lending requirements" but rather, "There's so many people out there we could sell loans to, if only they earned enough money to service the loans. There's no risk to us because house prices are going up and up and we will always end up with a valuable property if they can't pay the loan. We will insure against prices falling though by making borrowers pay for mortgage insurance which will cover any loss which may occur for us. Let's find a way to lend them money by not requiring them to show us earnings."

WHAT'S THE PROBLEM WITH THESE LOANS?

Now of course everything would have been just dandy had property prices continued to rise and banks had continued to lend but as with all Ponzi schemes, the wheels eventually come off when you can't borrow anymore to keep the thing going.

What the banks had in mind was that they would keep revaluing properties and lend more money against them each year, which would be used as a buffer to help the borrower cover the repayments.

In effect, people were being encouraged to use their house as one big ATM to live off when all of a sudden the machine was empty and they couldn't pull money out of it anymore. These people were not productive and had no income apart from the equity in their homes (which had run out) so they either had to sell en masse or wait for the bank to repossess their property. Hence the burst of the housing bubble and the credit bubble simultaneously. This bubble is still deflating and a lot of people have been caught short where they are "upside down" on their mortgages – they owe more to the bank than what the property is worth. They are stuck between a rock and a hard place with no exit strategy in this suddenly changed market.

WHAT IF YOU ARE STUCK WITH PROPERTY IN A SOFT MARKET?

I am not sure of the market in any given area in Australia at present or any given reader's individual circumstances, but I do know though that many people are stuck with negatively-geared properties which they cannot sell in a local soft market. You may or may not be a victim of predatory lending through a no or low doc loan as discussed above.

Most property investors over the last 40 years have had great success banking on capital gain and therefore were happy to suffer negative-gearing or short-term losses for long-term gain or increases in property values in the form of capital growth. As we have established though, things may have changed and what worked before will not necessarily work now. As we have said this is not a time to freeze with fear, but rather a time to pose the question: "What action is required here?"

A good strategy in this new market is selling some properties on a lease option or instalment contract in order to get some cash injections and boost cashflow. My personal recent experience and that of most clients is that the property market is challenged at present. People cannot get the loans to buy property as banks aren't lending, and the economic uncertainty in the world has made many people bearish. Having said that, you may be happy to hold everything and remain negatively-geared for the foreseeable future. If you want to have another iron in the fire though there is a way to turn your properties (or some of them) into positively-geared properties. There are other strategies which you may want to consider and which may help you towards achieving your goal. The problem is that the market has changed a lot in recent times and there are just not the buyers that there used to be so we have to think outside the square.

In the circumstances, it may be that you can look at a solution whereby you "park" some properties by selling them on vendor finance terms. A lease option sale is a quick fix which can put cash in your pocket, stop the monthly shortfall as well as stop the flow of money out in holding costs.

The upside of all this is that rentals are really quite strong at the moment. Additionally, a vendor finance arrangement or strategy will see you getting well above market rent. As banks won't lend, you are effectively the bank and will receive income from the purchaser like interest repayments.

I will give you some numbers by way of example. My husband and I have a house in Cairns which we purchased at below market price a few years ago for $313,000. We did a minor renovation and rented it for $390 per week so it was just cashflow neutral for us (maybe a little positive). When the Global Financial Crisis (GFC) hit we had to drop the rent to $350 per week. We put it on the market a couple of years ago. The agent told us it was worth $430,000. We have been burned by having property on the market for too long in the past so after one week we lowered the price to $410,000. There were a couple of nibbles at the open home that weekend but no offers. We dropped our asking price to $390,000 and whilst there was interest there were no offers for another few weeks. We bit the bullet and put a stop to all advertising and told the agent to ring up everyone who had been through and tell them we would take $370,000 there and then (well below market value). The agent came up empty.

Out of desperation we put an ad in *The Cairns Post* offering to sell the property at $529 per week as a vendor finance sale. At 8am the first day of the ad a lady rang up and paid us a $10,000 deposit and we ultimately sold the house to her on a two-year option for $410,000 ($420,000 sale price less her $10,000 deposit). During this time she pays us $529 per week. Our mortgage is $350 per week. She pays all rates and outgoings in respect of the property.

The agent came back to us a week later with an offer of $350,000 (the same agent who told us we could get $430,000). She said that this was now the market price in the current market (because of a variety of reasons).

You may want to look at doing something like what we did with our Cairns house to have your properties pay for themselves and support you rather than having to keep working because of negative-gearing. With this strategy you are, in effect, the lender or the bank, receiving monthly mortgage payments and you are no longer supporting your tenants by paying a shortfall and outgoings on properties that they want to live in but cannot afford to buy. You could try and advertise a property (in the local classifieds) as being for sale at maybe 10 per cent above market price and then sell it on a lease option. Your suburb may be an altogether different market (you would know best in this respect) but vendor finance deals are moving much faster than normal sales at present.

You should aim to get in at least a $10,000 cash option fee up front, followed by a significant positive cashflow from some of your properties throughout the option period (I suggest two to three years) with a balance payable to you at the end when the buyer refinances and pays you out. You will be up on sale prices in your area but it may pay to find out what rentals are going for. If it is something which appeals to you, this is a strategy which can be implemented cheaply and easily – just an extra iron in the fire as opposed to waiting for something to happen.

THE STOCK MARKET BUBBLE

In the 54-year period from 1928 to 1982 the stock market rose by 300 per cent. Stocks have always been seen as a vehicle for wealth-creation as it is a market which increases over time (as with housing). However those gains became artificially inflated in recent times. In the 20 years from 1982 to 2002 the stock market increased an astonishing 1,200 per cent (compared to 300 per cent over the preceding 54 years). The market grew four times as much in 70 per cent of the time. This would have been fine if there was real value and productivity to support such growth. Unfortunately, as with the housing and credit bubbles we have looked at above, this rapid price inflation was all artificial. The 1,200 per cent growth in the stock market came without 1,200 per cent growth in gross domestic product (the earnings of the country) or earnings of companies. As we have seen, Mr Market is like water – it eventually finds its own level and the false and inflated prices cannot be sustained.

THE PRIVATE DEBT BUBBLE

As we have seen above, the strong and growing economy we enjoyed over the last 40 years was a result of the combination of a credit bubble which fuelled housing and stock market bubbles. Because this boom went on for so long and created so much wealth, lenders (not just banks) began to feel very comfortable about managing risk. It seemed like crashing economies were a thing of the past and recessions may come but could be managed quickly and easily without too much fuss. It got to a point where all lenders felt that the risk of the economy failing had been eliminated - with the advent of modern economics there were no vagaries and governments could control anything. The risk of losing money as a lender in such an environment was perceived as being minimal. Private lenders took on a lot of debt in the false belief that there was no risk and that nothing could go wrong in the economy.

Lenders willingly increased the amounts they lent on credit cards, home mortgages, business and commercial loans – all types of loans across the board, in fact, on the strength of high asset prices, high employment and a strong economy. The private lending market was dependent on the housing and stock markets remaining at their high levels. When they fell, the private debt bubble burst.

THE DISCRETIONARY SPENDING BUBBLE

Consumer spending accounts for the lion's share of the Australian economy. A large proportion of consumer spending is optional and is known as "discretionary spending". Because we had a lot of bubble-generated income (for example from people easily drawing out their equity in properties and spending it) combined with easy consumer credit, lots of easy discretionary consumer spending was made possible at every income level.

As we now see the housing, credit, stock market and private debt bubbles deflate, people do not have ready cash to spend, they lose their jobs, earn less or fear the worst and begin to save. Either way they spend less out of necessity and discretionary spending is cut right back.

We have already seen the first four bubbles pop since the GFC hit in 2008. The final bubble may now be reaching critical mass.

THE GOVERNMENT DEBT BUBBLE

Governments around the world enjoyed the economic bubble that was the last 40 years along with the rest of us. When the other bubbles burst in the GFC, governments introduced various bailout and stimulus packages.

At the time of writing, in early 2012, the most vulnerable weak links remain the European nations affectionately known as the "PIIGS" – Portugal, Italy, Ireland, Greece and Spain. They are technically insolvent but are depending on further bailouts from the rest of Europe (or wherever they can get them) to stay afloat.

Where is the money to come from? The European Central Bank? The International Monetary Fund? The Germans? The powers that be are holding constant meetings trying to decide workable rescue plans. This affects Australian banks because they cannot borrow as much overseas and therefore the quantum of local funds available for lending tightens.

In a normally functioning financial system banks usually manage to fund themselves. At the end of each day, they tally up deposits and withdrawals and workout who has surplus fund and who is in deficit. The deficit banks borrow from the surplus banks at the interbank lending rate to balance the books. Then it's lights out and everyone goes home happy. Things get a little uncomfortable if a bank persistently finishes each day with a cash deficit. Its peers become a little suspicious. Perhaps the bank took too much risk and expanded its balance sheet a little too aggressively. Now, it can't satisfy customer withdrawal requests due to a lack of liquidity. Other banks are no longer prepared to lend to it in case they don't see their money again. So the bank in question goes to the central bank for a loan. This used to be a last resort for banks however today it is much different. Banks readily ask for bailout from the central bank all the time and it is not a matter of last resort. Of course, Australian banks are not going to fail tomorrow (and this book contains financing strategies that do away with banks altogether!) - but they will be impacted by world events.

WHAT DOES THIS ALL MEAN FOR YOU?

The purpose of this analysis is not to paralyse you with fear but to spur you into action; to convince you of the importance of acting now to protect yourself.

What this means for us as individuals is that the system we have become accustomed to for the last 40 years will unlikely exist for the next 40.

What will governments do? They may raise taxes and change laws, and European and American governments are already eyeing off superannuation funds as a massive pool of money from which to borrow. Just another reason why it's more important than ever to protect everything you have right now.

So you see, now is the time to adapt. As evolutionist Charles Darwin said:

"It is not the strongest or the smartest who survive, but those who are the most responsive to change."

So what must we do to change and protect ourselves?

THE ACHILLES HEEL OF PROPERTY INVESTORS

Most property investors or anyone who owns real estate will usually hold the title to that property in their own name. This means that any significant equity in property (the part that they own free of the mortgage to the bank) is exposed to creditors. The way that property works in Australia is that we have a Torrens Title system of registration in lands. Every single piece of land or real estate has a number and is registered in each state with the Land Titles Office of that state. Anyone claiming an interest in that land has to register the interest on the title of that property for it to be recognised. This is why banks will register their mortgage on your title and when you see a copy of your title deed or anyone performs a title search on your property they will see that it is subject to a first mortgage to the bank. Any other person who wants to claim security against your property can then register a second mortgage if you allow them or alternatively a caveat on the title to the property.

When you sell a property you need to discharge all debts on the title. This means that you have to pay out the first mortgagee for them to remove their mortgage. You'll also need to pay out anyone who has registered a caveat on the title in order for them to remove the caveat as the new purchaser will not want any debts on the title. They will want a "clear" title.

Where property owners can get in trouble then is that creditors or anybody pursuing them or wanting to target this significant wealth held in property can register a caveat on the title to that property.

We know that property is (and always has been) a great vehicle to hold and grow wealth. One drawback of property though is that it is unfortunately the most cumbersome of asset classes – it is easy to identify, being very much in the realm of public information on a national and readily accessible register, and it is difficult to liquidate. What this means is that in an emergency it is hard to hide and impossible to offload quickly. Unlike shares or cash property generally cannot be easily sold or traded in and out of. As we know, there are invisible costs like Stamp Duty, legal fees and other expenses involved in buying and selling property and additionally there is the time it takes to liquidate a property – you cannot just withdraw your equity at a branch or instruct your broker to liquidate. Most people need to appoint an agent, have photos and marketing prepared and it will take at least two weeks from the time you commit to selling to when the property is actually marketed. Standard settlement time is six weeks so even if you find a buyer immediately there is still some two months before you have your money in your hand (best case scenario), not to mention the invisible costs involved in commissions, advertising and marketing of a property. You cannot just quickly sell a house when you need to and the only way to speed up the process is to take a big haircut on the sales price. This means that if someone is chasing you for money you are a big target and cannot move quickly to evade them.

A creditor will always know if you own property because it is publicly available information and is easy to find out – it is the first port of call for all litigation lawyers. As a barrister working in the debt collection industry the first thing that I look at with a prospective defendant is whether or not they hold property in their name. I am delighted if I do a title search and find that my potential debtor owns real estate. Unfortunately for them it is publicly available information. I can run a search on their name across all Australian databases whilst I sit at home in my pyjamas on a Saturday morning, and will know in seconds the addresses of all properties they own or have an interest in, in Australia. I can even find out how much they owe the bank on the property. Indeed, in this information age, with another click of a button on my laptop I will know what their property is worth anywhere in Australia without having any local real estate knowledge. So I will know what their equity is and I can be sure that they cannot move quickly and that I can target that equity. The other thing that I can do, if I am worried that they will sell the property or try to evade me, is freeze that asset so that they are not able to sell it, mortgage it or otherwise deal with it.

Given that most of the very rich of the world store their wealth in property, there needs to be a way to reduce this exposure and potential loss of control as property investors. It does not mean that we become afraid and freeze up and sell all our real estate and bury the money in the backyard; it just means that we need to minimise the risk if we are going to hold our wealth in property. Therefore when I set out to reverse-engineer the debt collection process in order to create the ultimate asset protection system the first thing I needed to address was the vulnerability and exposure suffered by property owners.

So how do we get around this?

HOW TO PROTECT YOUR EQUITY AND PROPERTY QUICKLY, CHEAPLY AND EASILY

In order to practice what J.D. Rockefeller preached, that is, to own nothing but control everything, we need a legally viable vehicle with which to control our wealth. The technical legal answer is to form a trust. A trust is a legal entity which acts through a trustee. The trustee can be a corporate entity i.e. a company, or an individual. Anyone over 18 years can be the trustee of a trust. The beauty of a trust is that, whilst it can do anything a company or an individual can do and is a legally recognised entity, there is no register for trusts in Australia. Any information to do with your trust is therefore below the radar and is only available to you and those who you choose to allow into your circle of trust. That is the ultimate in control. It is not like a company or real estate ownership where creditors can access publicly available information through the Australian Securities and Investments Commission (ASIC) or the Land Titles Office to find more out about you or your company or your properties.

Okay, so how does this help you if you are holding property in your own name or under a company name where you or the company may be a target to creditors or others who wish to attack your wealth? As I said you don't want to have to sell and hide the money under your pillow, nor do you want to have to incur Stamp Duty just to change ownership over to a safe entity like a trust. Don't worry, there is a little-known secret that those in the know use to transfer their exposed equity in real estate over to a trust and give themselves the ultimate vehicle for control of that asset.

While devising my asset protection system I realised that banks and first mortgagees have the ultimate "box seat". When it comes to fighting over control of real estate assets a first mortgagee has the trump card. Even in a bankruptcy situation the first mortgagee does not have to cooperate with the trustee in bankruptcy as they are a secured creditor. Their power comes from the Torrens Title system of registration of lands that we have in Australia as discussed earlier and which I will explore further below. Under our Torrens Title system we have a concept of "indefeasibility" of title. This means that the first to register an interest in land will be ultimately protected and will stay on the title until their debt is paid out to their satisfaction or they otherwise elect to remove themselves from that title. Once an interest is registered it is indefeasible or final. This means that your first mortgagee is in a great position as against all other creditors. What we need to do then to protect ourselves is to create a trust whereby we essentially control that entity and that entity then registers an interest on the title to our property. This protects our equity. We are still the owners of the property however our trust holds an unregistered second mortgage and registers this interest on the title and that sucks up all the equity in the property.

HOW DOES IT ALL WORK?
Let me go back to the first principles briefly because if you understand the mechanics of the law, it will be easier for you to grasp the strategies I have developed and you can then assess their effectiveness as they apply to you and your ultimate goal.

If you know what can go wrong you will know where you are most vulnerable and you can set about fixing this.

DEBTS

The debts you have can be of two kinds, secured and unsecured. Secured debts are those secured by mortgage over the property you own, a mortgage over your real estate, a charge over your car or furniture if you have it on finance or a debenture charge over your company. If you borrowed money on a secured basis then your lender will have taken these types of securities from you as security for the loan. Your failure to pay an instalment is a breach of the loan contract entitling the lender to give you a notice to bring the arrears up to date or pay up the full amount of the loan account balance. Non-compliance by you entitles the lender to seize the goods and sell them and, in the case of real estate, to get a court order for possession of the property and evict you and then sell it.

Unsecured debts are those where the lender has provided you with a loan or supplied you with credit for which the lender has no security at all. In the case of credit cards, your obligation is to pay the lender the minimum amount each month that it stipulates, month after month. Your failure to pay an instalment is a breach of the loan contract entitling the lender to give you notice to bring the arrears up-to-date or to pay up the full amount of the loan account balance. Non-compliance by you entitles the lender to sue you by way of a Statement of Claim for recovery of the debt plus interest plus legal costs.

A third category of creditor is an unsecured creditor who sues you for an amount of money (for negligence or breach of contract or whatever) and gets a judgment against you. That judgment is a piece of paper, signed by a judge and stamped by the court, saying that you owe the money. The judgment creditor then proceeds to enforce that debt by going after anything you have of value – your salary, rental income, equity in properties and personal goods and effects.

WHAT CAN THE CREDITOR / LENDER DO?

SECURED CREDITORS

A. Real estate

If you default under your mortgage, the lender will post to you a statutory default notice under the property laws of the state where the property is located. The notice will give you 30 days to pay up the loan and non-compliance by you will entitle the lender to exercise its power of sale under the loan documentation. If you correct the arrears and things continue normally, should you default again, the lender does not have to issue another 30-day notice.

The lender will then make a Supreme Court application for an order for possession of the property, meaning, an order that you be evicted. The court application has to be served personally on each borrower. Personal service means that the Sheriff, Court Bailiff or a licensed commercial agent must physically hand a copy of the application to each borrower. The court papers will state a hearing date usually a month ahead. Unless you have a defence to the claim, you don't have to appear at court. The matter will be dealt with in your absence and in the usual course of events the court will make an order for possession and costs against you.

The Sheriff or the Bailiff will, in a few weeks, come to the property and serve a writ or a warrant for possession. Service can be personal but if you're not present when s/he comes, execution of the writ is effected by the actual document being taped or stuck to your front gate or door. The writ will tell you the date by which you must leave otherwise s/he will return with a commercial agent to physically take possession for the lender and a locksmith to change all the locks to bar your re-entry.

Once you've gone the lender will engage a real estate agent to list the property for sale by private treaty or by auction. Whichever they choose, you have no input. Following the sale the lender will pursue you for recovery of the balance of the loan account as an unsecured creditor, details of which are set out below. (Obviously this is unlikely to happen to you but you will see how the system fits together and will appreciate an understanding of the process). If you know the worst that can happen you can then set about guarding against it.

B. Cars, furniture and personal goods

Your car, boat, motor cycle, furniture or other personal property that you have under finance can be seized by the lender if you default under the loan contract. The first thing the lender will do is issue you with a statutory default notice under applicable state legislation. You will be told to pay out the account in 30 days. In the case of non-compliance the lender will make an application in a Magistrate's Court for an order for possession of the goods. This will entitle the lender and its commercial agent to come and take the goods and sell them. The Order for Possession usually goes further and authorises the lender to enter upon private property, using reasonable force, to seize the goods and remove them. If, for example, your car is parked in the street or another public place and the lender finds it s/he can simply organise a tow truck to hook it up and take it away. Obviously, this is very stressful if you come out of the supermarket and find your car gone. If the vehicle is in your garage or on other private property the lender cannot remove it without supervision which means that the local police will be in attendance. A common popular misconception is that the lender is obliged to get the retail value of the car or furniture in an auction sale. The reality is that the goods will be sold off by one of the auction houses listed in the Yellow Pages® where they will go under the hammer for or below the current wholesale price. For example, the car that you cherish and believe to be worth $50,000 could end up being sold under the hammer for $10,000 and there is nothing you can do about it. After sale the lender will become an unsecured creditor and be entitled to sue you using the devices set out below to recover from you the balance of the money due.

UNSECURED CREDITORS

As stated above, the balance of account on a secured loan becomes an unsecured debt after the security property has been sold off. Credit cards and personal loans entitle the lender to sue you for the balance of the loan account and as a general rule such claims are extremely difficult to defend because the courts take the simple view that the lender gave the borrower money to spend, the lender wants the money back and the borrower has not paid it therefore the borrower is guilty. Claims for unsecured debts are made through the courts by the lender issuing a Statement of Claim and unless you have a valid defence there will be no formal court hearing. It will be an administrative process in the court office where the registrar stamps the papers and enters a judgment against you for the debt, legal costs and interest.

With a court judgment, a creditor who is unsecured has five available remedies:

1) **Public Examination to obtain information about your current assets liabilities income and expenditure** - The lender can have you brought before the court to supply this information so they can calculate their next move.

2) **Writ of Possession of Goods** - The lender can have the court send the Sheriff or Bailiff to your home, place of business, rental properties that you have etc. to seize your furniture and personal effects and have them removed for auction.

3) **Writ of Possession of Land** - With a judgment the lender can issue a writ or a warrant and register this on the title to your real estate. If the property is not subject to a mortgage, the Sheriff or Bailiff can sell it by auction. If the property is subject to a mortgage then the writ or warrant will stay endorsed on the title to your property accumulating annual interest and you will have to pay it out when you either sell the property or refinance it.

4) **Garnishee** - A lender with a judgment can garnishee or intercept money due to you from other people. The most common garnishee is on wages where your employer is ordered by the court to pay you a specified minimum amount out of your wages with the whole of the balance of your pay being remitted to the lender. Bank accounts that you have can also be garnisheed and you won't necessarily know about it until your cheques start bouncing, as the court will order the bank to drain your accounts and pay the lender. Perhaps the least obvious garnishee that can harm you is where the lender intercepts rent due to you from your investment properties from your tenants or garnishees your real estate agent so that the lender gets paid and you don't. Without a cashflow from your investment properties you might be exposed to defaults under your other mortgages.

5) **Bankruptcy** - A lender with a judgment can go to the office of the Insolvency and Trustee Service of Australia (ITSA) and issue what is called a Bankruptcy Notice which is a procedure under commonwealth legislation directing

you to pay the judgment within a specified period and in the case of non-compliance the lender can then make an application to the Federal Court of Australia for an order for your bankruptcy. Unless you get yourself into a position to pay out the debt in full, bankruptcy proceedings are fatal because the courts always ultimately grant the Bankruptcy Order sought by a lender. The court will appoint a Trustee in Bankruptcy to administer your affairs while you are a bankrupt and this will either be a government agency, the ITSA or a court-appointed private chartered accountant. You have to have a meeting with the trustee and make a truthful disclosure of all your assets and liabilities, income and expenditures. The trustee will take title to all of your real estate and your personal possessions except for basic household furniture and tools of trade. Everything else you have will go to the trustee who will then distribute it among all of your creditors. Being a bankrupt is like being out of jail on bail; you can remain in society but there is very little you can do financially. The minimum period of a bankruptcy is three years but this can be extended if the trustee believes that you are hiding assets. Upon being declared bankrupt you have to surrender your passport and you cannot leave the country.

I am laying out the worst case scenario here – not that this will probably ever happen to you - but we are guarding against that one bullet in the game of Russian roulette and you need to know what can happen when things go wrong so that you can see how it is possible to block off all avenues any potential creditor may have at coming after you and everything you have worked hard for.

THE RECOMMENDED ASSET PROTECTION SYSTEM

You would probably not be surprised to learn that most people hold their most valuable asset, their property, in their own names. As we have learned, this means that our significant equity in our properties (which is usually the biggest chunk of our wealth) is open to an attack from creditors. As we have seen, anyone preying upon you can easily run land titles searches and will know that you own real estate. We therefore need to protect that equity.

Okay, so how does our asset protection trust operate in practice? As we know, with the Torrens Title system for registration of interests in land in Australia, anyone claiming an interest in land has to register that interest for the world to see. Anyone can do a title search on anyone else's property and will have notice of other interests. Competing interests work in terms of priority according to date of registration. That is, the date that the interest was created is irrelevant – the first to register the interest on the title to the property prevails and the concept of "indefeasibility" of title means that when someone registers an interest in land on the title to that property then that is final, no one can challenge or remove them from the title and their security over the property stands in order of the date they registered their interest. Therefore the first mortgagee goes first (as they are the first to register) then other mortgagees or subsequent registered interests line up in terms of their dates of registration.

Let's use an extreme example to illustrate the point. Let's say I own a property outright (there is no mortgage) and it is worth $500,000. Now let's assume that on Monday I go and borrow $300,000 from "Bank One" secured against the property. Bank One does a tile search and sees that I own the property unencumbered and there is no mortgagee on the title. They loan me the money there and then and I sign all the mortgage documents and deposit a Bank One cheque for $300,000 on the following day, Tuesday. On Wednesday morning I do a quick title search and see that Bank One still hasn't registered their mortgage on the title so as far as the rest of the world is concerned the property is still unencumbered. I go to "Bank Two" and borrow another $300,000. Bank Two gives me the money there and then on Wednesday as they do a title search and are satisfied that the property is unencumbered. On that Wednesday I sign a mortgage to the property over to Bank Two and they run directly to the Land Titles Office and register their mortgage. On Thursday, Bank One's filing clerk ambles over to the Land Titles Office and registers the mortgage which I signed with them on Monday only to find that Bank Two now has a mortgage registered on the title. I am probably in trouble for committing fraud and various other offences but at the end of the day, Bank Two's interest prevails – yes, Bank One lent the money first, but Bank Two registered first and the concept of indefeasibility of title means that they prevail. They can seize and sell the property if I don't pay the mortgage and they can take their $300,000 and be fully paid out. Bank One, having lent the money first but being second to register, will get paid out whatever is left after Bank Two helps themselves to whatever they require to discharge their mortgage. If it is not enough to pay out their loan that's too bad!

Most people know what a mortgage is – it is a debt registered against a property, usually because a lender advanced money for the purchase of that property and will register their mortgage on the title to protect their interest until the loan they gave the property owner is repaid. Sometimes it is paid off over many years and other times it is paid out when the property is sold. Usually the purchaser has their own lender advancing the purchase price of the property and they will pay out the owner/seller's loan and register their own mortgage on the title. Another common interest which may be registered on the title to a property which you may not have heard of though is a "caveat". Caveat is Latin for "beware". A caveat registered on a title to a property is a form of warning to anyone searching the title to "beware" or be warned that there is a debt owing to someone else. The caveat can be withdrawn by the creditor (the person who is owed money who registered the caveat) when the debt is satisfied.

PUTTING IT ALL TOGETHER: WHAT THIS MEANS FOR US AND OUR ASSET PROTECTION STRATEGY

What we want to do then with our asset protection is, in effect, mortgage all of your equity to a trust and that trust will then register a caveat on the titles to each of your properties to represent that mortgaged interest. The caveat (noting an "equitable" or unregistered mortgage) will sit there compounding and will soak up all remaining equity so that there is nothing else for others to take. Any other creditor who comes along and tries to attack your wealth or your equity will be in the same position as Bank One was in our example – they can take whatever is left after our trust (who registered earlier and has an indefeasible interest) has been paid out in full to its satisfaction.

WHY DO WE REGISTER A CAVEAT?

We register a caveat as opposed to a second mortgage because we want to "own nothing and control everything". Unfortunately we are vulnerable as things stand because we own the property and yet can lose control of it – anyone can register a caveat or writ on our title and we are powerless to stop this at present. If we grant an equitable or unregistered mortgage to our trust and the trust then registers a caveat on the title, we can prevent anyone else registering or claiming an interest in our equity. Indefeasibility of title means that once our trust registers on the title it can control the equity remaining in the property. What we are doing is asserting control and blocking out anyone else who wants to try and register on our title after us.

We can have our trust remove or replace our caveat at any time – for example, if we want to sell or refinance the property – and the first mortgagee lender will not be made aware of this so it will not cause any waves for you with higher ranking creditors. If we try and register a second mortgage the first mortgagee will know about it and in most states we will need its consent to do so which will be more trouble than it's worth and will result in us losing control by having to involve others (something we don't want to do as this is all about us gaining control). A caveat enables us to effect the ultimate control! It is quick and easy yet very, very powerful.

FREQUENTLY ASKED QUESTIONS

Do I have to pay Stamp Duty?

No, Stamp Duty only comes into play if the title is being transferred across to someone else. The ownership of the property still remains the same. All that we are doing is mortgaging the equity to a trust which is essentially controlled by us. It is a legal entity and a vehicle to hold and control our wealth. In effect what we are doing is mortgaging ourselves to the hilt so that we have two creditors. The first is our first mortgagee who, for most of us, is already registered on our title and has an indefeasible interest. We cannot get rid of them, nor do we want to; we know we owe them money – the amount our property is mortgaged for – but we are looking to protect our stake in the property after the mortgage is accounted for, our equity. The second creditor who is entitled to the balance of the equity after the first mortgagee is paid out is our trust. So that if anything ever happens our first mortgagee will get paid out first and so that our share is not exposed, our trust will get paid out second. We are a beneficiary under that trust so the money comes back to us.

Does my trust have to pay tax or have any accounting requirements?

No. Your trust is not trading or earning an income at all. It is merely a structure which is holding existing wealth. You pay your taxes as usual.

Who should I use as a trustee?

I suggest anybody over 18 years who you trust. Others have had success with parents, siblings, other family members or very close friends. Do not use a passing acquaintance or a professional. They will not want to do it. It must be somebody who you trust enough to ostensibly hand them the reins.

What if my trustee betrays me? I do not want to give control to someone else.

You would be the appointor under the trust. You have the ultimate power behind the scenes. You can remove a trustee or replace them at any time so you are not really relinquishing control. You are using your trustee in order to control your wealth. The trustee is essentially your puppet.

What if I cannot find a trustee or do not trust anyone enough to give them the role?

If there is nobody to act as your trustee then you can incorporate a company with you as Director and use this entity as your trustee. What this means is that your company is separate from you and your company is taking a controlling role with respect to your wealth. The goal is to separate you as owner of the wealth and turn you into a "man of straw". On paper you own nothing but behind the scenes you control everything!

If you need a corporate trustee you can incorporate a company online for $476 which may be cheaper than going through your accountant. The reason we would want a new and separate company is that we don't want a company which is trading – we don't want to expose your personal assets to business debts. You can set up companies as required online quickly and easily (24-hour turnaround) by going to www.ecompanies.com.au. They then email you all you need (incorporation certificate from ASIC etc.). Most people who are self-employed or financially independent run their businesses or earn their passive income through companies of which they are directors and shareholders. A company is a great vehicle which will enable you to "own nothing but control everything".

Why do I want to be a "man of straw"?

Put simply, if you have no wealth and no assets in your own name it means that there is nothing for anyone to take from you. We are trying to set up hurdles and barriers between you and your assets and potential future creditors by creating an asset protection trust. We want to divorce you as an individual from your wealth (so there is nothing for creditors to get at!). In order to protect our wealth we are putting it in a safe place and removing ourselves from the picture whilst we control everything from behind the scenes.

What happens if I want to refinance and borrow more money against my security property or I want to sell the property?

If we register a caveat on the title to your property in favour of your trust as a second mortgagee we can remove it at anytime by simply lodging a withdrawal of caveat so that any time we want to refinance or sell we can just remove the caveat. Again we retain ultimate control.

What about my other wealth?

Other forms of wealth are much easier to protect. Cash at banks, shares, personal items, chattels, cars and any other items of value including income and wages are easily protected through a simple legal document which can assign those assets or wealth across to the structure of the trust. These things are not as difficult to assign to a trust as property is because there is no public register where creditors can search ownership of these things. If a creditor is looking at you as a target for acquisition of wealth they will firstly run a land titles search – your kryptonite will be property. Beyond that they can legally intercept your income, earnings, personal goods and chattels and other wealth but there is no public register for such information so they will have to work hard to find and attack this wealth and it will usually not be as valuable as the wealth you hold in property. Through asset protection structuring and legal paperwork all of these items of wealth can be quickly and easily assigned across to your trust and there is no place to register this ownership in the public domain so proof of ownership will come from legal documents that you hold.

Can this be challenged?

Wherever there are asset protection structures there will always be creditors or others trying to attack them. No asset protection system can spruik itself as being impenetrable. Having said that, what we are trying to do is make it difficult for creditors to get at you. The more they have to prove, the more expensive it becomes and the more difficult the exercise. They effectively give up when it comes to throwing good money after bad.

The onus or burden of proof is on the creditor to show that what you have set up is somehow liable to be set aside by a court and available for them to take as creditors. This becomes very costly and difficult and can be an uphill battle because they have nothing to base their allegations on and you have all the requisite legal documents. Yes, they can get a court order that you produce documents but they need grounds for this and cannot just go on a fishing expedition hoping to dredge up something. In reality it is impossible to mount a challenge without ammunition and there is no way to get ammunition without some compelling evidence in the first place. It also becomes very difficult and costly for them to attack a registered interest on a title due to the concept of indefeasibility of title. Any challenge is a very expensive exercise and the legal cost alone to challenge such asset protection structuring would probably outweigh the debt that they are chasing. Put simply, it is a case of commerciality and the legal system is such that it just becomes uncommercial for creditors to challenge such asset protection structures.

This is what the very rich aim to do; have layers and layers of protection, companies within trusts within other companies. It becomes so convoluted and expensive to examine, analyse, prove and undo. Donald Trump famously once told his creditors: "You can sue me but I will hold you up in court for years and cost you more in legal expenses to fight me than what I owe you. I have the best lawyers and have tied everything up so tightly you will never ever unravel it."

CONCLUSION
This chapter contains information to build the ultimate system of asset protection. Those who don't know and use it will be massively exposed; those who do will be able to control their wealth and prosper in the current and future economic climates. Former US President, John F. Kennedy, perhaps best sums it up: "Change is the law of life. And those who look only to the past or present are certain to miss the future."

Chapter 7
TAX MINIMISATION

"We make the tax man work as
hard for you as you do."

ADRIAN HILL

ADRIAN HILL

Adrian Hill is one of only a few accountants talking the talk and walking the walk on the wealth-creation trail. A CPA accountant with 20 years' experience, he is constantly surprised by the amount of hard-earned money that people don't claim back from the tax office.

Adrian's wealth-creation journey began in 2000 when he started reading books and attending seminars on subjects including rental properties as well as share and option trading. He bought his first rental property in 2001 and has continued to buy property every year since then. He has traded shares and options over the years and in 2008 undertook a couple of subdivisions.

Adrian's mission is to minimise tax; he also strongly believes "the tax man should work as hard as you do". It has been his experience that if you don't have a rental property then you don't know the magic that can be achieved. Through learning tricks of the trade, you can legally use the tax laws to your advantage.

He is extremely passionate about properties, taxation reduction strategies and protecting your hard-earned assets. He loves to educate and will gladly spend hours assisting anyone who is willing to take steps towards financial freedom.

In 2004 he founded Superior Tax Solutions Pty Ltd to do just that, and so far has attracted 100 per cent of clients through referrals. Adrian's team is currently assisting more than 250 like-minded client groups to make the tax man work up a sweat!

TAX MINIMISATION

HOW TO GET WHAT YOU'RE ENTITLED TO

My story is a financial one but it begins in a very personal way. I met my beautiful wife Anita during the first subject of our six-and-a-half year degree at Monash University. We quickly fell in love and got married, then produced two wonderful girls who are the light of our lives.

Having a family of four at such a young age gave us some very sharp lessons in the difficulties of life. We struggled to save for our first home and, even with the help of our Nan who let us move in with her and live as cheaply as possible, it was a definite struggle. It was during this period that we learned the first of many key lessons that have helped us go from that precarious financial position to become millionaires: the only way to get ahead is to have a budget. Yes, I know many people consider the dreaded "b" word to be a dirty one but it taught us to respect money and to make sure we always know where it goes and what it is used for. In short, it put us in control of our own finances.

Our first home was a three-bedroom place in Cheltenham, 20 kilometres out of Melbourne. In hindsight, it would have been the perfect first rental property but at that stage we weren't yet able to recognise the fact. That first house was bought very much under the old school of thought, which basically states you have to work like a dog until you can afford to buy a house, then spend the rest of your life working to pay off the mortgage.

We always felt there ought to be more to life than that but it took us a long time to find the correct path. We would spend long hours walking the dog, talking and – both being accountants – crunching the numbers but we still couldn't understand why anybody would bother to own a rental property. The rent never covers the mortgage repayments, so what's the point of owning something that continually loses money?

Then we discovered two little words that changed everything: capital growth. In fact, they're so important I'm going to write them again in big capital letters:

CAPITAL GROWTH.

The basic principle behind this is that the property continues to grow in value while the loan always stays the same. It gives rise to another excellent word, equity, which pretty much means getting money for nothing. I can't think of anybody who would say no to that.

Of course, harnessing this principle relies on continued capital growth and having a stable or increasing income, plus you will need to build in contingencies to ride out the short-term market fluctuations.

Obviously one of the dominant forces behind capital growth is the scarcity of land. It's a commodity that everybody in the world wants and needs, yet it's the one thing they're not making any more of and never will again. The amount of land in the world today, being shared between seven billion people, is exactly how much 10 billion people or more will have to share in fifty years' time. In fact, if the experts are right about global warming and rising sea levels there could be even less.

Therefore, it's a good bet that any property you own will increase in value. The rate of the increase constantly varies as the market moves back and forth, up and down, but there are two things you should always keep in mind:

- historically it's been shown that over a period of time property will grow at two to three per cent above inflation;
- any fall-off in prices, which does happen from time to time, can affect all property values but more so those in the middle to high-priced property markets.

You can see, then, that owning rental property gives you a double bonus: income from rent in the short term and capital growth over the long term.

Of course, our path to financial freedom was not a straight one. Because we were feeling our own way through the dark and there was nobody out there to hand us the information we needed in a neat package, like this book is giving it to you, we had a few false starts that taught us some very valuable lessons. One of those came in the early 1990s when I was working in Collingwood. We decided to move to Park Orchards and bought some land there for $125,000 that we planned to build on. After six months, though, we realised we couldn't yet afford to build our dream home so we sold it for $200,000. In that situation our inexperience cost us twice over, as the property was re-sold again six months later for $300,000 when the Eastern Freeway opened.

There are two valuable lessons to be found in that experience. The first – and I cannot possible stress this enough – is that land will always go up in value. The second, though, is that land is also very expensive to hold onto if you're not planning to build a rental property in the near future. I'll get to the reasons for that in a short while but first I want to introduce you to one of the key principles that allowed us to go from being penniless university students to millionaires. It is simply this:

Money is a tool.

That's all. Again, it seems like a laughably simple concept, almost a trite statement really, but accepting it as a fact requires a fundamental shift in your thinking and a complete re-evaluation of your relationship to your finances. You need to see money as a means to an end, not an end in itself. Your ultimate goal is not to accumulate as much money as you can in your bank account before you die, it's to use the money that has passed through your hands in your lifetime to give you the best possible quality of life. Think of your life as a journey you are taking, a long distance car trip for instance, and money is simply the fuel that keeps you moving in much the same way as the food you consume gets you through each day. You need to be dispassionate about allocating appropriate amounts of money to your living expenses, home loan repayments, entertainment and so forth, always setting aside as much as possible for investing.

There are many different types of investing, with rental properties being the one we've dealt with most and gained the most profit from. The strategy we used worked for us because we were almost 100 per cent focused on building a business at the same time. Having read this far into the book, you would be aware of at least five other strategies to turbo-charge your wealth-creation from property.

However, there's one investment that needs to be your very first port of call on the journey to financial independence. Before you invest a cent in property, or anywhere else for that matter, you need to invest in yourself. By simply reading this book you've made an excellent start, trying as you are to benefit from the experience of those who have already made the journey you're trying to begin. Now I'll let you in on a little secret – that's exactly the same way that we started. Our practical education began back in 2000 when we started reading books just like the one you hold in your hands right now. As well as that we attended a number of seminars where we learned things they never taught us during our degrees or afterwards; we have spent close to $50,000 on self-education. It's certainly a lot of money but it's important not to dwell on that fact. The trick is to write the money off as a cost of business and think of it as an investment in yourself, which is easy for us to do as that money we initially spent has created a high enough return to make us millionaires.

It's amazing, really, to think of how much time Anita and I both spent in accounting firms without ever learning how to become financially free. You'd think it would be the first perk of a life spent juggling numbers for other people but none of our colleagues was asking the right questions and none of our superiors seemed to have the answers anyhow.

Of course, that lack of assistance turned out to be beneficial in one way, as it left us to learn everything the hard way. We passed through the school of hard knocks and picked up the skills we now have by actually doing things rather than simply observing or reading about them. For instance, nobody ever told us one of the most important equations for those undertaking a wealth-creation journey; we had to figure it out for ourselves.

It goes like this:

$$\text{Asset} + \text{time} = \text{wealth}$$

Or, to put it another way:

$$\text{Property} + \text{time} = \text{wealth}$$

WHY RENTAL PROPERTIES?

We settled on rental properties as our wealth-creation vehicle for a number of reasons including:

- the benefits of capital growth and equity;
- good debt versus bad debt (we wanted assets that appreciate and/or earn income, not those that depreciate and/or lose income);
- the tendency for rents to double every decade;
- the fact that 30 per cent of Australians currently rent with more likely to do so in the future;
- a high income is generally not needed to buy an income property; and
- value can be added easily by renovating.

But by far the best reason of all is that the tenant and the tax man – that's right, the tax man – help you pay for the rental property. Let's look at how.

HOW TO GET HELP OWNING YOUR RENTAL PROPERTY

If you keep the property in excellent condition you will get the maximum amount of rent from your tenant, which can be put towards paying down your mortgage. The tax man's part, though, is a little more complicated and can be a lot more profitable to your bottom line.

There are two things I should mention before proceeding: you should avoid buying vacant land, unless you intend to immediately build a rental property on it, develop it or add value in some other way, because unless your property is producing an income you won't get the many excellent tax benefits I'm going to spell out for you. Also, you should keep in mind that owning two smaller rental properties is better than owning one big one.

If you have a solid understanding of tax law or, even better, have a good accountant who knows it backwards, you can claim many tax deductions that will significantly increase your wealth and hasten your journey towards financial freedom. The key words there, of course, are "good accountant". You might think it's reasonable to assume that all accountants would know what I'm about to tell you but unfortunately that is not the case. The education received by accountants, both at university and throughout their on-site training, is patchy at best so you have to be extremely careful about choosing one that can not only talk the talk but also walk the walk.

It was this realisation that actually lead us to create our business, Superior Tax Solutions Pty Ltd, because we recognised a massive gap in the market that simply wasn't being filled by the majority of accountants who were out there.

It's not just an accountant that you need as you begin your journey to financial freedom, either. You need to build an entire team to support you along the way and help you reach your goals, each member of which will play a crucial role. Team members should include:

- accountant
- mortgage broker / financier
- property manager

- insurance broker
- solicitor
- quantity surveyor.

TAX DEDUCTIONS - GENERALLY

As accountants, there are lots of tricks we can share with you to help buy-and-hold your property, particularly in regard to maximising your tax deductions and asset protection. To start at the very beginning, an item is tax deductible if it is an expense incurred (that is, paid) while you were earning income. If you're not sure if an expense is tax deductible simply keep the tax invoice and seek your accountant's advice when your tax return is being prepared. The accountant should be on your side and will try to claim as much as possible to allow you to minimise your tax each year. It's their job to be proactive in this area and it's your right to claim everything you're entitled to.

RENTAL PROPERTY TAX ISSUES IN GENERAL

Rental income is, as you would expect, the income you receive in rent from your tenant each financial year.

> ### HINT FOR TAX RETURN
> If you do not receive your rent for June 2011 until 1 July, that rent is not income in the 2011 tax year but will be included in the 2012 tax year.

YOUR SHARE OF RENTAL INCOME AND EXPENSES

Your share of rental income and expenses is divided up according to who legally owns the property. For instance, property can be owned as:

- joint tenants, who each hold an equal interest in the property;

- tenants in common, who may hold unequal interests in the property. One could have an 80 per cent interest and the other 20 per cent.

HINT FOR TAX RETURN

Your rental income and expenses must be allocated to each according to their legal interest in the property, no matter what agreements they make between themselves.

RENTAL EXPENSES

You can claim a deduction for certain expenses you pay during the period your property is being rented or is available for rent.

There are three types of rental expenses:

1. Expenses that cannot be claimed as deductions;
2. Immediate deductions, which can be claimed in the financial year that you pay them;
3. Deductions expensed over a number of financial years.

1. Deductions that cannot be claimed

PURCHASE AND SALE COSTS

You cannot claim a deduction for the costs of purchasing or selling your rental property. However, they may form part of the cost base of the property for Capital Gains Tax (CGT) purposes. Below is an example that shows the kind of expenses you can claim as part of the cost base:

Purchase details:
Date of signing contract: 19 July
Date of settlement: 19 September

Purchase price	$300,000
Stamp Duty	$15,000
Legal costs	$1,000
Travel to purchase property	$2,000
Building inspection	$500
Pest inspection	$500
Buyer's agent fees	$6,000
Total Purchase Costs	**$325,000**

This means that when the above property is sold, $325,000 will be included in the cost base from which the amount of any capital gain or capital loss will be figured out.

> **HINT FOR TAX RETURN**
> The signing date of the contract is the triggering point for Capital Gains Tax purposes, while the settlement date is the triggering point for depreciation to start. Your total purchase costs, when you sell the property, may be reduced by depreciation and building write-off claimed.

2. Immediate deductions

Immediate deductions are those that can be claimed in the same financial year as they have been paid. Examples include:

- advertising for tenants
- bank fees
- body corporate fees and charges *
- cleaning
- council rates
- electricity and gas

- gardening and lawn mowing
- gifts to tenants and/or property managers
- in-house audio/video service charges
- insurance (including building, contents and public liability)
- interest on loans *
- Land Tax
- lease document expenses (including preparation, registration and stamp duty)
- legal expenses * (excluding acquisition costs and borrowing costs)
- mortgage discharge expenses *
- pest (annual check)
- property agent's fees and commission
- quantity surveyor's fees
- repairs and maintenance *
- security patrol fees
- servicing costs – for example, servicing a water heater
- stationery and postage
- telephone calls and line rental
- travel and car expenses for rent collection, property inspection and maintenance*
- water rates and charges.

Items marked with an asterisk (*) are discussed in detail overleaf.

HINT FOR TAX RETURN
You can only claim these expenses if you pay for them and are not reimbursed by the tenant.

BODY CORPORATE FEES AND CHARGES

Body corporate fees apply when you own an apartment, unit or any dwelling that has common property. The body corporate is responsible for the upkeep of the common property – such as lawns, driveways and lifts – as well as sometimes for the maintenance of external walls. It will usually issue a quarterly invoice to cover the costs of the above. These contributions are, in the majority of cases, covering a "general purpose sinking fund" and are fully claimable when paid.

A general purpose sinking fund is one that's established to cover a variety of unspecified expenses (some of which may be capital expenses) that are paid by the body corporate in maintaining the common property. This generally involves things like painting the common property and repairing or replacing fixtures and fittings. These are immediately deductible.

What is not immediately deductible, however, is if the body corporate requires you to make payments to a "special purpose fund" to pay for particular capital expenditure. A special purpose fund is set up to cover a specified, generally significant, expense that is not covered by ongoing contributions to a general purpose sinking fund. Most special purpose funds are established to cover the cost of capital improvement to the common property.

HINT FOR TAX RETURN
These special purpose contributions generally will be claimable at the rate of 2.50 per cent per annum.

INTEREST ON LOANS

If you take out a loan to purchase a rental property, you can claim the interest charged on that loan as a deduction. The important thing to be aware of here is that the deductibility of the interest depends entirely on what the money was used for. Incidentally, what property is secured against the loan is irrelevant when figuring out the deductibility of the interest.

While the property is being rented, or is available for rent, you may also claim interest charged on loans taken out for the following purposes:

- to purchase depreciating assets
- for repairs
- for renovations.

HINT FOR TAX RETURN

You have to keep your personal loans entirely separate from the loans you intend to be tax deductible. To give an example, if you buy a property for a total cost of $325,000 (which included a contract price of $300,000) the bank would normally give you an 80 per cent loan, secured against that property, of $240,000. You need to finance the remaining $85,000 from elsewhere. If you take out a loan for that amount, then make sure that no money for personal purposes is ever withdrawn or deposited into it; you can claim the interest on both loans against any rent received from the property.

Similarly, if you take out a loan to purchase land on which to build a rental property or to finance renovations to a property you intend to rent out, the interest on the loan will be deductible from the time you take the loan out. However, if your intention changes – if, for example, you decide to move into the property yourself or you no longer intend to use it to produce rent or other income – you cannot claim the interest after your intention changes.

> **HINT FOR TAX RETURN**
>
> Interest is not the only expense you can claim in the period between buying the land and building a rental property on it. You can also claim other holding costs such as water rates, land tax, lawn mowing, council rates and insurance.

Where personal and property loans are combined

The first thing I have to say about combining personal and property loans is that you shouldn't do it. Your accounting will be much simpler if you are able to keep the two entirely separate. For instance, if you take out a loan to buy a rental property and a private car you have to divide the interest on the loan into deductible and non-deductible parts depending on how much each item cost.

If you have a loan account that has a fluctuating balance due to a variety of deposits and withdrawals, and it is used for both private and rental property purposes, you must keep accurate records so you can calculate the interest that applies to the rental property portion of the loan. In other words, you need to figure out how much interest you paid as part of earning income through rent (which is deductible) and how much you paid as part of the personal loan (which is not).

> **HINT FOR TAX RETURN**
>
> You can see now why I always suggest keeping your deductible debt totally separate from your non-deductible debt. It is time consuming and costly for you or your accountant to determine the correct amount of interest claimable. It's an area where the tax office often finds errors and therefore it is crucial to get it right.

Example: Apportionment of interest

You decide to use your bank account to take out a loan of $355,000 from which $325,000 is used to buy a rental property and $30,000 is used to buy a private car. To determine the claim using a loan interest rate of 6.75% per annum, and assuming that the property is rented from 1 July:

Interest for year one = $355,000 X 6.75% = $23,963

Apportionment of interest payment related to rental property:

Total interest expense	X	rental property loan / total borrowings	=	Deductible interest
$23,963	X	$325,000 / $355,000	=	$21,938

Where you purchase a new home to live in and keep your old one to rent out

Some rental property owners borrow money to buy a new home and then rent out their previous home. If there is an outstanding loan on the old home and that property is used to produce income, the interest outstanding on the loan – or at least part of it – will be deductible.

However, an interest deduction cannot be claimed on the loan used to buy the new home because it is not used to produce income. This is the case regardless of whether the loan for the new home is secured against the former home.

Example – Old house rented

You bought your home five years ago for $275,000 (including all costs). The loan was $250,000 at the time of purchase but is now down to $100,000. The house is now worth $500,000.

You buy a new home for $450,000 (including all costs), using two loans to complete the purchase. One is for $360,000, secured against the new home, and the other is for $90,000, secured against the old home. You move into the new property and rent out your old home.

The only interest claimable is that from the $100,000 loan, which is being used for the purpose of creating income.

HINT FOR TAX RETURN
If I was purchasing a home in the future I would always utilise an offset account loan type, which is explained in greater detail a little further.

THE MAIN TYPES OF LOAN PRODUCTS UTILISED BY RENTAL PROPERTY INVESTORS

Line of Credit (LOC)/Redraws

A line of credit is a loan, similar to a credit card, which can be drawn up to a pre-determined maximum limit. Interest is only charged on the drawn balance and not on the available (undrawn) balance. For the interest to be deductible, you have to make sure there is a clear distinction between the business and personal uses of the loan.

For example, you might set up a $100,000 LOC, secured against your private home. If you use this to help you buy a rental property, the interest will be deductible against the rent received from your property. Your aunt passes away, leaving you $20,000 that you deposit into the LOC, dropping the balance to $80,000. You then dip back into the loan, taking $20,000 out to buy a boat for your personal use and bringing the balance back up to $100,000.

By doing this you've effectively created two loans, one of $80,000 that is tax deductible against the income received from your property and one of $20,000 that is not. You've turned $20,000 of deductible debt into non-deductible debt, which isn't good and demonstrates how careful you need to be when moving money around.

Making it even more difficult is the fact the tax office won't let you allocate repayments solely against the boat loan. If you choose to pay $1,000 into the above LOC it would be deemed to be reducing the boat loan by $200 ($1,000 x 20 per cent) and the rental property loan by $800 ($1,000 x 80 per cent).

Line of Credit (LOC) versus offset account

There is another way you could have proceeded with the previous example, one that would have been far more advantageous.

When you receive the $20,000 from your aunt's estate, instead of depositing it into the $100,000 LOC you could put it into a separate account held by the same bank. The bank can then "offset" the interest charged to you on the $100,000 loan against the interest they would pay you on the $20,000 deposit being held in the offset account.

Instead of paying the interest on $100,000 and receiving interest on $20,000, you will only have to pay the interest on $80,000. To put it another way, the $20,000 in your offset account gets subtracted from the $100,000 in your LOC before any interest in calculated.

You can then buy the $20,000 boat from the offset account, leaving the original $100,000 loan fully intact.

I favour offset accounts because they keep your interest deduction options as open as possible, particularly when you're going to pay a loan down by depositing money into it.

You should even set up an offset account on your private home loan, so you can maximise the interest deductions if you ever decide to rent it out in the future. Even if you don't think you will ever rent it out, you're keeping your options open and that's always a good thing.

LEGAL EXPENSES

Some legal expenses incurred in producing your rental income are deductible, such as the cost of evicting a non-paying tenant.

Most legal expenses, however, are of a capital nature and are therefore not deductible. These include the costs of purchasing or selling your property and defending your title to the property. It's not all bad news, though. Non-deductible legal expenses may form part of the cost base of your property for Capital Gains Tax purposes.

Example: Deductible legal expenses

In August 2011 your tenants moved out owing four weeks' rent. You retained the bond money and took the tenants to court to terminate the lease and recover the balance of the rent. The legal expenses are fully deductible because they were incurred while seeking to recover assessable rental income and you wished to continue earning income from the property.

> **HINT FOR TAX RETURN**
> You must include the retained bond money and the recovered rent as assessable income in the financial year received.

MORTGAGE DISCHARGE EXPENSES

These are the costs involved in discharging a mortgage other than through payments of principal and interest. Mortgage discharge expenses may include penalty interest payments, early termination fees or deferred establishment fees. They're claimable in the year they are paid.

REPAIRS AND MAINTENANCE

Repairs can generally be categorised into two types:

1. Repairs that are immediately claimable
2. Repairs that are depreciable.

Immediately claimable repairs

These repairs must directly relate to wear and tear or other damage that occurred as a result of you renting out the property.

They generally involve the replacement or renewal of a worn-out or broken part, such as guttering torn down during a storm or part of a fence that was damaged by a falling tree branch.

A repair simply restores the item to its original state prior to it needing to be fixed.

Some of the repairs you can claim deductions for include replacing broken windows, maintaining plumbing and repairing electrical appliances.

> ## HINT FOR TAX RETURN
> You need to consider how long you have been renting out the property before a repair is deemed to be from the wear and tear associated with the use of the tenant.

Depreciable repairs

The following expenses are depreciable at the rate of 2.50 per cent per annum:

- the replacement of an entire structure or unit of property, such as a complete fence or set of kitchen cupboards;
- improvements, renovations, extensions and alterations;
- initial repairs, which means fixing defects and repairing damage that existed in the property on the date you acquired it.

Example: Improvements

You've been renting a property out for a number of years when a section of the timber fence – not the entire fence but only part of it – comes apart and needs replacing. If you replace the timber fence with a Colorbond fence it is deemed to be an improvement rather than a repair.

Example: Initial repairs

You need to make some repairs to your newly acquired rental property before the first tenants move in. You pay an interior decorator to repaint dirty walls, replace broken light fittings and repair doors on two bedrooms. You also discover white ants in some of the floorboards, which requires white ant treatment and replacement of some of the boards.

It is considered that these expenses were incurred to make the property suitable for rental and did not arise from your use of the property to generate rental income.

GENERAL GUIDE TO CLAIMING REPAIRS

Repairs to a rental property will generally be claimable if:

- the property continues to be rented on an ongoing basis; or
- the property remains available for rent but there is a short period when the property is unoccupied, such as when unseasonable weather causes cancellations of bookings or advertising is unsuccessful in attracting tenants.

If you no longer rent the property, the cost of repairs may still be deductible provided:

- the need for the repairs is related to the period in which the property was used by you to produce income; and
- the property was producing income during the financial year in which you paid for the repairs.

Example: Repairs when the property is no longer rented out

August 2011 – Your tenants move out.

September 2011 – You discover the stove doesn't work, kitchen tiles are cracked and the toilet window is broken. You also discover a hole in a bedroom wall that had been covered with a poster.

October 2011 – You pay for this damage to be repaired.

Despite the fact that the property is no longer being rented out, you can still claim the repairs to the property. This is because the repairs relate to the period when the property was being rented and the repairs were completed before the end of the financial year in which the property ceased to be rented out.

```
┌ ■ ■ ■ ■ ■ ■ ■ ■ ■ ■ ■ ■ ■ ┐
      HINT FOR TAX RETURN
 You need to have some rental income in the same financial
 year that you claim the repairs. This applies even if you use
    the property as your home after the tenants move out.
└ ■ ■ ■ ■ ■ ■ ■ ■ ■ ■ ■ ■ ■ ┘
```

TRAVEL EXPENSES

You can travel to inspect, maintain your property or collect the rent and you may be able to claim the costs of doing so.

Potential claimable travel expenses:

- airfares (retain boarding pass and ticket)
- taxi, bus and train fares
- accommodation
- phone calls
- meals
- parking costs and bridge tolls
- car hire and petrol
- cents per kilometre usage of your own car.

Example: Cents per kilometre usage of your own car

Although your local rental property is managed by a property agent, you decide to inspect the property three months after the tenants move in. During the income year you also make a number of visits to the property to carry out minor repairs. You travel 162 kilometres during the course of these visits. At the rate of 74 cents per kilometre for your 2.6 litre car, you can claim the following deduction:

Distance travelled	x	rate per km	=	deductible amount
162 kms	x	74 cents per km	=	$119.88

On your way to cricket each Saturday, you also drive past the property to "keep an eye on things". These trips are not deductible in any way because inspecting the property is incidental to the primary purpose of enjoying the cricket.

Apportionment of travel expenses

You are allowed a full claim where the sole purpose of the trip relates to the rental property. However, in other circumstances you may not be able to claim a deduction or you may be entitled to only a partial deduction.

If you fly to inspect your rental property, stay overnight and return home on the following day, all of the airfare and accommodation expenses can be claimed as long as the sole purpose of your trip is to inspect the property.

Where travel related to your rental property is combined with a holiday or other private activities, you may need to apportion the expenses.

If this is the case you need to take into account the reasons for your trip. If the main purpose of your trip is to have a holiday and the inspection of the property is incidental to that main purpose, you cannot claim a deduction for the cost of the travel. However, you may be able to claim local expenses directly related to the property inspection and a proportion of accommodation expenses.

Example: Apportionment of travel expenses

You own a rental property in Cairns on the north coast of Queensland. You spend $1,000 on airfares and $1,500 on accommodation when you travel from your home in Melbourne, mainly for the purpose of holidaying but also to inspect the property. You also spend $50 on taxi fares for the return trip from the hotel to the rental property. One day of your 10-day holiday (10 per cent) is spent on matters relating to the rental property and nine days (90 per cent) swimming and sightseeing.

No deduction can be claimed for any part of the $1,000 airfares but $50 can be claimed for the taxi fare.

Given that 10 per cent of the holiday is spent attending to the rental property, a deduction for 10 per cent of the accommodation expenses ($150 in this case) would be considered reasonable. The total in travel expenses you can claim is therefore $200 ($50 taxi fare plus $150 accommodation).

PRE-PAID EXPENSES

If you pre-pay a rental property expense – such as interest – that covers a period of 12 months or less and the period ends on or before 30 June, you can claim an immediate deduction.

Example: Pre-paid expenses

In June 2011 you pay interest in advance of $16,000 on a loan for your rental property, which represents the interest you would pay in an entire year. Because you pay it in June 2011, and because it relates to a period of no more than 12 months, you can claim the interest in the 2011 financial year.

HINT FOR TAX RETURN

The interest has to actually be paid to the bank before 30 June to be claimed in that year. That means you will need to allow an appropriate amount of time for you to contact your lender, have your lender agree to this, send out the paperwork for the pre-payment and for the payment to be made.

Pre-payments can be made and claimed for rental properties owned by:

1. An individual
2. Individuals jointly or as tenants in common.

Pre-payments cannot be made and claimed for rental properties owned by:

1. Trusts
2. Companies
3. Super funds.

3. Deductions over a number of financial years

We've already spoken about deductions that cannot be claimed and those that can be claimed immediately. Now it's time to move on to those deductions you can claim over a period of time.

There are three types of rental expenses that fall into this category:

1. Borrowing expenses
2. Amounts for decline in value of depreciating assets
3. Capital works deductions (building write-off).

Each of these categories is discussed in detail below.

BORROWING EXPENSES

If the total deductible borrowing expenses are $100 or less, they are fully deductible in the income year they are incurred. However, if your total borrowing expenses are more than $100, the deduction is either spread over five years or the term of the loan – whichever is less.

These are some of the expenses directly incurred in taking out a loan for the property:

- loan establishment fees
- title search fees
- mortgage broker fees
- Stamp Duty charged on the mortgage
- valuation fees
- mortgage insurance.

HINT FOR TAX RETURN

If you repay the loan early and in less than five years, you can claim a deduction for the balance of the borrowing expenses in the year of repayment.

If you obtained the loan part way through the income year, the deduction for the first year will be apportioned according to the number of days in the year that you had the loan.

Example: Borrowing expenses
To buy a rental property for $300,000 you secure a 25-year loan of $316,000. You pay a total of $3,670 in various expenses, including establishment fees and Stamp Duty. Because these expenses are greater than $100 they must be spread out over five years or until the end of the loan, according to whichever comes first.

If you obtain the loan on 17 July 2010, you would work out the borrowing expense deduction for the first year as follows:

PRE-PAID BORROWING EXPENSES

Mortgage Stamp Duty	1,264
Registration fee	70
Establishment fee	700
Settlement fee	200
Mortgage insurance	1,436
	3,670

	Days in year	Claim	Balance
30 June 2011	350	703	2,967
30 June 2012	365	733	2,234
30 June 2013	365	733	1,501
30 June 2014	365	733	768
30 June 2015	366	735	33
30 June 2016	16	33	-
	1,827	3,670	

> **HINT FOR TAX RETURN**
>
> If you refinance the above property on 30 June 2012, the remaining borrowing costs yet to be claimed – in this case $2,234 – can be written off in full when the refinance happens.
>
> A new calculation (similar to the one above over five years) will also need to be done for the new loan that is going to pay out the old loan.

DEDUCTION FOR DEPRECIATING ASSETS

This is one of the most attractive benefits from a tax deduction point of view, particularly as it's one of those that is often overlooked even by professionals.

Depreciation is a tax deduction that you get each year, without having to spend a cent. It's built into the purchase price of the property.

Depreciation is meant to reflect the fact that the assets are worth less as time goes by, simply because of the "wear and tear" associated with having tenants use them.

Even if a property is 15-20 years old when you buy it there can still be some fantastic depreciation benefits available to you as the purchaser. It depends on how much you pay for the property and what plant and equipment are in it at the time of purchase.

Items of interest would include:

- stove
- oven
- hot plates
- hot water service
- curtains
- light fittings
- blinds
- ducted heating
- dishwasher
- ducted cooling
- stand alone heating unit
- stand alone air-conditioning unit
- security system
- carpet.

A quantity surveyor is the best option to determine your depreciation entitlements. The difference between a good quantity surveyor and an average one can have a substantial impact on the depreciation and building write-off that is claimable. This applies to both the level of detail provided in the report as well as the dollar value you can get out of a genuine professional.

Trust me, you will want to get a decent quantity surveyor. Valuers, real estate agents, accountants and solicitors generally won't have the skills and experience to get you everything you're entitled to.

A quantity surveyor's fees are also tax deductible in the year they are paid for.

Personal experience

I can speak from my own personal experience and say that
quantity surveyors truly are a gift from the tax office.

We had recently bought our first rental property and were
sitting outside one sunny afternoon reading *Australian Property
Investor* magazine when we came across an article about quantity
surveyors. We were stunned. Could the tax office really be that
generous? We were both accountants; why had we never heard
of this?

We researched the topic and, sure enough, discovered one of the
most wonderful little tools available. At the time we were both
working for a family company that owned 40 service stations
throughout Victoria, so we kept researching and discovered that
it applied to commercial property as well as residential. Some
time later we were able to give our employers an extra one
million dollars in their pockets after tax.

It made us realise there aren't many accountants out there who
know everything that will help you with your rental properties.
That's when Superior Tax Solutions Pty Ltd was created.

HINT FOR TAX RETURN

The tax deductions available through depreciation and
building write-off can significantly reduce the holding
costs of the property. This is one reason why Superior Tax
Solutions Pty Ltd amends, on average, 80 per cent of our
new clients' tax returns.

Amended tax returns are now restricted in the majority of
cases to two years, which is why it's imperative that your
accountant is looking after your interests.

Example: The difference a good quantity surveyor can make
One of my clients commissioned an average quantity surveyor who was relatively cheap. They got the following results:

- property purchased for $150,000 in January 1997
- has three bedrooms and a study, as well as ducted heating, dishwasher, carpet, curtains, stove, oven, range hood, etc.
- built in 1987 and still had all original fixtures and fittings
- total depreciation calculated by quantity surveyor: **$13,639**
- total building write-off calculated by quantity surveyor: **$45,354** ($1,814 per annum).

I, on the other hand, spent a little extra money and commissioned a good quantity surveyor to achieve the following results:

- property purchased for $210,000 in June 2001
- has three bedrooms and a study, as well as ducted heating, dishwasher, security system, carpet, curtains, stove, oven, range hood, etc.
- built in 1987 and still had all original fixtures and fittings
- total depreciation calculated by quantity surveyor: **$53,615**
- total building write-off calculated by quantity surveyor: **$12,873** ($1,126 per annum).

Given that approximately 60 per cent of depreciation is claimed back in the first five years, the above example means the following:

Average quantity surveyor – Claims over five years:

$13,639 x 60 per cent	=	$8,183
$1,814 x 5	=	$9,070
Total Claims		**$17,253**

Good quantity surveyor – Claims over five years:

$53,615 x 60 per cent	=	$32,169
$1,126 x 5	=	$5,630

Total Claims **$37,799**

Difference in claims over five years = **$20,546**
Tax savings foregone at 31.50 per cent = **$6,472**
(Cashflow lost by average surveyor)

This clearly highlights the importance of a good quantity surveyor but, even more than that, it shows the cost of not using a quantity surveyor at all.

How do you work out your depreciation deduction?
There are two methods of calculating depreciation:

1. Diminishing value method
2. Prime cost method.

The **diminishing value method** assumes that the decline in value each year is a constant proportion of the remaining value, thereby producing a progressively smaller decline over time.

For depreciating assets bought after 10 May 2006, you generally use the following formula to work out the decline using the diminishing value method:

$$\text{base value (asset's cost)} \quad X \quad \frac{\text{days held}}{365} \quad X \quad \frac{200\%}{\text{asset's effective life}}$$

Example:
You buy a dishwasher for $1,000 on 1 August 2011. Assuming its operational life expectancy is 10 years, it has a depreciation rate of 20 per cent under the diminishing value method.

Year 1
$1,000   x   334/365   x   20%   = $183 ($1,000 – $183 = $817)

Year 2
$817   x   365/365   x   20%   = $163 ($817 - $163 = $654)

Year 3
$654   x   365/365   x   20%   = $131 ($654 - $131 = $523)

The **prime cost method**, on the other hand, assumes the value of a depreciating asset decreases uniformly over its effective life. The formula for working out decline in value using the prime cost method is:

asset's cost   X $\dfrac{\text{days held}}{365}$ X $\dfrac{100\%}{\text{asset's effective life}}$

Example:
You buy a dishwasher for $1,000 on 1 August 2011. Assuming its operational life expectancy is 10 years, it has a depreciation rate of 10 per cent under the prime cost method.

Year 1
$1,000   x   334/365   x   10%   = $92 ($1,000 – $92 = $908)

Year 2
$1,000   x   365/365   x   10%   = $100 ($908 - $100 = $808)

Year 3
$1,000   x   365/365   x   10%   = $100 ($808 - $100 = $708)

> **HINT FOR TAX RETURN**
> Due to the fact that rental properties usually cost more to hold in the first few years, we recommend using the diminishing value method as this will maximise your depreciation claim each year and increase your tax refund.

Effective life
Generally, the effective life of a depreciating asset is how long it can be used for a taxable purpose.

Immediate deduction for certain non-business depreciating assets costing $300 or less
You can get an immediate deduction for the cost of an asset if its purchase price was under $300. This deduction is available if the asset meets all the following tests:

- it cost $300 or less
- you use it mainly for the purpose of obtaining rental income
- it is not one of a number of identical, or substantially identical, assets that together cost more than $300 (example below).

Example: Immediate deduction
You buy a blind for your rental property at a cost of $70. You can claim an immediate deduction as the blind is used to obtain rental income.

Example: No immediate deduction
You buy four blinds costing $90 each for your rental property. You cannot claim an immediate deduction for any of these because they are identical, or substantially identical, and the combined cost is more than $300.

> ### HINT FOR TAX RETURN
> In the previous example, you should have bought three of the blinds in one year and one in the next year. Then you could have fully claimed them in the respective financial years they were bought and paid for.

Low-value pooling

A low-value pool is a simplified method of depreciating any assets that cost less than $1,000 per item. These assets are allocated to the pool each year and stay there once they've been added. The pool shows one cumulative dollar value for all the assets inside it, along with one depreciation amount for the entire pool.

This compares to the traditional method of showing a depreciation schedule with individual assets listed separately, each with its own depreciation calculation per year.

For the income year you initially purchase an asset, you work out its depreciation at a rate of 18.75 per cent. For the following years the deduction uses a diminishing value rate of 37.5 per cent.

Example: Depreciation claim – low-value pool

On 1 August 2010 you bought a blind for $400 and two air-conditioners for $900 each on 30 June 2011.

2011 financial year depreciation claim:

$400	x	18.75%		=	$75
$900	x	18.75%		=	$169
$900	x	18.75%		=	$169
Total Depreciation Claimed				=	**$413**

Low-value pool totals are:

Total items bought during year	$2,200
Less: Depreciation claim per above	($413)
Closing Value Of Pool	**$1,787**

2012 financial year depreciation claim:

Opening Value Of Pool			=	$1,787
$1,787	x	37.50%	=	$670
Total Depreciation Claimed			=	**$670**

Low-value pool totals are:

Opening Value Of Pool	$1,787
Total Items Bought During Year	$ 0
Less: Depreciation Claim Per Above	($670)
Closing Value Of Pool	**$1,117**

HINT FOR TAX RETURN

It does not matter if an asset costing under $1,000 is bought at the start or end of the financial year because the depreciation claim will be the same. A good accountant will be vigilant in moving applicable depreciation items to the low-value pool to maximise your depreciation claims each year.

CAPITAL WORKS DEDUCTIONS (BUILDING WRITE-OFF)

You can claim building (construction) expenditure over 25 or 40 years.

Examples of building expenditure include:

- plumbing
- electrical
- roofing
- slab
- carpentry
- bricklaying
- architect's and engineer's fees
- frame
- a building or an extension, such as adding a room, garage, patio or pergola
- alterations, such as removing or adding an internal wall
- structural improvements to the property, such as adding a gazebo, carport, sealed driveway, retaining wall or fence.

Examples of building expenditure not included:

- the cost of the land on which the rental property is built
- expenditure on clearing the land prior to construction
- expenditure on landscaping.

HINT FOR TAX RETURN

No claim is available until the construction is complete and you can only claim deductions for the period during the year(s) that the property is rented or is available for rent.

The claim percentage available is determined by figuring out when construction was first started. That means, from the date the foundations were laid.

Summary of building write-off claim percentage

Date construction started	Percentage rate of claim each year
17 July 1985 – 15 September 1987	4 per cent
After 15 September 1987	2.50 per cent

Estimating construction costs

Where a new owner is unable to precisely determine the construction costs of a building, an estimate from an appropriately qualified person may be used. As discussed earlier, this person would ideally be a quantity surveyor.

A WORKSHEET EXAMPLE TO HELP YOU CLAIM EVERYTHING YOU'RE ENTITLED TO FOR YOUR PROPERTY

You are now in a position to put together all the information you need for your tax return, as well as to determine how much you have made from your rental property in a year and how much you've paid to hold onto it.

Income	$
Rental income	14,500
Bond money refunded in lieu of rent	800
Gross rent	**15,300**
Expenses	
Advertising for tenants	98
Bank charges	100
Body corporate fees and charges	600
Borrowing expenses **	359
Cleaning	200

Council rates	800
Depreciation claim **	3,896
Gardening/lawn mowing	450
Gifts to tenant/agent	400
Gas and electricity	200
Insurance	695
Interest on loan(s)	12,475
Land Tax	300
Legal expenses	250
Pest control	150
Property agent fees/commission	1,200
Quantity surveyor's fees	660
Repairs and maintenance	1,500
Building write-off claim **	3,745
Stationery, telephone and postage	80
Travel expenses	536
Water charges	250
Sundry expenses	195
Total expenses	**29,139**
Net rental loss ($29,139 – $15,300)	13,839

** These items should be worked out each year by your accountant

Note: All the above expenses are inclusive of GST as no GST claims can be made on residential rental properties.

SELLING YOUR RENTAL PROPERTY - CAPITAL GAINS TAX (CGT)

Our strategy has always been to buy-and-hold rental properties. However, no rule is without its exceptions and on two occasions it was the right decision to sell properties.

As a result we needed to work out how much money we would make on the sale (known as a capital gain) or what loss, if any, was incurred (known as a capital loss). This applied to us because we had purchased our property after 19 September 1985. If you bought your house before this date you would be exempt from Capital Gains Tax in the majority of cases.

Capital gain basically means that you receive more money from the sale of your rental property than the total you paid for it. A capital loss, on the other hand, means that the base cost of the property exceeds the amount you ultimately receive for it.

If you are a co-owner of an investment property, your capital gain or loss will be figured out in accordance with the percentage of your ownership interest in the property.

Here is our most recent capital gain calculation as an example:

Purchase details:
Date of signing contract: 19 July 2005
Date of settlement: 19 September 2005

Purchase price	$300,000
Stamp Duty	$15,000
Legal costs	$1,000
Travel to purchase property	$2,000
Building inspection	$500
Pest inspection	$500
Buyer's agent fees	$6,000
Total Purchase Costs	**$325,000**

Sale details:

Date of signing contract: 19 June 2011
Date of settlement: 19 August 2011

Sales price	$500,000
Sales commission	$(15,000)
Advertising	$(3,000)
Legal costs	$(1,000)

Total Net Sales Proceeds   **$481,000**

Net capital gain is:

Net sales proceeds		$481,000
Less:		
Total purchase price	$325,000	
Less: depreciation and building write-off claimed *	$(23,000)	$302,000
Net capital gain		$179,000

As we owned the property jointly between ourselves, the net capital gain was reduced by a 50 per cent discount from $179,000 to $89,500. We each declared Capital Gain Income of $44,750 in our respective personal tax returns.

*   Building write-off and depreciation claimed during the ownership period is $23,000

HINT FOR TAX RETURN ONE

Depending on who owns the property – if, for instance, it's owned by an individual(s) or a trust – the net capital gain can be reduced by a 50 per cent discount. To get the discount the property needs to be owned for more than one year from purchase contract date to sales contract date.

If a company owns the property it is not entitled to the 50 per cent discount.

HINT FOR TAX RETURN TWO

Most accountants don't believe in the benefit of claiming the depreciation and building write-off, as they are both added back at the time of sale as shown above.

However, we believe that as long as the property is held, from purchase contract to sales contract, for at least one year, you will always be in front by claiming your entitlement. To demonstrate using facts from the previous example:

Depreciation and building write-off claimed for the period of ownership	$23,000
Depreciation and building write-off added back at sale	$23,000
Less: 50 per cent discount available at sale	($11,500)
Actual amount added back at sale	$11,500

Therefore, you are $11,500 better off by claiming your depreciation and building write-off.

HOW TO DEFER YOUR CAPITAL GAINS TAX

Using the previous example, because the sales contract was signed in June 2011 the capital gain needs to be declared as income in the 2011 tax year. This is despite the fact that the sale did not settle until August 2011.

It would have been better to move (defer) the capital gain into the next tax year. As the capital gain is taken from the date both parties sign the contract and not settlement, it would be great to lock the purchaser in to the deal but defer the gain until next year.

You need to contact a solicitor who understands this type of transaction. You enter a simultaneous put and call option contract that works as follows:

- you give the buyer a put option to sell your property to the purchaser, which is not exercisable before 1 July and expires by the end of August;
- the buyer takes a call option to be able to purchase the property from you after 1 July but they must exercise the option by the end of August;
- the normal sale of property contract is attached to the option agreements;
- you now have the right to sell your property after 1 July and the purchaser has the option to buy the property after 1 July;
- when either party exercises their option after 1 July, the contracts are officially signed and dated by each party;
- therefore, the contract date now falls after 1 July and into the next tax year.

KEEPING RECORDS - CAPITAL GAINS TAX

You must keep records relating to your ownership of the property, including all the costs of acquiring and disposing of it, for five years after the date it is sold.

You must keep records that include:

- the date you acquired the asset
- the date you disposed of the asset
- the date you received anything in exchange for the asset
- the parties involved
- any amount that would form part of the cost base of the asset
- whether you have claimed an income tax deduction for an item of expenditure.

KEEPING RECORDS - GENERALLY

You should always keep records of both income and expenses relating to your rental property, for at least five years after you lodge your tax return.

Records of rental expenses must include:

- name of the supplier
- amount of the expense
- nature of the goods or services
- date the expense was incurred
- date of the document.

If a document does not show the payment date you can use independent evidence, such as a bank statement, to show the date the expense was incurred.

ISSUES TO CONTEMPLATE FOR FUTURE YEARS

Rental property ownership is a long-term strategy. Buying and holding is the common strategy for passive investors like the majority of us. Given that it costs around five to six per cent of the purchase price to buy and around three to four per cent of the sales price to sell, property needs to be held long-term to allow these costs to be absorbed by the property's growth in value.

Sometimes, though, a property will need to be sold if it was bought in error. The error could be that over an extended period of time it has not grown in value or that it's costing more to hold each year than you can afford to pay.

The good news is that when the economy struggles and the majority of the world is either in recession or close to it, there is no need to change your buy-and-hold strategy. Try not to read the papers or watch television, with their doom and gloom reports, and try to speak only to fellow investors rather than family or friends who are not in the market. The important thing is not to get caught up in the market bumps, interest rate adjustments and government changes along the way.

To quote a great man, *Think and Grow Rich* author Napoleon Hill, "You become what you think about" and "Every person is what they allow to occupy their mind".

History says that well-positioned property, bought for the long-term, is a great investment. Property will always appreciate in value over time.

OVERCOMING FEARS

There are a number of fears you will need to overcome during your journey to wealth, the chief among which is the fear of poverty. It's the most common fear among those of us who are rental property investors.

Common symptoms of the fear of poverty are:

- **Procrastination** – The habit of putting off to tomorrow what you can do today. This is a major cause of failure to achieve your goals. You may think about purchasing property but you find excuses and place obstacles in your own way so that nothing is ever done;

- **Over-caution** – Looking for the negative side of every situation leads to you thinking and talking about failure instead of concentrating on success;

- **Indecision** – Permitting others to do one's thinking and "sitting on the fence" means you become overwhelmed by other people's opinions and take no action.

CONSOLIDATION / REVIEW PERIOD

We're nearing the end of this chapter now, which makes it a good time to go over some of the things we've discussed in a way that will hopefully make the most important parts stick firmly in your mind.

First of all, it's always a good idea to have an available line of credit to take care of unexpected rental property expenses. However, you should never over-extend yourself with too high a level of debt. Constantly review the interest rates and fees you're paying and compare them to those offered by other financiers in the market. Consider refinancing to a lender with a lower interest rate, as long as the savings in interest rates are more than the cost of changing lenders. This applies to both your rental properties and private home.

Consider the purchase of a positive cashflow property to help defray the holding costs of your negatively-geared one(s). The trade-off with these properties is that the capital growth is often lower over the long-term.

We recommend that at the end of each year you reflect on what you have achieved during the past 12 months and whether you are closer to your goal of financial freedom. Also, plan your goals for the coming 12 months and five years. Be aware, though, that it's common to underestimate what can be achieved in five years and overestimate what can be achieved in 12 months.

Ensure that your credit cards are paid off in full each month and try to only put expenses on the credit card you can afford to pay in cash. Credit card interest rates are very high and can quickly bite into your cashflow.

Consider consolidating any other private debts or loans you have – such as car, boat, caravan or furniture loans – that have higher interest rates than your private home loan. This will also save cashflow.

OPPORTUNITIES TO PURCHASE PROPERTIES

The right time to purchase a rental property is always right now. If you take a long-term buy-and-hold approach then there's no such thing as the perfect time. It is time in the market that counts.

There are, however, some conditions for purchasing and holding rental properties that are especially favourable. These include:

- low interest rates
- residential rents increasing
- low rental vacancy rates.

THE BENEFITS OF HOLDING PROPERTY OVER TIME

Investors who have owned their properties for several years generally find their negatively-geared properties become positively-geared. For instance, we bought a rental property in Ringwood for $210,000 in 2001 that was paying a rental of $220 per week. This represents a gross rental yield of 5.44 per cent ($220 x 52 = $11,440 / $210,000).

In 2011 the property was paying a rental of $420 per week. This represents a gross rental yield of 10.40 per cent ($420 x 52 = $21,840 / $210,000). Our current interest rate payable on the loan for this property is 6.86 per cent per annum.

The property would therefore now be positively-geared.

CASHFLOW SUPPORT STRATEGIES

Consider the use of debt to help with funding the costs of holding rental properties each year. Each of the following four strategies can help you hold your rental properties when times are tough and cashflow is restricted. Feel free to use them but keep in mind that each strategy involves increasing your level of debt to assist with the holding process. This will eat into future capital growth (equity) of the property(ies).

Example 1: Holding costs of rental property each year

- **Rent received for year** $15,000

- **Less : Cash expenses**
  Bank fees $300
  Body corporate fees $1,200
  Council rates $1,100
  Insurance $700

Interest paid	$16,000
Property agent's commission	$1,200
Repairs	$1,000
Water rates	$400
Total cash expenses	($21,900)

CASH SHORTFALL	**($6,900)**

- The cash shortfall each year of $6,900 can be funded by a line of credit. The line of credit must not be mixed with private funds to maintain the loan's 100 per cent deductibility.

- The interest on the cumulative balance of this LOC would also be claimable. Here is an example, using 10 per cent interest per annum to keep the calculations as easy as possible:

Year	Shortfall	Claimable interest	LOC balance
1	$6,900	$690 ($6,900 x 10%)	$7,590
2	$6,900	$1,449 (($7,590 + $6,900) x 10%)	$15,939
3	$6,900	$2,284 (($15,939 + $6,900) x 10%)	$25,123

- This interest would be claimable against the property outlined above each financial year.

- According to the conclusion in PBR 69725 you are not required to fund the investment property cash shortfall with personal funds. This means you do not have to use your salary to pay the shortfall of holding costs each year.

- You can choose to use this personal money (that you do not need to utilise to fund holding the property) to pay down your non-deductible private home loan.

Example 2 : Claimable interest when building a rental property

The land costs you $240,000, including purchase expenses, while the building costs you an extra $200,000. The timeframe to complete construction is anticipated to be 12 months and it's expected that roughly $22,000 in interest will be paid during this time.

A line of credit for $462,000 can be established to fund the total cost of land and buildings ($440,000) as well as the $22,000 interest payable during the construction period.

As the intended use of the property is for rental purposes, and has been since the land was first purchased, any interest paid from that date is claimable.

Example 3: Rising debt scenario for retirement

Just imagine it is now 2014 and neither of us is able to work. How will our decision back in 2001, when we first commenced purchasing property, help us in retirement?

Let's see where we are now and where we may be in the future.

Year	Purchase price	Rent at start	Rent 2011	Value in 2011	Value in 2014 (est.)
JUN 2001	$210,000	$220	$420	$500,000	$650,000

Purchased two other properties in 2002 but sold them for a small profit.

Year	Purchase price	Rent at start	Rent 2011	Value in 2011	Value in 2014 (est.)
AUG 2003	$258,000	$250	$350	$420,000	$500,000
NOV 2004	$256,850	$250	$340	$420,000	$515,000
SEP 2005	$196,240	$210	$335	$350,000	$420,000
SEP 2005	$276,290	$260	$360	$450,000	$550,000
NOV 2006	$296,993	$380	$400	$500,000	$600,000
TOTALS	**$1,494,373**	**$1,570**	**$2,205**	**$2,640,00**	**$3,235,000**

So in 2014 the debt hasn't changed, it is about $1.5 million, and the equity is roughly the same. Therefore the properties should have just about broken even and will cost us nothing to hold.

If we are unable to work and need to draw out the equity to live off, this will amount to $100,000 a year over ten years. That's a million dollars tax-free.

Even if interest is at 10 per cent, which is way over the top but will show you that it still works in a high interest environment, we'll have approximately $500,000 over the 10 years in capitalised interest.

That gives us a total of $1.5 million over 10 years.

Of course, by that stage the properties will have doubled again in value (even at a conservative estimate) and will be worth $6 million.

> ### HINT FOR TAX RETURN
> The interest on the money drawn out to live on is not tax deductible as it is private. A separate loan should be set up for the yearly drawings plus the interest.
>
> The interest on the original debt for the rental properties remains fully tax deductible.

Please note that despite drawing out money to live on, plus paying the appropriate interest on the money drawn, the equity we have after 10 years has still doubled.

Some people may not like the rising debt scenario but at least we have been able to manage, which is something we may not have been able to do without our property investments.